9 ELEMENTS OF FAMILY BUSINESS SUCCESS

A PROVEN FORMULA FOR IMPROVING LEADERSHIP
& RELATIONSHIPS IN FAMILY BUSINESSES

9 ELEMENTS OF FAMILY BUSINESS SUCCESS

ALLEN E. FISHMAN

New York   Chicago   San Francisco   Lisbon   London
Madrid   Mexico City   Milan   New Delhi   San Juan
Seoul   Singapore   Sydney   Toronto

1 2 3 4 5 6 7 8 9 0   FGR/FGR   0 1 5 4 3 2 1 0 9 8

ISBN   978-0-07-154841-0
MHID   0-07-154841-6

The Alternative Board, Strategic Business Leadership (SBL), Pocket Vision, and TABenos are trademarks of TAB Boards International, Inc.

McGraw-Hill books are available at special quantity discounts to use as premiums and sales promotions, or for use in corporate training programs. To contact a representative, please visit the Contact Us pages at www.mhprofessional.com.

This book is printed on acid-free paper.

Dedication

To Judi, who understands all too well the challenges of being married to an entrepreneur. We married young and had to carefully watch our dollars. Dinners out were rare, and the book *165 Ways to Cook Hamburgers* got a lot of use! Judi has understood and supported the financial risks that business founders often have to take and the time that needs to be dedicated to both launch a business and make it successful. It isn't always easy being married to someone who, at times, obsessively focuses on creating something new or solving a challenge. Thank you for your love and support and the great gift of our two wonderful daughters.

In Memoriam

Many of us would feel blessed to have trusted relationships in our lives—people in our camp to support us, defend us, and believe in us with a depth of passion reserved only for ourselves. I was lucky to have this relationship with my brother, Jack Fishman. Jack and I were not only able to share the simple pleasures of life together such as movies, swimming in New Zealand, and wearing outlandish outfits in Mexico, but as a family-member employee of businesses I ran for over 35 years, Jack and I had the dual roles of being brothers and being in business together.

Yes, balancing familial and business roles can be awkward at times. But family business relationships can also be greatly enriching by allowing family members to share something that is meaningful. Jack shared a sincere enthusiasm for the businesses. During our frequent phone calls, walks, or workouts together, he often voiced his concerns over business issues as well his excitement regarding achievements—his and mine.

When I started TAB, we talked about the many people we knew who didn't believe that the business would ever launch successfully. Jack believed in the idea—and in me—and he was incredibly proud of TAB's increasing success. He showed an immense sense of accomplishment when something he participated in was achieved and acknowledged. He demonstrated the kind of dedication that is rarely seen by someone other than a relative in a family business.

He always showed unwavering support of my business vision for TAB. He generously expressed to me his love for me. I miss his terrifically harsh slaps on the back and the strength of his bear hugs as he kissed me goodbye.

Contents

Foreword

Wa hat a powerful, greatly needed, and comprehensive book on all the issues confronting family businesses!

When we mix emotional and economic criteria, we open a Pandora's Box of problems. Few family businesses are spared these unique challenges. Many of these problems have ultimately torn their families apart. How sad. But how unnecessary.

Deathbed research shows that those "passing on" don't wish they had spent more time at the office or watching TV. They talk about their loved ones. They realize that no other success can compensate for failure in the home and that the most important work we will ever do is in the four walls of our own home.

This marvelous book is so vital and timely in dealing with the tough issues all family businesses face so as to preserve our most precious relationships and develop prosperous contributing businesses.

The book organization covering the nine elements is so wisely sequenced, starting with sharing Personal Vision Statements. These are the most important decisions simply because they govern every other decision. Putting together the family team, determining compensation, selecting and grooming family-member successors, dealing with spouses and non-family-member employees—all become so vital in cultivating healthy, positive, synergistic family business cultures.

Chapter 6 on building and maintaining a happy family culture in a family business is worth the entire book by itself! The 11 Cultural Potholes are so common and so realistic, and the prescriptive analyses and recommendations are brilliant, wise, practical, and very doable.

And, finally, one of the most challenging issues: how do you transition the business ownership to family members?

Seriously, this book goes into depth on almost every conceivable, relevant issue. This book is a "must read" for all those transversing the emotional-economic chasms in the perilous journey to the family business Mount Everest, the top of the world.

But just think of the powerful lessons taught and the character growth that flow throughout the entire family on such a magnificent journey. Primary greatness is character. Secondary greatness is worldly success. Character is destiny. Also, think of the transcendent contribution the business makes—such as The Alternative Board does—and how children and grandchildren learn that contribution is ever more important than achievement, that they can be happy for the success of others rather than so pretending but eating their hearts out, that integrity to principles is the essence of loyalty rather than loyalty being greater than integrity. Unbelievable character growth!

Family members, business involved or not, don't grow up in a comparison-based culture where the true identity theft happens. The cultural DNA is aligned with the immortal spiritual DNA, unleashing the greatest potential of each family member and reaffirming his or her true worth and identity, unconnected to net worth.

Few family businesses achieve such heights. Sadly so. But by following these wisely sequenced nine principles, this can happen for your family.

How I've wished I had these materials in so many situations over the years with family businesses who struggled profoundly with such unusual challenges. I commend Allen E. Fishman on such a marvelous contribution, and I know you will profit from the reading and from applying these principles as much as I have.

Dr. Stephen R. Covey

Preface

The greatest gift in my life is family. Thoughts of my family guide me through the tough times, and those same thoughts bring me deep contentment when I'm sitting on the porch, gazing out at the Rockies while my horses graze nearby, just thinking about all the good stuff life has brought my way.

Some fortunate turns and a hearty dose of hard work afforded me a level of business success that allows both my family and me to enjoy life fully. Every day I am thankful for all we have. Knowing I created something that right now, and in the future, will support and nourish future generations of my family, both financially and emotionally, is for me a great honor—as a business owner, a father, and a grandfather.

The nine elements of family business success that I describe in this book have not only helped TAB bring financial benefit to our family; they have also become a wonderful part of our family relationship dynamics. The meaningful relationship I have with my son-in-law, Jason, and the opportunity to watch him grow to become an outstanding president and COO of TAB bring immeasurable enjoyment to my life. I can only hope my mentoring brings equal enjoyment to Jason's life.

My succession planning has me secure in the knowledge that TAB will stay in the family at least into the next generation. I'm often asked if TAB will go on to a third-generation family business leader. The truth is that I don't know if any of my grandchildren—Daniela, Jake, or Pierce—will grow into adults who want to become a part of TAB. If they do, that would be wonderful, but if not, that would be okay too.

I just want my grandchildren to find their passions and enjoy life doing work that is meaningful to them: work that provides happiness and fulfillment. My hope is that each of my grandchildren embarks full force on the journey to their respective dreams. In my mind, this is the best that can be wished for anyone.

Allen E. Fishman

Acknowledgments

I want to thank my daughter, Michele Fishman, for the many hours she spent asking me questions and shaping my responses—bringing life to so many of the stories in this book. Michele has been involved in a number of our family businesses, and she is currently the executive vice president of one of them, Direct Communications Services, Inc. Because she has been exposed to family business discussions since she was a child, her insights came naturally and are an invaluable part of this book. It is fitting that my daughter was involved with me in writing this book on family business. I so enjoyed being able to work on this book with her.

Thanks to Lyn Adler for assisting me with the editing. Heartfelt gratitude also goes to Dana Besbris for handling the administrative challenges of putting this book together, as well as coordinating the resources we have used, taking dictation, and keeping me on track.

After I identified the easy-to-use "Nine Elements" formula for those who want family business success along with enjoyable family dynamics, I wrote out my techniques and stories for addressing the challenges. I then sent chapters to Larry Amon, Kevin Armstrong, Barry Arnold, Sharon Bolton, Carol Crawford, David Cunningham, Steve Davies, John Dini, Jan E. Drzewiecki, Bruce Gernaey, Jackie Gernaey, Bruce Healy, John Keener,

Blair Koch, John Lybarger, Harlan Oelklaus, Don Schlueter, Cheryl Swanson, Ben Sweeney, Oswald Viva, Bill Vrettos, Stevan Wolf, Sheelah Yawitz, Joe Zente, and Jason Zickerman. These outstanding professionals were generous with sharing their powerful insights into solving the special challenges of family businesses and helping to create a book that is right on target on how to handle these needs. Without their contributions this book would be missing so much of the power it has to help family business leaders, family business employees, and non-family-member employees. Sincere thanks to these family business experts who shared their experience and advice.

In this book the actual names of business owners are used only where I have been granted permission to do so. Otherwise, in order to respect and ensure the confidentiality of the families and their businesses, I have used fictional names, companies, and business fields for the stories and examples provided in the book.

List of Abbreviations

FBL (Family Business Leader)   The leader of a family business.

FME (Family Member Employee)   A family business employee who is usually related to the FBL.

Non-FME (Non-Family Member Employee)   A family business employee who is not related to the FBL or FMEs.

PAVE   Passion, Aptitude to be the future business leader, Vision of the Big Picture Potential, and Empathetic personality match with the leadership personality needed.

SWOT   Strengths, Weaknesses, Opportunities, and Threats.

TAB (The Alternative Board)   The world's largest business peer board and coaching franchise system.

9 ELEMENTS OF FAMILY BUSINESS SUCCESS

Introduction

The joys and the challenges of family business are in my blood; they drew me in with great fascination as far back as I can remember. My father, Herman, and my uncle Willy (who was my father's brother-in-law) were equal partners in a couple of successful businesses. One of the earlier businesses involved fabric recycling. I remember when, as early as five years old, my mother would drive me to visit with my dad at work; he worked long hours, and we would visit him during the day. I would walk in with a big grin on my face because I was absolutely mesmerized by the whole, loud process of the roaring conveyor belts that loaded the materials from the docking stations. How I enjoyed being allowed to manually manipulate the elevator levers to go up and down the different floors. I felt such pride! This was *my* family's business!

Years later, my father and uncle owned a pillow manufacturing business, which was located down on the Mississippi River in the Laclede's Landing warehouse district in St. Louis. My strongest memories of that manufacturing plant are the acrid smells of the chemicals that were used to dry out the feathers for the pillows. When I was 15, my father and uncle worked out a deal with me to sell some of the low-end pillows door-to-door. A friend of mine had a car so he and I worked out a partnership. Over time, one of my cousins and my brother joined the family pillow business as full-time employees, setting the stage for the second generation of the family company.

Our family and my uncle's family were constantly in each other's homes, and we often vacationed together. Surrounded by the smell of the men's thick cigar smoke, I listened and hung on their every word that involved the business. My father especially enjoyed sharing business stories with me. What I heard and what I witnessed gave me at a very young age invaluable insights into business workings. These experiences provided me with a strong advantage when preparing my own businesses that would eventually become family businesses. I recognized the benefits of being raised in a family in which business was a way of life, and I also learned that it is possible to have a family business while maintaining a strong, positive family dynamic among both the family members working in the business and those not working in the business. My son-in-law, Jason, is the president of The Alternative Board (TAB), which is the family business I founded in 1990 of which I am still the CEO. Jason and I live the same family business philosophy and believe in the same formula for family business success that I was raised with—and it is the same formula upon which this book is based.

In the early 1980s I formed a consulting company, Allen Fishman Business Consultants (AFBC), which helped small and midsize businesses. I needed to bring on consultants who were experienced in family business matters. I met with several prospects, and I was surprised to find that most of them were very uncomfortable getting involved with family-member dynamics. During lunch with one of the prospects, he boldly acknowledged that he was actually afraid to enter into any discussions that involved family-member relationships. "These issues are just too *touchy-feely*," he said. "There are just too many gray areas unlike purely business matters such as how to improve sales or whether the business should borrow money. I don't want to get involved in all of the messiness of the emotions."

As a result of these unsuccessful interviews, it occurred to me that family businesses had such special needs that I would form a division of AFBC that would focus solely on helping family businesses with family dynamics challenges. In the course of developing this division of AFBC, the more I worked with family businesses, the greater my understanding and appreciation became for their unique business situations. In many cases, the businesses were underachieving because of family business dynamics that went unnoticed and/or unaddressed. In other cases, the businesses were financially successful, but they were failing from a family relationship standpoint. I recognized that these family businesses had common challenges that fit one or more of the *Nine Elements* shared in this book and that they could be helped with the specific strategies discussed in conjunction with the *Nine Elements*.

Because of the national media exposure I had received relating to some of my business successes, I was asked by Tribune Media Services to write a weekly newspaper column, *Business Insights*, which they nationally syndicated. Many of the questions that readers sent in involved the impact of family dynamics on their family businesses. I wasn't surprised that I received such a large number of family business–related questions, given the great number of family businesses in the United States. As of 2007, there were estimated to be over 24 million family businesses in the United States, which accounted for 89 percent of all business tax returns. And 82 million people were employed by these family enterprises—that was 62 percent of the workforce!

When I entered into discussion with McGraw-Hill, which had published my *Seven Secrets of Great Entrepreneurial Masters* in 2006, about writing my next book, they asked me to pick a topic for which I felt the most passion. The discussion took place during a period of time in which I was feeling really great about how I had been able to help several family members who were involved in family businesses. It was rewarding to see the dramatic positive benefits my program had brought to their lives and businesses. I started thinking, "Hmm, when I give my hourlong talks to audiences, I can reach only so many people and give them only an overview of the formula and highlight only some of the important issues." It would be a great opportunity to have the book format because not only could I reach more people with this formula but I could also dive into a greater depth of discussion.

One of my objectives for this book is to bring to life the so-called gray areas that the consultant I mentioned earlier said he feared. I am not interested in presenting textbook types of theories; the formula and material presented in this book are based on real people and real situations. Here I share with readers the procedures, methods, and techniques for resolving and eliminating the family-related problems that keep so many family businesses from achieving success. I provide an arsenal of tools for family business success—tools that allow everyone connected to a family business to better understand the often difficult dynamics involved. Together, the principles, techniques, and tools that make up the *Nine Elements* formula will improve leadership and relationships in every family business. The formula is easy to understand, and it reveals a correct path for family members to take if they wish to help their family business achieve greater success and stability—while also enjoying life both from within and outside the business. It's this same formula that has helped TAB to grow into the world's largest franchise system that provides peer board advisory and coaching services for business owners and leaders.

Issues around management and leadership take on a higher degree of complexity in family businesses. There is a level of subjectivity with which nonfamily businesses do not normally have to contend. Decisions are often made in unique ways when family-member dynamics are involved.

In successful publicly owned companies, all efforts concerning the business are typically focused on maximizing the profits of the company and the return on the stockholders' investment, while using the top management affordably. In a family-owned business, maximizing growth and profits may not be the primary direction desired. The family business leader (FBL) may want family members to be involved in management even if they are not the best-qualified candidates for the roles.

One of the special challenges of a family business is running it in such a way that it creates the least amount of family stress possible. Family life already involves many day-to-day stresses, but when you throw in the business, the complexities increase. If family issues are left unaddressed, family members employed in the business will not feel satisfied, and they will drag the business down in spirit, and maybe even in body.

Don't kid yourself: family relationship dynamics will intrude in the family business relationships. This book provides more than a process; it brings to the forefront the emotional factors and hot buttons that can make or break the family business. The *Nine Elements of Family Business Success* will not only keep your family business on the fast track moving forward toward increased business success, it will also reinforce and strengthen relationships within the family.

Yet, while it is easy to get caught up in discussing the pitfalls or the negative impact of having family members involved in family businesses, it's important to remember that this is only part of the story. The best part of the story is that when things are going well, you can share the joy with those people you really care about. Conversely, when business is going through challenging times, you have those people around you whom you can trust; you have your family to rely on. Ultimately, it is my hope for every reader of this book that the *Nine Elements* will allow you to reach the kind of family business success of your dreams—not just financial success but also that level of success wherein all family members feel purpose, self-worth, and the joy of working together.

I'd like to clarify in advance that, as defined by the parameters of this book, a *family business* is one in which one or more family members are employed full-time by the business. Moreover, it is a company that is owned, controlled, and operated by one or more family members. A family business can be a corporation, a partnership, or one of any number of other legal structures. Also, a family business may involve more than one family, with each segment having family-member employees. Possible combinations can be as straightforward as spouses or siblings, or they can extend to include cousins, nieces and nephews, stepchildren, and beyond.

CHAPTER 1

THE FIRST ELEMENT
Creating and Sharing Personal Vision Statements

When I give my "Nine Elements" talk to audiences of those involved in family businesses, I ask the family-member employees (FMEs)—other than the family business leaders (FBLs)—whether they have a written statement concerning their Personal Visions and whether they have shared this with the FBL in their company. Out of the thousands of audience members I've spoken to, no one has raised a hand indicating a positive response. Having family-member employees provide their own Personal Vision Statements, as well as having the FBLs do so, is one of the many untraditional strategies that the methodology of the *Nine Elements of Family Business Success* provides.

As Steve Davies, a TAB facilitator-coach in Long Island, New York, said to me, "The problem is that family business owners are asking their family-member employees to live the owner's vision of success. Seldom is the family-member employee allowed to live or even explore the vision of which he or she may dream. But in order for the business to ultimately succeed, FMEs too must be allowed to live their dreams within the family business construct. Otherwise, their passions will be quashed and they will not have the level of motivation needed to bring about the kind of results for the company that leads to the business owner's vision of success."

If you, as the FBL, want to capture the passion of your FMEs, it's critical to identify and acknowledge what your FMEs' dreams for the future look like and to explain how working for the family business can help them reach these Visions. Conversely, if you want your business's FMEs to work toward the future of your dreams, you need to share your Vision for the future of the business with them. This includes explaining what your future plans are for your involvement of the company. The only proven way of doing this is by identifying in writing and sharing with all the FMEs your long-range (5 to 10 years or more down the road) personal and business dreams, which I refer to as "The Personal Vision," as you see them today. These writings become the Personal Vision Statements.

It is for these reasons that the formula for improving family business leadership and relationships begins with the first element: Creating and Sharing Personal Vision Statements. In this chapter, we explore the ways to develop and share these written Personal Vision Statements. These statements are important because, in order to have a cohesive workplace with a positive family business culture that includes FMEs who are passionate about their roles in the future of the business, there must be compatibility between the Personal Vision Statements of the FBLs and FMEs.

Before moving on to specific issues involving Personal Vision Statements, I'd like to express how strongly I feel about the benefits of sharing those aspects of the Personal Vision Statements that can impact upon the business and/or the desires both for the business and the roles within the business. There *are* many elements of Personal Vision Statements that FBLs and FMEs do *not* necessarily need to share with one another. Those involve non-business-related desires such as the desire to spend more time after work playing tennis or learning to sculpt. They are not crucial to the business functions. On the other hand, I want to tell you about *Pocket Visions*. These are elements in a Personal Vision Statement that some people feel they simply cannot share. These are the desires that they want to keep close to the chest, in their "pocket" for safekeeping, away from the eyes of others.

I'd like to share with you the story of a family that suffered greatly when the FBL kept crucial aspects of his Personal Vision Statement from his son, the president of his company. The FBL knew he eventually wanted to sell the family business to outsiders, and he stated this in his Personal Vision Statement. He planned accordingly by making certain budget decisions for the family business. One decision was to start getting audited statements versus unaudited statements, and this increased the business's accounting costs. He did this in order to improve the credibility of the business and put the company in a better position to be sold in five years. Additionally, his Pocket Vision also involved reducing the company's dependence on him, which he knew would result in slowing down the business's profit growth temporarily. He hired two outside executives for key positions who took over many of his sales responsibilities to his major clients. An outside company would feel more confident with nonfamily executives since it would be safe to predict that those executives would be unlikely to leave the company after it changed ownership.

The FBL explained to some of the people involved in this transition that he didn't want to let his son in the loop because he didn't want to lose the son's efforts before the potential sale. Not surprisingly, this caused his son to feel a great amount of resentment, which would not have taken place if the FBL had been open and trusted his son. Because the FBL kept his motives in his pocket, his son was highly confused and bitterly angry by his father's actions, and the family is estranged to this day.

In general, I think it is wise to share all of the important business-related issues, but if you feel that sharing some of them might have a negative impact, you can offset some of that impact with positive incentives.

When the Personal Visions of the FBLs and FMEs are out of alignment and neither party is willing to make changes that address the conflicts, it leaves the door wide open for trouble to develop. This is especially true when the conflicts directly affect the business. Writing, sharing, and creating compatibility among Personal Vision Statements will guarantee dramatic improvement in the success of your family business and relationships among FMEs. These Personal Vision Statements will become the foundation for the personal plans that FMEs use to synergistically work together and lead the business forward.

There are seven Vision Essentials common to most Personal Vision Statements. Let's begin by taking a look at them and how they may apply to you and your FMEs.

Vision Essential 1. Material Desires

In this book, I share many experiences that involve my son-in-law, Jason Zickerman, who is the president and COO of TAB, because they illuminate many of the *Nine Elements*' points. For example, when Jason first came on board at TAB, we discussed my dreams for the income that TAB should be generating in the future, and he shared his income expectations for the upcoming years. I needed to understand his long-term expectations if I wanted to create plans to move the company in a direction that would satisfy his material desires. It is important for FMEs to know if their income desires are consistent with the long-term expectations of the FBL for the FME because, ultimately, income decisions are in the FBL's hands.

Jason's Personal Vision Statement includes the following: "I want to own my dream home, one that has plenty of land and a great view overlooking the mountains. I envision this home being in a convenient location so that our boys can attend the schools my wife and I approve of, and, for me, I want to live close to some really awesome rock climbing locations." The first time I saw this, I laughed and said, "What the heck?" but then I thought about it and realized that this type of material desire was very realistic, and it did fit with my dreams for the future of TAB.

In contrast, Joe, who owns a furniture importing company, had a written Personal Vision Statement specifying a desire to grow the business so that it would provide an income of $100,000 a year for his son. Like many FBLs, Joe's material desires relating to the business are not limited to his own needs and wants. The problem was that Joe's son thought $100,000 wouldn't be enough to enable him to live a life he desired 10 years down the road. "My dad doesn't seem to recognize how expensive it is for me to send my kids to college." When they went over their Vision Statements together, they recognized their different views had to be reconciled because they dramatically impacted plans that had to be made for the company. The company would have to grow significantly to support both of their income desires. Joe wasn't thrilled, quite frankly, about the extra work and risk involved in a more aggressive expansion, but he committed to doing it because he wanted his son to be happy and stay in the business.

In a family business, the business itself is usually the most important factor affecting the family's material lifestyle, and that is why desired income and net worth should be included in Personal Vision Statements. This information shared between an FME and FBL can be a critical influence on company decisions, such as how aggressively to expand the business.

Jacob, who is an FBL of a retail chain, included in his Personal Vision Statement having a minimum net worth outside the company of $1 million. To do this, he had to distribute more money out of the business to himself personally than he had been taking out in the past. This money could have been used to expand the business. His daughter, who had given up her law practice to join the family business, was not exactly happy about Jacob taking out so much money to fund his retirement investments. Jacob did not foresee this conflict with his daughter until they shared their written Personal Vision Statements.

The resolution involved spinning off to Jacob certain real estate that was company owned. This passive rental income helped satisfy his desire to have a minimum net worth outside his company of $1 million. At the same time, it allowed an increase in cash flow to be allocated to the business, thus satisfying the daughter's desire to expand the business.

Vision Essential 2. Amount of Time to Spend Working in the Family Business

After I had finished giving a talk in Detroit about my last book, *Seven Secrets of Great Entrepreneurial Masters*, I was greeting some of the audience members, and one TAB member came up and said, "I want to thank you for something wonderful that's happened in my life because of your program. Do you have a few minutes?" and he asked me to sit down. He told me how creating his Personal Vision Statement had changed his life and how much more he is enjoying it. "I wanted to spend fewer days and weeks working, quite frankly, and I wanted to take more time from the office to go to the gym. I finally got these ideas down in writing, and I realized I had to make some changes." He told his son-in-law about his dreams, and his son-in-law was thrilled because he wanted to take on more responsibility. "After we talked about it, we set up a plan in which my son-in-law will become the COO of the company after a three-year transition period, and during that time I want to phase out my day-to-day involvement in the business." He smiled proudly: "Business is doing better than ever, and you know, I'm really enjoying having time to be away from the office, time to think and not being involved in the daily operations. I'm living my dream."

While it may seem like a contradiction, when the FBL spends less time involved directly in the family business, it does not necessarily mean results will go down. Many FBLs, just like the one I met on my book tour, have surprised themselves by earning more than they had while working long hours. Their companies actually tend to do much better because they are making "big picture" contributions that were out of reach because of distractions of day-to-day business problems.

It is equally important for FMEs to identify in their own Personal Vision Statements the balance they'd like to strike in their business life versus their nonbusiness life relating to factors such as how much time they want to devote to their work. I get some of the greatest stories on trips. One time while in Port Douglas, Australia, while in the hotel swimming pool, a man who looked to be in his seventies struck up a conversation with me. We ended up talking for quite a while. Tony is the second-generation owner and CEO of his family's produce business. He grinned largely and proudly told me that he is still at work at six in the morning till late in the day, seven days a week! After he introduced me to his daughter-in-law, he explained that her husband, his son, was back in Melbourne running the business. "My wife had to drag me to take me on vacation! I'm the one who's first to the office and last to go. Yeah, my boys do the same thing." He told me that he also believes that FMEs should keep their vacation time to a minimum. He operated this way when his father ran the business, and he expected the same from his two grown sons, who were both employed in the family business.

Tony's sons, however, have different Personal Visions as to the kind of balance they want between work and personal life. Both sons love the family business and even hope that some of their children will become fourth-generation FMEs. However, Tony's expectations on the number of hours the sons would work each day and each week was causing problems for his sons. They had been missing their kids' activities, such as baseball games and school conferences, and the sons had started to resent it.

This situation had persisted for many years, and Tony's sons had been discontented, but they had no way of letting Tony know. Inevitably, the situation drained the sons of some of their passion for the business. The problem did not get resolved until they sat down with their dad and shared their Personal Visions. Tony told me how one son said, "I love you, Dad, but I get really resentful that I haven't been able to make *one* of my oldest son's Tai Chi belt awards. You should want me to spend more time with my boys, your grandchildren. I don't want to work every day and the hours you work." Tony explained that he lightened up on pushing them to follow his lead in always being at work early in the morning and staying late seven days a week. "I had to do what I've done, because they wouldn't stay in the business if they had to put in the kind of hours I do.

Vision Essential 3. Role in the Family Business

All family members employed in the business should identify their long-term work desires of what role they want to be performing in the business. The problem of working in roles for which there is no passion is more common with FMEs in the Second Reign and Dynastic Stage. The *Second Reign* is usually run by the founder's child or children; so often, a Second Reign generation is usually run by siblings. The *Dynastic Stage* is the third generation and later generations running the family business. This means that at the Dynastic Stage, the business is often run by cousins. The FBL may feel trapped in his or her position as the "leader." In many cases, the FMEs and the company itself are overly dependent on the founder. In turn, this feeling of being absolutely needed feeds into the founder's overinvolvement in every aspect of the business, which leads to communication problems developing between the FBL and the FMEs. All too often, the FBL has one idea of what the long-term role should be for an FME, but that role is not the one the FME wants, and the FME thus feels trapped in it and unable to express his or her feelings to the FBL. One reason FMEs may hesitate to speak up is that they don't want to antagonize the FBL because what they have in mind as their role includes what may be substantial parts of the FBL's role, and they don't want to step on the FBL's toes.

How do FMEs determine and get into the correct role? Matt's experience serves as an example of how this type of shift can be accomplished. Matt's father started and ran a distribution business, and Matt's role was to run the operations for the warehouse. The problem was that Matt loved the rush that selling can offer, and he felt he had natural persuasion skills, while warehouse operations did nothing for him; he was just going through the motions. It was suggested to Matt that he put his desire into his written Personal Vision Statement and then share it with his father. When his father read the statement, he explained to Matt that being in charge of the operations was the best possible training for moving Matt into becoming the future COO of the company, which is what his father saw Matt eventually moving into. Unfortunately, Matt didn't enjoy managing people, and his father had a very hard time understanding this. It took the involvement of an independent coach to develop a career path for which Matt could feel passion. Ultimately, his dad had to come to terms with the fact that Matt would not be the successor to the family business; he would have to find an alternative.

My own Personal Vision Statement reflects my desire to focus on the strategic aspects of TAB and also to continue working on Big Picture projects that I enjoy and that could have a great impact on TAB. This focus allows me to continue with my passion for developing programs and tools for TAB facilitator-coaches who would, in turn, provide additional value to TAB members. I have also added to my Personal Vision Statement a desire to write books, like this one, that allow me to share my experience, to help other business leaders.

Vision Essential 4. Emotional Rewards from the Family Business

The emotional rewards and happiness gleaned from business success often have a personal meaning beyond mere financial success. I had a dream that TAB would own and occupy its own building upon achieving certain milestones. I knew I would receive psychological rewards when we found and financially secured such a building, and years ago I identified this in my Personal Vision Statement. I discussed this aspect of my Vision with Jason, and I found he was totally in sync with it, and together we made it happen. I cannot describe the joy I felt the first time Jason and I sat down in the family-owned building that was almost 30,000 square feet large.

One contrasting situation took place between an FBL and his two sons, who worked in a family-owned manufacturing business. The FBL's long-term Company Vision included relocating the manufacturing plant within 10 years to a significantly larger plant that the family would own. When he shared this part of his dreams for the company with his sons, both of his sons expressed displeasure. They wanted the business to be operated more conservatively, and they did not want to increase expenses in order to cover the mortgage and additional utility and operating costs that would be involved with a significantly larger manufacturing plant. They were shocked to hear of their father's Vision because he had never discussed it with them before.

The father had spent a lot of personal time looking at real estate. When he met with his sons to discuss what he had found, they gave him a litany of reasons why they didn't see any value in owning the building in which the company operated. Owning the building meant a great deal to the FBL, but his sons didn't want to take the risk. Their fear was that the company could get hurt over the long term if the family was responsible for this building in the event of "a downturn in the economy."

The FBL and both sons shared their differing Visions as to the emotional reward of owning a building in which a company would operate. Both sons were adamantly against owning a building with its related debt and risk factors that could come into play if the company did not achieve the projected growth. After several meetings, the father gave up the dream of owning a company building.

Another FBL passionately loves art and being recognized for having his art collection. His Personal Vision included a desire for his professional services business to purchase and display an impressive art collection. He used company funds to have the company buy investment-level art to display in a prized gallery at the company office. As his three sons, one by one, joined the business, the practice of adding to the company art collection was a use of company funds that did not exactly match the sons' Personal Visions. They wanted the money to be reinvested in the company and used for maximizing company growth, but they were hesitant to confront their father about their unhappiness.

Only after sharing Personal Vision Statements did it come out that the sons resented company funds being used for art when it should have been, in their minds, used for company expansion. Their father explained to them his belief that his impressive art collection was a symbol of his company's success. He pointed out how over the previous decade the art collection had gone up in value.

The sons finally found the opening for discussing what they felt was a poor use of company funds. Their opinions were difficult for the FBL to deal with because the art gallery at the company offices was such an emotional factor for him. The sons politely explained that the gallery might make the FBL feel good, but it wasn't the best use of company funds.

At first, the FBL was unmovable on this point, and he told his sons that, even though it was a family business, he was the owner and so he viewed all of the funds as his personal money. He explained that if he was not investing in the artworks, the amount of money he would be drawing out of the business would be increased dramatically. The sons did understand the FBL's "emotional" views on the subject. Finally, the man and his sons compromised on an amount that would be used to add paintings to the art collection every two years. But the amount was much less than the FBL had been spending. Getting their emotional rewards from the business consistent with each other removed most of the sons' resentment over the issue.

Money in the bank is just that, and as we all know, you can't take it with you. Psychological reward may directly or indirectly benefit you and your family, but its motivational impact usually far outweighs its financial impact. What serves as a psychological motivator for FBLs and FMEs is a very personal thing.

Vision Essential 5. Semi- or Full Retirement

At some point, FBLs need to consider and put into their Personal Vision Statements their views on retirement. If you are an FBL, there are likely to be health issues, financial issues, and changes in FME dynamics that can lead to fluidity in the aspect of your Personal Vision relating to retirement. It's important that this Personal Vision be shared with FMEs and that they are in alignment with your plans. Your views on retirement can change as your personal life changes and as the dynamics among FMEs change. One business owner had wanted to work full-time in his business forever—he loved it. But after his two heart attacks, he made a decision to take it easier and to turn more responsibility over to his daughter. He greatly changed this factor in his Personal Vision. Fortunately, his daughter wanted to assume the role of president, and they shared their Personal Visions relating to the man's semiretirement.

The more common scenario, however, involves FBLs who do not want to give up control of their companies, much to the consternation of the next generation in the business. John, with the help of his three grown sons, runs a manufacturing operation. One day, he called an extended lunch meeting with his sons away from the business. John announced he wanted to share his own long-range dreams for both his life and the business with his sons. He handed each son a printed copy of his Personal Vision Statement, which he had created over the previous month with the help of his TAB facilitator-coach.

John shared his dreams for being the CEO of the company 10 years into the future and being in the office most days of the workweek. John asked his sons for their comments concerning his written Personal Vision Statement. After what had started as a restrained conversation, which in no way represented the sort of open and honest talk John had wanted to generate, he told them he really needed to know what they thought about his desires. Upon being prompted to be honest, his oldest son stated his surprise that John was going to stay in the CEO position so long. Weeks of discussions followed, however, and John was eventually able to get their buy-in to his Personal Vision by promising that the company's functions would be separated into three different divisions with each son becoming the COO of one of the three divisions yet still reporting to John.

As part of identifying the long-term future desires for retirement or semiretirement, it's critical to first consider the income that will be needed for successful retirement. As I will discuss in more detail later, in family businesses the responsibility for generating the income needed for retirement often falls on the back of the family business, and this must be accepted by the FMEs who will be remaining in the business and generating the money for the retirement.

Family members coming into the business can change retirement plans. Before Jason joined TAB, my Personal Vision Statement reflected my desire to retire from TAB by selling the company or taking it public when I reached a certain age range.

But when Jason first came to work at TAB, we agreed to hold off on discussing the long-range view for the future of the company until he had been with the company for a year. We met after his first-year anniversary, at which time we were both confident he would remain at TAB. Jason had demonstrated the intellectual ability, personality, and passion needed to one day become the leader of TAB.

Based on Jason's entrance and proving his abilities, I changed my Personal Vision to reflect keeping TAB as a family business. It also now reflects my desire to one day serve in a pure CEO role and to mentor Jason, who will be running the business. Personal Vision Statements are long term in nature, but, as with my Personal Vision Statement, they do change over time because factors affecting the statements change. A scheduled review, which you will learn about later, will make certain these changes are acknowledged and addressed.

Ultimately, it is entirely at the discretion of the FBL to decide how much importance he or she wants to give to the Personal Vision Statement of each FME as it relates to the semi- or full retirement of the FBL. Concessions and changes to the FBL's Personal Vision Statement may or may not be made in order to accommodate the dreams for the future of family members.

Vision Essential 6. Compatibility of Company Vision Statements with Personal Vision Statements

One reason so many family businesses underperform is that they lack strategic direction. Having a strategic direction requires a written Company Vision for the long-range (5 to 10 years) future of the business. The individual Personal Vision Statements of FBLs and FMEs typically include factors that should influence the written Company Vision Statement. But the written Company

Vision Statement is the pinnacle to which the company as a whole should be aiming for. It is the foundation for the plans of the family business, and it should reflect the future picture of the company as the FBL has deemed his or her long-range dream. Every family business should use the unique set of dreams of the FBL to pave the way to the future of the company. If the company's overall plan is compatible with the dreams of the FMEs, the stage will be set for stronger relationships both in their business and personal lives.

The written Company Vision Statement should reflect the FBL's dreams as to long-term levels of the company's sales and revenues, but not with any specific quantification. These levels are more conceptual than measurable standards. Other factors commonly included in the Company Vision Statement show the long-term picture for the types of products or services to be sold, the quality of the products or services, the positioning of the company in its respective business field, and the company's geographic (local, national, or international) presence. The Company Vision Statement should include a desired long-term size for the company such as its being the biggest in its business field. Many family businesses have Company Vision Statements that reflect the FBL's desire for the business to service certain types of customers or clients or for employees to enjoy certain levels of compensation or challenge.

In order to find compatibility, the Company Vision Statement has to be shared with the FMEs. Many times, FBLs will delay sharing the Company Vision Statement with the FMEs so long that when they do eventually share it with them, the fireworks start. The FMEs begin to worry about the changes soon to occur without their having time to prepare mentally and emotionally for them: "Wow, I had no idea about that!" In a family business, unlike other businesses, there is a need to at least consider the views held by FMEs regarding the long-term future of the business.

When I first created TAB, an important part of my Personal Vision Statement was that TAB would become the largest franchise system in the world that provided peer board and coaching services. This desire is reflected in the TAB Company Vision Statement displayed at the TAB office entrance, which reads as follows:

> To be a leading international provider of peer advisory and coaching solutions to leaders of privately held businesses. Based on real-world experience, we will encourage and empower our members to achieve their business and personal vision.

At lunch one day, I asked Jason to tell me, in one sentence, what he saw for the future of TAB. After reflection he said, "I want TAB to be an important factor for privately owned businesses in countries worldwide." You can see that his dreams were fully consistent with my TAB Company Vision Statement. Jason and I agreed to not distribute a lot of the company profits during certain years and instead use the money to make significant investments in TAB's infrastructure so it would position TAB to more quickly become a leading international provider of our services. We have never regretted choosing this option as the results enabled us to achieve our shared Company Vision for TAB.

Joan is an FBL who developed her first draft of her Company Vision Statement. She showed it to her son and daughter, both of whom worked in the family business, and she asked for their comments. Her Vision Statement included a 3 percent per year growth factor that caused her children to express their concern to her: "This is much slower growth then we envisioned for the company." Joan responded, "I'd love for there to be higher growth, but in order to really increase the growth, I'm afraid I would have to work a lot harder than I want to; I would rather spend more time enjoying life and playing with my grandkids."

There was almost a sense of "ah-hah" that flowed through the room. For years, her children had been confused as to why she'd so often vetoed their ideas for growing the business. They had harbored an underlying anger due to their unsettling impression that their mother had found their ideas for growth to be too weak. Consequently, within weeks of their gaining a new understanding of Joan's conservative long-term Vision for the company's growth, both children independently came to her and said, "You know, Mom, I'm going to find some other opportunity that gives me a better shot at making the kind of money I want to make." Joan's daughter said that she had been thinking about starting her own business before she heard about the Company Vision Statement because she was tired of Joan's constantly dismissing her ideas for growth. Joan didn't want to lose her children's involvement in the family business because they were talented and she enjoyed working with them. So she decided to deal with the situation head on. The final version of Joan's Company Vision Statement thus reflected a compromise between her children and her in which it was stated that there would be a significantly greater but not recklessly aggressive company growth of 5 percent a year. Joan's writing the Company Vision Statement and sharing it with her children working in the company may have saved them from leaving the business. It brought to the forefront issues that hadn't been discussed and were festering.

The younger generations typically are more aggressive in terms of what they'd like to see in the long-term growth of the business. FBLs often feel like, "I've already been through that, and the business can grow a little slower now. Let's distribute more of the profits instead of keeping the money in the business to speed up the growth."

Seeing the FBL's Vision for the future of the family business in writing will open up an objective assessment by the FMEs of whether the Vision for the future of the company will meet the primary needs of the FMEs. Gaining the buy-in of all the

FMEs to the Company Vision Statement can have a profoundly positive impact on the success of the family business and on family relations. On the other hand, if an FME is unhappy or bitter about how the Company Vision Statement will affect him or her personally, it can be very harmful. Without a clear understanding of the Company Vision Statement, FMEs may be rowing their oars in a different direction than the FBL and/or from each other. Talk about counterproductive.

The Company Vision Statement should be discussed with, understood by, and supported by all FMEs. FMEs who don't understand, accept, and support the Company Vision Statement can be destructive and undermine the attitudes of management and practices of the business. It does not always happen on purpose, but sometimes counterproductive actions are made out of outright vindictiveness. The bottom line is that FMEs who cannot support the Company Vision Statement should find other employment.

Vision Essential 7. Compatibility of Co-FBLs' Personal Vision Statements

You know the old saying, when there are too many cooks in the kitchen. . . . A company with more than one FBL has a recipe for problems. When I refer to "co-FBLs" or "family partners" in this book, I am referring to situations in which the company has more than one person with an equal amount of control in running the business. This definition is not limited to legal partnership relationships but is instead intended to include co-FBL situations in which the company is a corporation or any other legal entity.

When there are co-FBLs who share control of a business, it is common for conflicts to exist between the partners' Personal Visions as they relate to the co-FBLs' dreams for the future of the family business. Most commonly, one co-FBL's Personal Vision for a desired long-term expectation of what the business will look like differs from the other co-FBL's Vision for the business. Sharing the written Personal Vision Statements as they relate to the co-FBLs' dreams for the future of the business typically reduces the tension arising from the differences in the co-FBLs' perspectives on the direction of the family business. When there are major differences between the Personal Vision Statements of family partners and those differences are known by the partners, it is more likely that the family partners can overcome the problem.

Resolving these differences starts with establishing an understanding of each other's dreams for the company. Then the family partners must explore ways in which the company can meet the dreams of all the partners. When conflicts are left unresolved, the company will underachieve and there will be a resounding negative impact upon family relationships.

In the Northwest, a coach was working with the eldest brother, Seth, who was a co-FBL with his two younger brothers. His father, who had founded the company, had passed away a few years earlier, and he had left all three brothers control of the ownership of the business. By the time Seth discussed his predicament with his coach, he and his brothers were no longer talking, and they ignored each other when they saw each other at work. This was a highly charged environment, and many employees felt as if they were walking on eggshells. "At this point, we speak to each other only when we have to," Seth told his coach.

The main problem was that the three brothers are very different in nature, and this was reflected not only in how they operated day to day but also in how they interacted with personnel. Most problematic, they had their own visions for the future. They had radically different notions about such things as the growth of the company and the amount of risk it should take on. They had completely different Visions for the company and different ideas on how to run the business and even on what their individual commitment to the business should be. Seth wanted to be very aggressive. His middle brother wanted to be conservative but steady, and the youngest brother wanted to take no chances. Seth also felt that his middle brother worked hard enough, but he was not totally dedicated to the business, and Seth couldn't figure out why this was. When it came to the youngest brother, Seth would whistle through his teeth and shake his head; he felt the youngest brother was not working out at all.

Seth's coach recommended that a good starting point would be for each of the brothers to write his Personal Vision Statement. Then the coach got them to share their Visions with each other. They were asked to share only those parts that related to the family business, which would include their desired long-term involvement with the company, what they felt their role within the company should be, what kind of money they wanted to take out of the business, and what desired growth they wanted for the company. They were not asked to share what they wanted to do with their free time, in nonbusiness activities.

Their Personal Visions Statements showed an incredibly high level of incompatibility. There was a tremendous amount of conflict between what they wanted for the business 10 years down the line and what they desired for their own individual commitment. Some major changes would have to be made for their father's desires for equal ownership and coleadership to succeed.

Not long after, the youngest brother sold his share to his older brothers, and he went off to start his own company. Unfortunately, the relationship with the youngest brother has yet to be repaired as there is still so much resentment. The two older brothers, now without the added pressure of the youngest brother, have redeveloped the closeness that they had as kids; they often have lunch together and get their families together.

When co-FBLs have trouble creating a Company Vision Statement that is mutually acceptable to all of them, negotiation among the co-FBLs typically ensues. Co-FBLs should put in writing their rationale for their long-term Vision of the company. Resistance from other co-FBLs to a mutually acceptable Company Vision Statement can often be overcome by presenting a well-reasoned case. If negotiating among the co-FBLs becomes necessary, each should be prepared to make a thorough and unemotional case. The focus should remain solely on the facts that support each side's positions. If, despite negotiations, the co-FBLs are still at an impasse, the use of a neutral and independent professional to mediate or facilitate a discussion between or among the co-FBLs relating to the Company Vision Statement should be considered. A third party often brings about a mutually agreeable statement because he or she has the ability to objectively ease the amount of emotional baggage brought to the table by the co-FBLs.

Conclusion

A Personal Vision Statement should clearly outline every essential aspect of the FBL's and FMEs' dreams for the future. There is no right or wrong dream for the future; we all have different dreams. Sharing written Personal Vision Statements is indispensable in getting all family members involved in the business working on the same page. It's extremely important for the success of the family business and family relationships.

Left unaddressed, nonalignment of Personal Visions tends to impact not only the results of the company but also the quality of family dynamics. It can dictate how effectively family members work and how well family members interact both inside and outside the work environment.

Sometimes FBLs will find their dreams are closely in line with their FMEs, but not every family business is so lucky. Personal Vision Statements include a wide range of family business and personal factors, and each person's dreams will be unique. FBLs must consider seriously each FME's dreams for the future to maintain the peace and the passion in the company.

FBLs and FMEs must be committed to discussing each others' Personal Vision Statements, including those critical factors in the statements that are in conflict between the FBLs' and FMEs' Visions. Sometimes this discussion brings about significant changes to someone's Personal Vision Statement. Remaining ignorant of or ignoring these conflicts will only open the gates to bigger problems down the road.

Now that you understand the importance of creating and sharing written Personal Vision Statements and the importance of creating a minimum level of compatibility between these dreams, you are ready for the second element in the formula, which is developing a policy for hiring and firing FMEs.

Checklist for Creating and Sharing Personal Vision Statements

Before we move to Chapter 2 on the second element—Hiring and Firing Family Members—let's recap some of the factors that should be considered when creating and sharing written Personal Vision Statements:

• Make sure that your Personal Vision Statement reflects your long-range dreams.
• Ask yourself what family relationships in your personal life are important to your happiness.
• Determine what balance must exist between your personal and work lives to bring you happiness.
• Figure out what emotional rewards you hope to gain from work.

- Understand what types of work involvements (roles) will give you the most pleasure.
- If you are an FBL, you should be very clear as to your dreams for retirement, succession, anointment, and transitioning of the business ownership.
- Create a Personal Vision that is realistic and achievable.
- Determine and clearly mark the parts of your written Personal Vision Statement that make up your Pocket Vision—that is, those items you choose not to share.
- If you are an FBL, you should share the business-related factors in your Personal Vision Statement with your FMEs.
- If you are an FME, you must share the business-related factors in your Personal Vision Statements with the FBL.
- Whether an FBL or an FME, you must work to resolve conflicts between your Personal Vision Statements.
- If you are an FBL, your Personal Vision Statement must include your dreams for the family business, and those Visions will in turn be incorporated into the written Company Vision Statement for the family business. The Company Vision Statement must be compatible with the FBL's Personal Vision Statement.
- If you are an FBL, your draft of the Company Vision Statement must be discussed with all of the FMEs and take their dreams into consideration.

CHAPTER 2

THE SECOND ELEMENT
Hiring and Firing Family-Member Employees

The expression "It's just business—nothing personal" does not apply to family businesses' hiring practices. It's family so it's personal. Hiring and firing practices in nonfamily businesses typically reflect an objective hiring philosophy that aims toward the best interests of the business. It is usually quite different when it comes to the hiring and firing of family members in family businesses. According to a research survey by Laird Norton Tyee, which is the oldest and largest privately held wealth management company in the Pacific Northwest, most family-owned businesses lack any qualification requirements for family members to become employees. Family-owned businesses tend to gear hiring/firing philosophy to the best interest of the family as viewed by the FBL rather than the best interest of the business.

Even new-hire application processes tend to be different for family businesses. Family members with dreams of joining the family business usually are not required to go through a formal application process. Often, the process of bringing on family members starts years before they are ready for employment. It can start informally with a young family member expressing at the dinner table his or her interest in someday joining the family business. Then at some time in the future, there is a family conversation on whether the young member is ready.

Family relationship problems often stem from bad hiring decisions relating to family members. The greater the number of FMEs in the business, the more likely there will be new issues and problems within the family unit and/or with non-FMEs. To lessen the chances of hiring a new FME who creates a nightmare for the FBL and the family business and the chances of the family business having to deal with the issue of dismissing an FME, there need to be clear hiring/firing policies in place including those discussed in the first section of this chapter:

1. Family-member-employee eligibility
2. Evaluation of potential new family-member hires
3. Dismissal of FMEs

I recommend that you cover these factors in a written policy for the hiring and firing of FMEs, which can be handed out and discussed before any commitment is made to a family member to become a new FME. Putting it in writing will help to avoid hard feelings on the part of a family member who wants to become an FME but does not meet the qualifications of the written policy. Having the written policy will help to prevent potential hard feelings and other problems stemming from hiring and firing decisions before they have a chance to occur. But my experience has been that it is easier to get FBLs to think about these factors and create guidelines in their minds than it is to get them to put the policies in writing.

The second section of this chapter is aimed at those family members who are considering whether or not to join the family business. It shows such family members how to go into this important decision with their eyes open, considering the nature of the FBL and the other FMEs already in the business. It will help prospective family members identify key areas such as expectations of FME work ethics and the FME long-term role and financial future, which are too often ignored until it is too late.

Section 1. Hiring/Firing Policies

Factor 1. Family-Member-Employee Eligibility

Before determining your policy about family-member eligibility to be employed by the family business, as an FBL, ask yourself what it is you hope to achieve by bringing family members into the business. Is it a matter of wanting to work with those you can trust? Is it a succession issue? If succession is a major reason for your bringing a family member into the business, is it because you desire to create a legacy? Or is it simply that you want to give an employment opportunity with income support to family members who you feel need this help?

Most eligibility decisions involving the hiring of family members are not made because they satisfy business goals but rather because they satisfy some emotional or psychological desire on the part of the FBL. The motivations behind these FME hiring decisions are usually found in the long-range personal dreams of the FBL for the FBL's business and family. Many FBLs dream of a future that includes family members working in the family business and the FBL seeing them blossom into whatever they have the capacity to become. Many want to see their children or the spouses of their children join the family business and even eventually take over its leadership. These FBLs enjoy keeping their families tightly knit, and when this happens, it gives them great happiness and personal satisfaction. These factors are often expressed in the FBL's Personal Vision Statements. For example, I had a desire to ultimately have the role of mentor of one of my family members. This desire was a major factor in my bringing Jason into TAB.

All these motivational areas affect whether or not an FBL elects to make family members eligible for hiring and, if so, with what requirements. FBLs need self-awareness in terms of their motivations behind hiring family members before they make any decisions regarding whether family members are eligible for employment.

There are six Eligibility Questions that you, the FBL, need to answer to assist you in making decisions regarding family-member eligibility. How you answer the following six Eligibility Questions can make all the difference in the world when it comes to achieving good family relationships:

1. Should I employ *any* family member?
2. Which family members qualify as potential FMEs?
3. What, if any, outside employment experience is required?
4. What, if any, is the required minimum age?
5. What, if any, is the minimum requirement for formal education?
6. What, if any, policy should govern reemploying a family member after he or she has quit the family business?

Eligibility Question 1. Should I Employ Any *Family Member?*

Many FBLs want as many family-member employees in their business as possible. One of the best things about being a business owner is being able to choose the people you work with. The type of people we employ, because we spend many hours working with them, will greatly affect our work enjoyment level. If your dream is to have a relative join the business, you need to be mindful that you will be spending many, many hours with the person you are bringing into the business. If this works right, it can bring about a lot of joy.

A friend of mine, whom I respect enormously, has very strong feelings about not wanting his children, or any other family member, working in his physical training business, even though three of his children have expressed an interest in working in the business. As he has stated, "Here is my simple policy on my family working for me: No family members will be employed in my business, period." He does not want to deal with the problems or challenges associated with FMEs. He learned about the problems that can occur when he was in his twenties and was employed by his father's family business. The FMEs of his father's company were always at each other's throats. This negative experience was very important in his decision to not allow family members to be eligible to work for him.

Often there is a love/hate relationship that FBLs have with the experience of having FMEs. There are times when it is wonderful. But there may be times when all sorts of things happen that may have negative family relationship results and the FBL wonders if having FMEs is worth it. Each FBL has to answer this question for his or her own business. Because the challenges of employing family members can be intense, it's not surprising that many business owners have policies against hiring family members. Many owners of businesses have decided that under *no* circumstances will they hire family members. They recognize that when you add a family member to the business equation, you bring in a new set of family dynamics and family history to business decisions, and they don't want this to happen.

Eligibility Question 2. Which Family Members Qualify as Potential FMEs?

If the owner of a business wants the business to become a family business, it does not necessarily mean that he or she is open to employing all immediate or even nonimmediate family members. Is eligibility limited to immediate family, or should in-laws or even distant cousins be eligible? The question of which family members are eligible should be reflected in the written policy.

As I have mentioned before, my son-in-law is president of TAB. My daughters work in other companies that are part of our family businesses. I do not want any family members, other than Jason and my grandchildren, to work at TAB in long-term career positions. The policy is restrictive relating to employing other family members such as nephews and nieces because I do not want to deal with hard feelings about their pay level or advancements. Consequently, our TAB policy prohibits nonimmediate family members, such as nephews and nieces, from long-term career jobs at TAB. We have and will continue allow nonimmediate family members to be employed in temporary (summer) positions or intern capacities and fill available entry-level positions for up to one year, if they have the ability and desire to help TAB. But they are not eligible for long-term track positions. The purpose of this policy is to help qualified nephews and nieces get needed short-term work experience, which can help them launch their careers in many other places.

Eligibility Question 3. What, If Any, Outside Employment Experience Is Required?

According to the *Family to Family: Laird Norton Tyee Family Business Survey 2007*, nearly 64 percent of family businesses do not require family members entering the business to have the related experience or qualifications needed to be successful in the family business. One main reason for this is that FBLs of very small businesses may desperately need the help of a child in the business. The FBLs of these businesses may not be able to wait for children to get experience by working outside of the family business for several years. Too often in these situations, the new FMEs join the family businesses before building confidence from succeeding outside the family business womb. One FBL told me he does not care if family members choose to travel after high school or college instead of achieving substantive work experience on the outside. He says, "As long as they are a minimum age, I can find some kind of job for them."

In contrast, with most successful family businesses, it's common practice to require applicants who are family members to have worked in the outside business community for some period (three to five years is most common) before getting a full-time career position with the family business. Typically, FBLs have a policy that family members must have experience at an outside company before being hired for long-term positions inside the family business. (These policies, however, usually do allow family members to work at the family business in the summer or part-time during formal schooling years.) Requiring potential FMEs to gain outside business experience before joining the family business allows them to learn how other organizations are run; it provides them with a reference point as to how the business world runs outside of the family business.

When family members are required to get work experience outside the family business, they can often bring back to the family business new ideas, knowledge, and approaches. One of the best places to gain these advantages is with a competitor in another part of the country. John Dini, a TAB facilitator-coach in San Antonio, told me about an FBL who runs a $50 million plus family business and maintains relationships with other family-owned businesses around the country. He sends his family members who are prospective FMEs to work for them.

Often, outside experience allows family members to gain knowledge and experience in many areas that may not be available through the family business. For a few years after getting my law degree, I worked for a multi-billion-dollar publicly owned company. I learned ideas, processes, and management methods in a way that I would not have been exposed to in a small family business.

One FBL of a construction company cherry-picks the most qualified prospective FMEs based on whom he sees as having achieved the most during the five years he requires that FMEs have worked in other companies. Those that cannot meet his stiff "prove you can succeed elsewhere" requirements do not get offers to work in the family business. He believes his system reduces resentment and accusations of nepotism.

Some family businesses require that family members work in a management-level position for an outside company before being considered for full-time management within the family business. This forces the family member to prove his or her ability to do well outside the family business in other circumstances. When given a promotion by a nonfamily business, family members know they can do it on their own without being dependent on the family business. This instills a sense of self-worth and confidence that may not be gleaned working in the family business.

Working for an outside business gives potential FMEs a much better perspective on whether they want to join the family business. It gives them a chance to get away from the family and determine, with less family pressure, what they want to do with their lives. If and when they join the family business, they will not be doing it because they feel that they can't make it anywhere else. Obtaining outside management experience also gives the rest of the family, and the non-FMEs of the business, more confidence that the FME has earned his or her spurs and is not being employed by the family business just because of nepotism.

This outside experience can also help potential FMEs appreciate the benefits of working in a family business. As one son, who spent several years working outside his family's business, shared with me, "I was finally able to appreciate how good I would have it when I started working at the family business!"

Jason's previous work experience was an important factor in my decision to bring him into TAB. He had already demonstrated confidence in his management ability through various management roles in accounting, finance, and operations in New York and California. He had served for years in management positions with large staffs and budgets. He also had an accounting career at Ernst & Young after he graduated from college, and, while this was not a requirement for employment, I knew that his experience in this area could only help TAB. There was a lot of transference from Jason's experience managing and being responsible for budgets involving several millions of dollars to the skills needed for TAB. If one day potential FMEs want long-term careers with one of my family businesses, they will need a minimum of three years' experience working for a firm other than one of the family businesses.

Requiring the outside experience may result in losing a potentially great FME who decides he or she likes working for another firm. John Dini related to me a story about a family business with a policy requiring at least five years' experience working at an outside business before joining the family business full-time. The business owner has a very bright nephew whom he saw as a potential successor. This potential successor gained employment in a related line of business as required by the FBL's policy. The nephew was tremendously successful in the career he established outside the family business. When the five years had passed by, the uncle urged the nephew to take a close look at the benefits of working for the family business before settling down to work elsewhere, but the nephew had found working for the outside business so attractive that he declined the offer to work for his uncle. Sometimes you lose the gamble!

Eligibility Question 4. What, If Any, Is the Required Minimum Age?

Most family businesses that have made it past the Founder's Stage do have a clear minimum age requirement for a family member to be considered for full-time career-level employment. Many in the other stages of family businesses have minimum age requirements as well. One metal fabricator will not bring in any FMEs under the age of 25 other than between semesters at school. She believes her family members are more likely to be settled down by 25 and that they are also more likely to appreciate the benefits of working for the family business. Whatever policy the FBL decides upon regarding the minimum age for potential family hires should be incorporated into the written hiring policy.

Eligibility Question 5. What, If Any, Is the Minimum Requirement for Formal Education?

I believe education requirements should not be applied in a blanket manner but instead should be viewed in a job-specific manner. For example, a potential hire for a telemarketing position may need only a high school degree. One family service business requires any family member interested in joining the company to first obtain a college degree in a business-related area. Other family-owned businesses specify that the candidate has to reach a certain minimum degree level, such as an undergraduate degree, without requiring that the degree be in a specific field of study.

Eligibility Question 6. What, If Any, Policy Should Govern Reemploying a Family Member after He or She Has Quit the Family Business?

It's not uncommon for FMEs, for any of a variety of reasons, to quit the family business to try other work opportunities or even start their own new businesses. Many family businesses have in place a policy that if the request for reemployment does not take place within a stated time, the opportunity for reemployment is closed. Ideally, family members should understand these rules before they become FMEs.

I believe that the eligibility for reentry after departure is best handled on a case-by-case basis. Rehiring an FME who can ultimately play a major role in the family business may be addressed differently from a situation in which an FME is not likely to be able to do so.

Factor 2. Evaluation of Potential New Family-Member Hires

One of the challenges FBLs face when looking at potential new FMEs is identifying the traits and capabilities that those family members actually have versus what the FBL, looking through his or her rose-colored glasses, wants them to have. The process of doing an objective evaluation of a prospective FME takes a lot of time but only a small amount of money. You wouldn't buy a house or make a real estate investment without first having the property inspected. And yet most FBLs do not take much time getting objective evaluations of the family members they are considering hiring.

Ideally, each decision on whether to hire a family member should be viewed in light of whether that family member is likely to be a valuable employee with great company spirit. But the reality is that many FBLs hire family members who would not otherwise be the ideal candidates for the jobs. Family-member employees come in all types, shapes, and sizes, and they do not need to have the potential to be a great leader in order to bring value to a family business. With some FMEs, all you will ask for is that they always give 100 percent because you do not believe a substantial position for them within the company is in the cards. In such cases, it is important that these FMEs know the limitations you see for their futures in the family business so that they do not feel entitled to greater positions just because they are family members. If FMEs are promoted to positions for which they are not qualified, this situation can cause a lot of internal unhappiness among other more qualified nonfamily employees.

As I mentioned earlier, family members typically don't go through a formal application process. Instead, the ball often gets rolling by a senior family member asking the family member if there is an interest in joining the family business, or the family member expresses his or her interest to the FBL or some other senior family member. In most cases, a decision is made by the

FBL without the level of evaluation that would be required with a nonfamily member. However, because of the family dynamics involved, an even higher level of evaluation than that used for non-FMEs should be conducted on the prospective FME.

Evaluation Area 1. Written Personal SWOT Statements

One effective tool for evaluating a prospective FME is requiring him or her to create his or her written Personal SWOT Statements. SWOT is an acronym for "Strengths, Weaknesses, Opportunities, and Threats." The FBL should review the FME's written SWOT Statements. Then a discussion of these SWOT Statements should be scheduled for the FBL and the potential new FME.

Reviewing the SWOT Statements opens up the door for a discussion of the differences in how things within the business are perceived. This often results in the FME revising or changing altogether his or her SWOT Statements. There should be mutual agreement between the FBL and the potential FME as to the content of the SWOT Statements before any decision is finalized for the future employment of the family member in the family business. These SWOT Statements for each potential new family-member hire provide great insight into the area of responsibility, if any, within which the family member will best perform in the business. Giving a family member responsibility in a business area that is outside of his or her strengths in aptitude and personality will lead only to frustration and likely failure.

During the time that Jason and I were discussing his joining TAB, Jason agreed that as part of his evaluation as a potential new employee, he would complete and share with me his written Personal SWOT Statements. Jason has been kind enough to share his 2001 SWOT Statements with you, which you can find in the Appendix as Exhibit A.

The evaluation of a prospective family member requires much more than reviewing his or her written Personal SWOT Statements. The question that needs to be answered is whether the prospect has the needed mental aptitude for the job.

David's son Byron had been working in the family company for a year. "What am I going to do? I think I made a big mistake bringing Byron on. Even when I hired him I wasn't sure he was the right person for the role." David dropped his head into his hands. "I needed executive material; I don't think Byron has it. He doesn't think things through." It was easy to see that this was causing David a great deal of heartache. "I couldn't discuss it with my wife; she wouldn't hear me. She automatically defended Byron, said I was being too hard on him." David explained how things had recently come to a head when one of the firm's top three customers stopped doing business with the company because of Byron. It was recommended to David that he have his son complete a "G test." The G test is a general intelligence test. The results showed that Byron might not have the aptitude for the position he had already been placed in. David had to fire Byron, and the repercussions of that action hit very hard at home. David said that he wished he had never brought his son into the business.

Evaluation Area 2. General Intelligence Tests

I asked Jason if he felt comfortable taking an intelligence test (the Wonderlic G test), and he said he did. The results of Jason's test reinforced my belief that he has the needed thinking ability to lead TAB.

Many successful family businesses have been harmed, or even destroyed, by family members' being hired for key positions for which they did not have the ability to handle the responsibilities. Recognizing that a family member lacks the right skills for the family business before employing him or her prevents major trouble down the road.

Evaluation Area 3. Behavior Surveys

The third evaluation area involves gaining an understanding of the natural personality or behavior of the family member. Giving a family-member candidate a personality or behavioral survey can be done in minutes. The results of this simple survey will show the natural behavior of the family member, which will help you understand what the probable behavior patterns of that person will be in the family business. Surveys based on the DISC assessment model that give a printed analysis can be administered quickly and inexpensively using any one of the many computerized surveying programs currently available. The acronym DISC represents Dominance, Influence (originally called Inducement), Steadiness, and Conscientiousness (originally called Compliance). See the Glossary for a more detailed description of the acronym's meaning.

Prior to starting work at TAB, Jason completed a behavioral survey that gave me a better understanding of his basic nature. Jason's DISC behavior survey showed that he was high in Dominance (D) and Influence (I). Since I also have a high D and I, we had to discuss if we would feel comfortable and get along well in the business despite these shared personality traits.

One FBL who requires all non-FMEs to complete DISC types of surveys told me that he didn't need to have his son complete the survey because he already understood his personality. Months later, after his son had started working for the company, the FBL admitted he had greatly misread his son's controlling nature and wished he had gone through the time to give him the testing. Every potential hire, including those who are family members, should be required to complete a behavioral survey.

The closer you match people's jobs to their natural behaviors, the less the likelihood of stress or burnout in the job. As a relative, you may think that you know the drive level of the FMEs, but you may not be very objective in making this assumption. One reason why Second Reign Stage businesses so frequently destroy formerly successful family businesses is the successors lack the ability or drive to maintain that success. Furthermore, the likelihood of your interacting in a more positive way with FMEs will also be greatly improved if you know and accept the FME's basic behavioral nature.

You may think your child is a lot like you, but when it comes to the family business world, "It's not often that the apple falls close to the tree" would be a more appropriate saying than the traditional "The apple doesn't fall far from the tree."

Factor 3. Dismissal of FMEs

What a conundrum it is when you have to let a family member go from the family business! As every FBL knows, a good working relationship with FMEs can bring a great amount of happiness to life, whereas having to fire an FME can bring about pure misery. As you can imagine, a difficult situation with an FME is often fraught with challenges. You can count on the fact that FME firing decisions will impact the FBL's relationships with relatives inside and, in many cases, outside the business. Family events such as Thanksgiving dinner are far more enjoyable if you don't have to sit across from a family member you have fired.

There is the possibility that even if you have taken all the right steps in evaluating a family member before hiring him or her, the person may still be intolerable and unacceptable as an employee. Think long and hard before offering a position to any marginal family-member-employee candidate. Bottom line: don't hire people if you can't fire them.

Bill Vrettos, a TAB facilitator-coach in Grand Junction, Colorado, feels not holding family employees accountable is one of the most common reasons for the failure of family businesses. Bill says, "Every family member in the business needs to know he or she can be fired. Most FBLs deal with family employees as relatives and not as employees. So FBLs must make their expectations clear and be sure that FMEs know what is unacceptable in their performance and know that they will be discharged if their performance continues to be unacceptable." The long-term survival and success of the family business are based on the fact that it is a "team" business—that is, it is based on employees' contributions to the total results, not on employees' getting to keep their place on the team.

Before hiring an FME, it should be clear that one of the conditions for employment is that tenure and family relationship do not guarantee advancement, just opportunity. If the FME does not meet expectations, he or she will be fired. Communicated properly, this can be understood up front without creating an uncomfortable situation in which the FBL is loathe to sit across from the former FME at Thanksgiving dinner.

Even when FMEs are on the payroll primarily for the sake of collecting a paycheck, they are expected to get some level of results. To increase the likelihood of this happening, performance evaluations need to be conducted on a regular basis. New FMEs should be told about the performance evaluations and how frequently they will be made. It should be clear before hiring that after a specific review date, it may be necessary to part ways in the family business if the expected results have not been achieved. In effect, the family member starts on a probationary basis with a clearly established point at which the position is to be made permanent or terminated.

Before Jason was hired, I told him that we should both look at his move to join TAB as a one-year commitment. We agreed that at the end of the year, if either of us thought he was not able to do the job or that working together was hurting our family relationship, Jason would move on to something outside TAB. Some time after Jason came to TAB, he told me that the agreement to review after one year took the pressure off of him and helped him make the decision to join TAB. He knew that after one year, we would take a look and determine it if was a good fit for him to be with the company.

Many FBLs are often reluctant to fire FMEs because of concern over family repercussions. Even if it is clear that a family member is not performing as needed for a position, it may cause a family relations mess when you fire him or her. The reality is that some relatives might not see it your way no matter how much the FME deserves to be fired. Needless to say, this can put a chill on family gatherings.

When I reflect on how hard it is for some people to fire a relative, I think of the following story related by Carol Crawford, a TAB facilitator-coach in Grand Rapids, Michigan. During a time of success for the business, against her better judgment, the FBL of a third-generation family business acquiesced to family pressure: she hired a brother as a potential successor. The FBL decided to conduct only verbal discussions with her brother regarding the expectations and requirements for employment. Unfortunately, her brother felt that, as the boss's sibling, he was not required to do boring work, hard work, or much work at all. In attempts to correct the situation, the FBL engaged an outside coach and even enrolled her brother in a management class, but neither step achieved positive results. To avoid further family negative discourse, the FBL ultimately sold the family business rather than fire her brother.

Larry Amon, a TAB facilitator-coach in Naples, Florida, told me he hired all three of his children to work for his company partnership. His partner's wife and daughter also worked for the company. He had to fire one of his children. Larry said, "It was so hard to do because I had no clear guidelines for firing in place when I hired my children." You can avoid much of the problems that Larry faced if before hiring your new family-member employee, your grounds for dismissal are presented in writing and formerly acknowledged by the family member. One family business states in its written hiring/firing policy, "Family members employed in the business must conform to the highest level of confidentiality since they may have access to information that cannot be revealed to nonfamily employees. If a confidentiality breach takes place, it will be grounds for dismissal."

If you do have to fire a relative, it's usually money well spent for the family business to engage and pay for an outplacement firm to help the relative find a new job. It will give the FME less fear about the probationary period, and it will also create a more positive atmosphere within your family.

Section 2. Considering the Pros and Cons before Saying Yes to Becoming an FME

Peter shared the following story: "I was just out of college armed with a degree in journalism, and I could not wait to get out and work overseas in journalism. Except my dad, who founded the family firm, well, he had other ideas for me. He couldn't see it any other way than for me to one day run his company—which I'm still doing. There was a lot of pressure to join the family company from my mom too. There isn't a day that goes by that I am not wishing I were doing something else, that I had followed my dreams. Thirty years later, and I'm still regretting that I gave in. I'm not angry with my dad; he did what he knew, and he wanted to provide me with the best he could. It's just that most days, I *dread* going into the office." Peter's story should be considered before you let pressure from a family member sway you to join the family business.

If you are a family member considering employment at the family business, recognize the benefits, but don't ignore the potential liabilities and obligations involved in working in the family business. "Will working for the family business be worth it, let alone something I can tolerate?" Try to be honest with yourself about the pros and cons of working for the family business. Understand the special challenges that you may be facing in your particular family business with your particular FBL before committing to being hired. Before joining the family business as a family member, you need to do some soul searching about whether it will be the right situation for you. Ask yourself, "Is this the situation that will be best for me in the long term?" The following six factors will help you find the needed answers.

Factor 1. Motivation to Join the Family Business

When I first discussed with Jason my thoughts about the opportunity for him at TAB, he told me that he did not know if he was interested in becoming employed by TAB. At the time, Jason was working in a high-ranking managerial position in the St. Regis Hotel in Aspen, Colorado, which required working evenings, weekends, and holidays. He laughed and said, "I'm hesitating here . . . because I'm not sure how I feel about working for my father-in-law, and right now my priority is to have a happy marriage. I'm not so sure about how working for her father might affect that." We both decided to leave the subject alone for a while.

Not long after these discussions began, Lynette, his wife and my daughter, became pregnant with their first child. He wanted to be very much involved in his children's activities, and he knew it would be impossible working in his then current position to be the kind of involved father that he wanted to be. He and Lynette decided it would be worth exploring the opportunity to join TAB, and Jason told me that he wanted to reopen our discussions about the TAB opportunity. We subsequently met to look more closely at the possibility of his joining TAB. Jason and I talked about what we both would need to address to ensure that working together would not hurt Jason and Lynette's marriage. Then I asked him what interested him most about the TAB opportunity.

He answered, "I know TAB is going to give me the opportunity to be with my family; it'll allow me to be financially independent and do something where I can grow with the job."

Next, we discussed my dreams for the future of TAB. I had to be comfortable that he could easily get behind my vision for TAB in a very dedicated manner. Jason smiled and said, "I really think working for TAB will give me the chance to have positive, life-changing impact on many people, not just my family. That would make me feel amazing to help people change their lives for the better." I left the meeting with Jason convinced that he was highly motivated to join TAB.

It's important for the FBL to know if the potential family-member hire is truly motivated to become a new employee of the family business, and if so, why. This is why the potential FME should ask himself or herself the following questions:

- Why do I want to join the business?
- What are my goals and objectives in the company?
- What do I think I can bring to the family business?
- What can the family business bring to me?

Factor 2. The FBL

Is your FBL a tyrant or bully? If this is the case, you might want to find work elsewhere—a position with the family firm is not worth receiving abuse. When the topic of working for an abusive FBL comes up, I think of Tom's story: Tom was married to a woman whose father, Garth, owned a family manufacturing business. The first day Tom started working for Garth, Tom knew that Garth's employees were often the target of Garth's wrath. Garth yelled and belittled his employees and, in general, terrorized them. The employees stayed with Garth only because he paid well. Tom told his coach that "it wasn't long after I started working for him that *I* became his verbal punching bag!" When his coach asked Tom why he stayed in the business, he answered flatly, "So that my wife and I can maintain our lifestyle." The response of his coach was to ask, "Is it worth it?" Surprisingly, the answer was, "I guess so."

If the FBL seems to be on an emotional roller coaster, displays paranoia, or seems at times to have irrational behaviors outside the business, these behaviors may be worse in the business because business pressure often brings out the worst in people. The potential for unhappiness working for this type of FBL is high. Ralph is miserable working for his father, the FBL of a very successful family retail chain. Before Ralph joined the company, Ralph knew his father's moods would swing dramatically, and sometimes this resulted in his becoming extremely aggressive. He knew his father was highly mistrustful of others, particularly those who challenged his opinions. After joining the business, Ralph realized his dad was much worse at work. At times, Ralph felt his father could become downright irrational, even paranoid. "He goes on and on about how this employee's going to stab him in the back, how that one can't be trusted at all. I don't know what I was thinking . . . that somehow he would act differently if I came on board? Yeah, I guess I figured that. I was pretty damned naive."

Even if these types of behaviors are not present in social family situations, you should look, before joining the family business, at how the FBL operates at work. With many FBLs, it's as if they are two different people. Sally's mom, Jenny, was a Dr. Jekyll and Ms. Hyde. Jenny was very sensitive to her family's needs at home. Sally figured that her mom's way of interacting at work would be the same way they interacted when they were at home. When Sally started working for the family business, however, she found that Jenny was a tyrant to her employees. Jenny seemed totally incapable of seeing her employees as *real* people with *real* needs. Sally discovered that Jenny wouldn't listen to any of her employees, and she answered in a vicious voice when her orders were questioned. "Good Lord, it was worse than I expected. The first time my mom was so hostile to me at work, I was shocked. She yelled at me from down the hallway—where all of the other employees could hear her!" Sally then recounted, "I looked my mom straight in the eye, and I told her, 'The next time you treat me like that again, I am out of here!' She started up with me again in the same yelling way just a few days later, and I packed up my things and walked out." Sally and her mom are still estranged. How often I've heard FMEs complain of the "I love you at home, but as soon as we step into the office, this different person comes into the business relationship" scenario.

Is the FBL the type who will listen to your ideas and give them reasonable consideration? Many people are not happy working in an environment in which their ideas are not given reasonable consideration. Is your FBL the type who does not encourage and use ideas from others? "I can't get Dad to take my ideas seriously" is a frequent complaint of new FMEs. How open the FBL will be to hearing new ideas offered by the potential new FME is foreshadowed by how the FBL currently operates at work with other employees. Are problems solved by a team approach at the business or unilaterally by the FBL?

If the business already has other FMEs, you should consider asking the FMEs if they feel they are appreciated and rewarded for their accomplishments and rewarded by the FBL. Ask these FMEs, "Are the current FMEs' feelings of hurt or anger dealt with fairly and compassionately by the FBL?" How much trust is there and how strong are the lines of communication between the FMEs and the FBL?

Factor 3. The Other FMEs

If there are other FMEs in the business, ask yourself how you will fit in at work with the other FMEs and what you may be getting into if you join the business. Family tensions can increase and relationships with other family members already employed in the business can change when another relative starts working with the company. Normal sibling or cousin rivalry can be hyperaccentuated because of the dynamics of the family business. Even a congenial sibling or cousin relationship can be difficult to maintain under the strain of the family workplace.

Ask yourself the kind of questions that will bring issues to the surface such as, What are the current dynamics among the FMEs? Is winning individual battles more important to one or more of the other FMEs than keeping peace in the family? Is there a tendency for the FMEs currently in the business to shift blame to someone else? How much trust is there, and how strong are the lines of communication between you and the other family members active in the business?

Factor 4. Life Balance and Work Role

Most FBLs expect FMEs to have the highest standards of conduct and the best work ethic in the company so as to be an effective model for the rest of the company. They believe that since FMEs set the tone for non-FMEs, they have to be good examples, not excuses for bad behavior. But what does this mean to you as far as specifics for work hours and days at work? Will you be expected to become a workaholic? These are things that need to be discussed with your FBL, particularly if the FBL has an extremely high work ethic and expects the same from you in the business.

After getting the answer from the FBL, ask yourself if the expectations of working hours for the business will lead you to good long-term relationships with your family in which conflicts are kept to a minimum. If having a different life balance is important to you but is not what the FBL has in mind for you, express your desire to have a more balanced life, and try to reach an understanding that is based on each of you compromising.

Marcus, an FBL, was having some serious physical challenges that made running the business difficult. He asked his sister,

Danielle, to move back to their home city and help him with the family business. Danielle was a high-level executive at a public company, and she had not worked in the family business since she was in her early twenties, a few decades ago. She asked Marcus to define the specific role and responsibilities he wanted for her, and he responded that he wasn't sure. During the time they spent working on a job description, it became apparent that the ideas that Marcus had relating to what the business had to offer Danielle did not match what interested her.

Ask for a written job description for your first position before agreeing to start with the family business. You may not have full knowledge of what you are getting yourself into, in which case, the job description would help you. Job descriptions often bring to the surface responsibilities and expectations that if not mentioned at the outset, would later be surprises. Discuss with the FBL your projected short- and long-term roles in the business, including the type of work experience within the company you will be getting before moving on to your eventual role. What does the FBL see as your eventual role if things work out well? This will help you determine if there is a match with your motivation for joining the business. Failure to discuss and clarify short- and long-term roles at the time of hiring is a formula for creating future feelings on your part of being misled. You may decide not to join the family business if the short- and long-term roles do not match your expectations of tenure.

In most family businesses, one of the rewards for FMEs is the knowledge that when they compete with non-FMEs of equal skill and attitude, they will get the promotion. In some businesses the reality is that they will get it even if the non-FME is a better candidate. Ask your FBL to discuss his or her philosophy on this subject. You need to know what expectations of performance level will be needed for you to move into the future role and what amount of time is expected for you to work in other areas of the family business before a promotion can occur.

Factor 5. The Finances of the Business

Before committing to joining the company, it is important to also clear up any misunderstandings or misperceptions about the finances of the company. It is surprising how many people join family businesses in key positions without asking the FBL to share financial statements.

If the position you are considering is at a management level, ask to see the company's recent balance sheet and P&L statements. This is particularly important if you will have to leave an executive position to join the family business. Don't assume the family business is in a strong enough financial position to handle your compensation and provide for your financial growth. Be very realistic about whether the current size of the business can handle the added cost of your proposed starting compensation and the range of compensation for future roles without negatively impacting on the family business or other FMEs. A review of the financial information of the company has a way of bringing these types of things to the front.

Factor 6. The Bias of the Non-FMEs against Nepotism

Make your decision with an understanding that it is very common for non-FMEs and customers involved with the business to look for signs of incompetence in new FMEs because many people have a bias against nepotism. You have to be up to handling this pressure and know, in advance of starting employment, that a major slip-up will cause those inside and outside the business to judge harshly, to a disproportionate degree, your capabilities in the business. There is likely to be resentment from them; so you must be prepared to confidently, but humbly, show your moxie.

Jason and I had many discussions about the opportunities and challenges that went along with a son-in-law's coming into a family-owned business. I pointed out that most of the employees of TAB, as well as most of our facilitator-coaches, would likely view his being hired as pure nepotism and resent his joining TAB. I told him that "most of the employees will believe you were hired solely because you're married to my daughter. They will probably hold this against you at first and will look for, and maybe even hope for, you to fail." He was prepared for the resentment. It was there. He faced it and overcame it.

Conclusion

Each FBL has his or her own set of relationships with others in the family, and each relationship has a unique set of dynamics. When family members become employees of the business, it becomes a new journey for the family, and everyone in the family enters into this journey. Even under the best circumstances, having family members in the business creates pressures that you would not have with nonfamily members. It's very hard to leave the family relationship at the door when you come to the business in the morning. You should ask yourself, "Will hiring family members be best for the business and my relations with my immediate family and our relatives in the long run?" If the answer to that question is yes, then you need to create a written policy for hiring and firing of FMEs.

Most FBLs know years in advance of the interest of family members in joining the business. Do not consciously or sub-consciously try to influence those family members not interested in becoming employees to change their minds because it may be viewed by those family members as your putting unfair pressure on them. This is not to say that you shouldn't try to encourage your family members to be interested if you want them to join the business. Jason and I have been talking about our family businesses—sharing stories and positive experiences—with my grandchildren from the time that they were very young. You could even say there is a subtle grooming process going on for the grandchildren's eventual entry into one of the family businesses. It would be exciting for me if one or more of my grandchildren would like to pursue careers at TAB. If that is the case, they will have to satisfy certain requirements that are discussed in this chapter.

Checklist for Hiring and Firing FMEs

- Every family business needs a clear, written policy for hiring and firing FMEs.
- Family members must consider all the unique challenges presented by the family dynamics before agreeing to take a position.
- Evaluation of a potential new family-member hire must be made to determine his or her qualifications. SWOT Statements, general intelligence tests, and DISC Profiles are basic tools for determination.
- The terms for dismissal must be presented in writing to family members considering employment.
- The motivation behind a family member's desire to join the family business must be determined to make sure it is in sync with the FBL's expectations.
- The company's or FBL's expectations for employees' work ethics must be made clear and be agreed upon by potential family-member employees before hiring decisions are made.
- Family-member employees must be fully aware of their potential long-term roles and financial future in the company, including any limitations that may prevent them from achieving those ends.

CHAPTER 3

THE THIRD ELEMENT
Compensating Family-Member Employees

During a midmeeting break at one of my TAB board meetings, five of my members, all FBLs, remained seated at the board table. The topic of discussion was, "Of all the issues you deal with as an FBL, which would you consider to be the most difficult and emotionally charged?" The members looked at each other knowingly and, almost simultaneously, said, "Compensation!" One member added with a wry chuckle, "Without a doubt, compensation is what gave me the most anxiety when my daughter joined the business. And then—oh boy—it became even more complex when my son started working with us."

The compensation policy for FMEs does not have to be, and often is not, a policy that leads to maximizing the company's bottom-line profits. The variables surrounding compensation of family members are quite complex and viewed more subjectively than compensation of non-FMEs. The topic is potentially fraught with conflict and underlying bitterness. My objective in this chapter is to point out some of the most common reasons for compensation unhappiness among FMEs and show you how to avoid these problems.

Reason 1. Equal Pay FME Compensation Policy

During a TAB board meeting on one hot July day, a member explained how salaries for his family business were about to go up by $60,000 per year because his granddaughter would be attending a highly prestigious private middle school. His fellow board members shot him confused looks that communicated what they were thinking: "*What middle school on earth could have tuition of $60,000 a year?*" The member laughed and said, "I've just given my daughter Sarah, who you all remember is employed as my head buyer, a $20,000 raise. Sarah's daughter is starting a private school, and Sarah needs this much, after taxes, to pay for her daughter's tuition. This means I have to give similar raises to my two sons. . . . I don't want them to resent the raise I gave Sarah!"

"It would be better to pay the tuition as a gift and offer a similar program for your other grandchildren," one member suggested. Because of the advice he received, the board member decided to not go ahead with his original idea of giving equal raises and instead put into effect the same offer to gift the tuition for any of his five grandchildren enrolled in private schools. There is a lot of potential for FMEs to feel poorly treated by raises that equalize FME compensation.

It would be very unusual for all FMEs in a family business to bring the same value to the business in terms of their innate gifts, learned skills, and dedication. However, many FBLs choose to pay them equally, and this policy is ripe with potential for creating family dissension. In response to the issue of equal pay for all FMEs, Milwaukee-based TAB facilitator-coach Jan E. Drzewiecki says, "This is done because the FBL believes he or she needs to keep peace in the family by keeping the wages of the FMEs equal, or very close to equal, regardless of job performance or position held."

Unequal pay level does not indicate unequal love. By attempting to keep the peace with equal pay for unequal contributions, you are actually providing fuel for future conflicts among FMEs. Equal pay practices reward underachieving FMEs who are not doing their jobs satisfactorily. Moreover, FMEs who contribute more resent the company's rewarding them the same as it rewards those who do not contribute as much. Those FMEs who perform above and beyond expectations feel especially resentful. The negative impact that this peacekeeping-through-equal-pay approach creates has resulted in many high-performing FMEs leaving family businesses. And in the case that the high-achieving FME decides to stay, often their frustration has led to indifference and a downward slide in their performance. Ask yourself how you would feel if your compensation potential was being stifled by having to be "in line" with every other FME regardless of performance. You would probably think, "Well, my siblings can get away with this and they make as much money as I do. Why should I work this hard?"

Sometimes it takes the parent to see the need to change the equal pay policy. TAB facilitator-coach Carol Crawford in Grand Rapids, Michigan, coaches Greg, who partners in a business with his sister, Tonia, who, like Greg, owns 45 percent of the business. Their father owns the remaining 10 percent. Greg, at 45, has developed a "business owner" mentality. He thinks about long-term strategies for the organization; he develops growth plans; and he works on expanding the company's services. Tonia does not think like an owner but more like a "good employee." Greg told Carol, "I'm still earning the same as Tonia even though I'm the one carrying the entire management load of the firm." Their father was unwilling to exercise his 10 percent to support his son's desires for greater income explaining that he does not want to show favoritism between his two children. "I get that my dad doesn't want to hurt Tonia's feelings, but if I can't get my dad to see this right, I'm going to have to leave the business." For the sake of trying to salvage the situation, Carol asked the father to meet with her in private, and when they were together, Carol asked him to momentarily imagine a scenario in which his children were not his children. Would he pay them equally? He quietly said, "No." Finally, he took off his blinders and saw the picture in a clearer light, and he did the right thing by changing their compensation to more correctly reflect the difference in their contributions.

Sometimes the key is taking the policy problem off the back of the parent by getting the siblings to see things the same way. Samuel founded and owns a clothing distributorship business that his son Kendall joined, and Kendall was put in charge of the warehouse. Within a few years, Thomas, Samuel's other son, joined the business. From the day Thomas started working at the family business, he worked longer hours than Kendall, and he spent a lot of time with his father away from the office talking about the business. In contrast, Kendall approached work as an eight-to-five job. Due to Thomas's dedication, ability, and positive impact on the business, within five years of starting with the business, he was promoted to president while Kendall stayed in charge of the warehouse.

Samuel compensated them equally. Thomas felt that equal pay with Kendall was not fair. After being appointed president, Thomas strongly expressed to his father that he should be compensated much more than his brother. After Samuel explained that he was very uncomfortable having any discussions about compensation, Thomas's resentment reached full pitch.

The solution to the problem was my meeting at the end of business one Friday, at the request of Thomas, with both siblings present to discuss Thomas's resentment, but without the father present. I was able to keep in check the emotional responses by the brothers so that we could focus on the equal compensation policy. Each time the discussions started to get emotional, I executed a recap of facts that reduced the emotions. When things were apparently not getting resolved, I finally asked Kendall whether he believed, as did his brother, that the future success of the company was dependent on Thomas. Kendall paused, looked down at his lap, looked up, and said, "Yes." I then asked how he felt the business would be impacted if Thomas were to leave the business. Kendall responded that if Thomas left, the business would be badly hurt. I would love to say that the issue was resolved right there and then. But it wasn't. In spite of the logic, Kendall explained his perspective by saying, "We both have the job because Dad owns the business so the only fair pay is equal pay," and he did not budge during the meeting. Interestingly, Kendall walked into Thomas's office the following Monday and acknowledged to him that he understood a change in compensation was in order and that he and his brother would no longer be paid equally.

Having the decision made by the brothers took the pressure off Samuel. Within a week, a revised compensation arrangement tied part of Thomas's compensation as the president to the future increased profits of the company over an agreed-upon benchmark. Every year since the change, bonuses earned by Thomas have resulted in his earnings being substantially more than Kendall's. The business has succeeded, and the family ties have stayed strong.

The question of fairness with respect to compensation among siblings, not to mention the challenge of compensating FMEs from different generations, is an issue faced by most FBLs when there are multiple FMEs working in the business. There are bound to be hurt feelings and jealousy when some FMEs perceive that other FMEs are overpaid for a position in relationship to their contributions to the business. The way to bring this to a head is to get buy-in from either or both the FBL or the other FMEs through a nonemotional discussion rather than using the "stick your head in the ground" approach that too often leads to blow-ups.

Reason 2. Lack of a Clear, Deliberate, and Consistent Compensation Policy

As the FBL of a family business, I faced the same family-member compensation question relating to how my son-in-law should be compensated at TAB that all FBLs face. In 2001, Jason and I spent a good deal of time discussing this, and we came up with a formula by which Jason's compensation is a mathematical percentage of my compensation. My compensation is tied to a formula relationship with the highest-paid non-FME at TAB.

Dealing with FME compensation is much easier to do if there is only one FME and much more of a challenge if there are multiple FMEs. The first step to avoid compensation conflict with multiple FMEs is to acknowledge that compensation issues are bound to occur and to develop a policy, preferably a written policy, for how FME compensation will be handled. The more the compensation is in line with salaries, promotions, benefit packages, and performance bonuses and perks appropriate to the industry based on position and performance, the less reason any FME has to complain. Only after acquiring this outside market knowledge should the FBL decide what FME premium, if any, should be paid to an FME for participation in the business. If the compensation policy is based on an objective, clear, deliberate, and consistent standard, there will be fewer instances of family-member emotions getting involved and there will be fewer conflicts.

It would be best if even during the Founder Stage, the family business developed its employee compensation policies to approximate the industry levels to some degree. The reality is that the great majority of businesses that are founder controlled have only informal and unwritten compensation policies for their FMEs. These unwritten policies lean toward the FBL's subjective values, beliefs, and cultural upbringing. Implementing a formal written and objective compensation policy tends to become a more common practice with each succeeding stage of the family business. Often the founder looks at what his or her FMEs need in order to live a certain lifestyle or what they may have been earning elsewhere, rather than what the founder would pay a non-family-member employee. Replacing the common Founder Stage seat-of-the-pants approach to compensating FMEs with a written compensation policy takes away the mystery and compensation unknowns among FMEs that lead to the majority of FME compensation conflicts.

It's not at all uncommon for family businesses to employ family members for more than the "going rate." Your compensation policy should address it if FMEs will generally be getting paid more, sometimes called a "family premium," than experience or market rate would dictate. In most cases, the FBL's desire is for FME compensation to be above market value for the particular position. This can create resentment with non-FMEs who know the policy but in reality might not like it and so might start looking for other employment. Fighting a stated policy is as productive as trying to squeeze water out of a stone.

A consistent compensation policy does not exclude exceptions for unusual circumstances. For example, Tom, a retail chain founder, hired his son-in-law to start at an assistant buyer level in the business with the hope he would become the future FBL. This was a little unusual in that his son-in-law had been a practicing attorney and did not have any retail experience. Tom convinced his son-in-law to give up practicing law and go into the family business by offering him the same salary as he was making practicing law. Tom explained to his other FMEs that his son-in-law needed to start at an assistant buyer level as a step to one day running the business. He told them that his son-in-law was being groomed and that with his business law background, he would become an outstanding leader of the family business in the future. Basically, Tom wanted his son-in-law to come on board and was willing to pay a major premium to do so. After five years, the son-in-law became president of the company. In this case, Tom's decision to "overpay" his son-in-law for his entry-level position was justified.

Dealing with the FME who is coming in at an entry level is a common compensation challenge. The compensation policy should be clear that if the entry position is, in essence, a training program for a future role, the pay may be based on the role for which the FME is being trained—a role that has more importance and so warrants greater compensation. As with Tom and his son-in-law, the policy should take into consideration the fact that a family member may be coming in with a strong education or experience but is being slotted into a lower-level job to gain specific experience before being moved up.

Reason 3. Desires for FME Material Lifestyle

Lawrence is the FBL of a janitorial service company, and he has developed a highly creative approach to compensation. He started with the base philosophy that he wants all of his children to maintain a certain material lifestyle. Then he created an advisory committee to which all his children belong, regardless of their importance within the company. The advisory committee meets monthly, and all his children receive $25,000 per year for serving on the committee. This amount is totally separate from the compensation they receive for the jobs they do in the family business, which Lawrence bases on what the FME would be compensated on the open market in the area in which his company is based. Lawrence's FMEs both respect and appreciate this policy.

There are many reasons why FBLs pay excessive compensation to FMEs; they do not do so always out of a sense of pure familial love. The key to evaluating whether the reasons justify the actions is to understand the reasons for the overcompensation. One reason is that for some FBLs, employment of a family member is just a means of giving the family member a way to collect a paycheck even though it wouldn't make good business sense to employ the person if he or she were not a family member. FBLs who employee FMEs based on these "support reasons" usually determine the amount of compensation based on what the FBL sees as the needs of the FME instead of the fair market value of that position.

Another reason an FBL might overcompensate an FME is that the FME has been with the company for many years and goes into semi- or full retirement. The FBL wants or feels the need to help financially with the retirement by continuing the FME's full or a substantial portion of his or her full-time active-level compensation. This practice can lead to resentment among the still full-time FMEs and among non-FMEs as well. In other common situations, FBLs feel compelled to meet the demands of FMEs who simply feel entitled to excessive compensation, perks, and benefits.

Guilt has been known to play a big part in some FBLs' decisions to overcompensate. One FBL explained that he hired his son-in-law to work at the family business and then paid him double what a non-FME would receive. It took a while for the FBL's son, Mark, who was also employed in the family business, to understand the root cause of why his brother-in-law was being overcompensated. Eventually Mark realized that his father was doing this to make up for how he had mistreated Mark's sister when she was growing up.

Control is another reason for FME overcompensation. Yes, as sad as it may be as a reason, many FBLs use compensation as a means of keeping their family members under their control. For instance, Brady worked for his wife's father's law firm. His wife, Kim, decided that she wanted to buy a house that cost almost $1 million. Brady felt that they shouldn't become overextended; he felt they could be very happy in a less expensive home. Kim took the argument to her parents, and Kim's dad, who was Brady's FBL, made it imminently clear to Brady that Kim deserved the more expensive home. He told Brady, "And I certainly pay you enough to take on the mortgage. If you've got a problem with it, you should sacrifice in some other way." The FBL clearly had control of the "purse strings" of his children's lives. Eventually, Brady's resentment about the fact that he and Kim could not live a life independent of her parents' meddling became one of the factors responsible for their divorce. When he filed for the divorce, one of his first steps was to take a job working for another law firm.

Decisions by the FBL regarding compensation, including benefits, often are motivated by what the FBL wants as the *image* of success for his or her family members. Freedom to travel to nice places with times that tie in with business meetings or other business activities, which allows the business to pay for a large part of the travel and accommodation expenses, is another perk that many FBLs offer their FMEs with much generosity. This reason impacts on more than just the salary overcompensation. The total benefit package of the FME, including common prestige types of perks such as company cars, athletic club memberships, and substantial entertainment allowances, reflects the image that some FBLs want their FMEs to have. Many family businesses allow the FME in an executive position to take his or her family on business trips, and they place no limit on the amount of vacation days the FME can take as long as the FME feels the time away is not hurting the business.

Carol, who is a petite Chanel-wearing FBL, is generous with her FMEs' benefits and perks. She typically insists that the company pick up the bill when her FMEs entertain business clients. In passing, Carol mentioned that her company had just leased a Lexus sports car for her son, who in his early twenties had just joined her company. Carol admitted that she had detected resentment coming from non-FME executives as well as from her other two children who had been working as FME executives for years. She was interested in what her TAB board members felt about the situation. One of her fellow board members asked, "Carol, what has your son done to deserve a Lexus?" Another member wondered, "Are you doing something positive for him by giving him a car he possibly doesn't need or deserve? Where does he go from a Lexus sports car when later on he deserves an image car?" Much to the disappointment of her son, Carol exchanged the Lexus for a much less expensive car, and she explained to her son that he could earn the use of a Lexus sports car but he should not have one now because of the resentment it was causing.

This type of resentment about image benefits is not just a problem with non-FMEs. Shawna is a 35-year-old vice president of a manufacturing company that her father, Joe, had started. Her younger sister was an FME, but she was simply filling a mostly "phantom" position within the company so that she could earn enough to get on her feet financially, and she was rarely even at work. Shawna, who at the time had been at the family firm for 10 years, told her father, Joe, that she was extremely resentful that he had given her sister a company car comparable to her own. "I don't think it's right for her to come in, not put in as much effort, and then get the same level car as I get." Joe listened and then took the matter up with his youngest daughter realizing that it was his ego or desire for her to be seen in a certain type of car that was responsible for leasing the car for her. He sold the car from the company to her and gifted the money to her to make the payments. Shawna was happy to see that the family business profits were no longer impacted by the lease and upkeep of the car.

You as an FBL need to decide what image, if any, you want for your FMEs and recognize what it costs to sustain that lifestyle.

Philippe brought his son, Gaston, into the family company at an entry-level position making $40,000 per year. Gaston, who was in his midtwenties, had been out of college for only two years. He had turned down other job offers where he could make more because he wanted to work for the family business. Unfortunately, after joining the family business, he lived like he was making much more, by purchasing on credit such things as an Armani tuxedo that he used for only one formal event. Within a year of joining the family company, Gaston was $15,000 in debt. When Philippe asked Gaston why he had allowed himself to get sucked into such debt, Gaston replied that he was used to living a certain lifestyle, and he stated that the material level of the lifestyle he enjoyed was the one in which Philippe had raised him.

Philippe realized that he had encouraged a high lifestyle for Gaston, and he liked seeing his son move in the expensive circles of those who had gone to the same private school to which he had sent Gaston. He also took into consideration that Gaston could have been earning higher compensation working outside the family business. He increased Gaston's pay so it was more in line with the job offers Gaston had turned down in order to join the family business, even though it meant that Gaston would be paid more than the market rate for the job he was currently doing for the family business. After a lot of thought, he also bailed Gaston out of debt this one time with a loan that required monthly payments. He increased his pay while making it clear to Gaston that he had to learn to live within his means, based on this higher but not extremely high new compensation, from that point forward.

Frequently the reality is that the children of very successful business owners are generally not able early in their careers at the family business to live at as high a standard as they did while being raised by their parents. In such situations these FMEs might need some additional compensation. Compensation policies should take into consideration the current material needs of those family members with the potential to be the future leaders of the family business. These are the FMEs who will be the future FBLs, and you need to make an investment to keep them in the business.

Reason 4. Resentment of Family Members Not Active in the Business

Another source of potential resentment about perceived over-compensation of FMEs may be family members who have ownership in the company but are not employed by the business (that is, investor family members). Many investor-family-member stockholder lawsuits are based on the argument that the FBL is avoiding dividends by paying FMEs more than they are entitled to be paid as employees of the business. Investor family members often believe that the total compensation of FMEs is too high, and it is thereby reducing or even eliminating the amount of profits available for payment of dividends to the investor family members. Use of objective standards for compensation can dramatically reduce the chances of such lawsuits taking place. I need to caution you that making sure your investor family members are "in the know" does not always solve the problem of investor family members resenting FBL or FME compensation. But generally speaking, the "unknown" of keeping them in the dark is more dangerous than the "known."

This type of family quarreling often occurs when a business owner gives ownership equally to his or her children or grand-children but only some of them become FMEs. The greater the number of family members ("investor family members") who have ownership but not jobs in the business, the more likely there is to be unhappiness regarding compensation, including fringe benefits, of FMEs. The negative dynamics that result in resentment about FME compensation are particularly strong when there are substantially different material standards of living among the family members not employed in the business and the FMEs.

One FBL has three of her four children working in the business. By his own choice, her younger son Charlie was not employed in the family business, but he did, like each of the other siblings, own some company nonvoting stock. Charlie admitted to his mom that he felt angry about the big compensation of his older brothers employed in the business. Charlie resented their big homes, luxury cars, and expensive lifestyles because he felt that these were worth more than what he felt the business should be paying his brothers. Furthermore, at the same time, he had not received a dividend payment from the family business in over 10 years. She asked him how much he thought his older brothers were paid. His answer revealed that he had an exaggerated view of what his brothers were being paid, but it was true that their compensation was still very high compared to the going market rate for the jobs they were doing. Upon hearing the truth, his anger diminished, but it did not stop. She finally eliminated the resentment by, with his approval, converting Charlie's stock to preferred nonvoting stock to provide him with a guaranteed dividend each year.

Often investor family members do have rightful concerns about unfairness in this area, and these concerns need to be addressed. Terrance, the founder of a construction business, gifted 20 percent ownership of the business to both his grandson and granddaughter by putting the stock into trusts for them. Three of Terrance's children worked for the construction business as did his granddaughter, who came to work for the business after college. Each drew a significant income and an annual bonus based on Terrance's philosophy of distributing all the profits of the company in the form of annual bonuses paid to his FMEs. The business showed very little income at the end of each year and paid no dividends. Several years after receiving stock in the family business, the grandson, who did not work in the family business, started to complain to his grandfather that the end-of-the-year bonus program to the FMEs was eating up the profits while he received nothing each year as dividends. Terrance saw no value in discussing the issue with his grandson, whom he now considered ungrateful. He recounted this conversation with his grandson in which Terrance said: "You don't work in the business, and you're not entitled to anything." His grandson told Terrance that he should be treated equitably according to his position as a stockholder and that he had legal rights as a stockholder. Terrance did not eliminate all the annual bonuses, but he did reduce the amounts of the bonuses so that significant dividends began to be paid annually. This solved the conflict with his grandson, but it did not make for a good relationship between the grandson and many of his other family members.

When there are investor family members and the FME compensation—whether salary, bonuses, or perks—is above the market value compensation average, it's important to explain to the investor family members why the policy exists. Let's look at what Lawrence, who is the majority owner of a chain of bakeries, did when his investor family members expressed concern that the business was providing increased distributions to the FMEs employed in the family business. He had heard that a couple of the investor family members were ticked off because they thought Lawrence's son, Brad, was earning much more than he would be if he worked outside the family business. Lawrence proactively called together a meeting among his FMEs and the investor family members. Lawrence informed the group of his compensation policy for his son: his policy was to pay a premium of 20 percent *above* market value, based on a similar size company in their market with comparable profits, for FMEs, including his son, in the business. The 20 percent premium reflects the additional obligations and responsibilities FMEs assume, and it rewards and maintains the FMEs' extra loyalty and focus. He told his family members about the extra obligations and responsibilities that the

FMEs have in the family business. Investor family members often are not aware of the amount of time an FME spends occupied with business matters—even if not physically at the office. Upon hearing the facts and reasoning presented in a logical and calm manner, the investor family members accepted this philosophy.

Spouses of FMEs make up another group in which resentment about compensation of other FMEs is common. Two brothers, each in their fifties, were FMEs of a retail chain run by their father. The brothers were not being paid the same amount. These brothers, who had been very close growing up, were driven apart by their spouses, who did not work for the family business. Each of the wives felt her husband was the one responsible for the success of the business. Each complained to her husband that the other brother should be paid much less compensation than her husband. The resentment built up to a point where it spilled over into tense and uncomfortable moments at all family social gatherings. The final blow-up took place at a Fourth of July party that resulted in the two women shouting at each other across the dinner table over some minor thing that had nothing to do with the business compensation. They still treat each other with a coldness that makes it uncomfortable for other family members to be around.

The interesting thing about this story is that to a large extent, the problem was caused by the FBL's unwillingness to share with the spouses his reasoning for the amounts of compensation he was paying to his sons. The spouses were out of the loop when it came to understanding why each of the brothers was being paid what he was being paid.

Some family businesses have created a Family Council in which what is happening in the family business and such matters as FME compensation are discussed. Such discussions usually bring about better understanding. Family Council meetings help to eliminate any resentment that might take place based on false assumptions. For years my family has had Family Council meetings to discuss what is happening in the businesses, and we have shared information including that about compensation matters. Each of my children has substantial ownership in each of my businesses and has an interest in knowing what is happening. I believe the Family Council has been good for our family, as it is for many other family businesses. Sometimes investor family members of Family Councils are paid to attend meetings, but typically there is no compensation paid to an FME on the Family Council since he or she receives income from his or her employment with the business.

Reason 5. FME Compensation Underpayment

Although FMEs are typically compensated more generously than are non-FMEs doing the same job, there are those FMEs who feel that because the FMEs are family members, they do not have to be competitively compensated for the work they *are* doing. FMEs, who are not adequately rewarded for performance, often stay on because the carrot is held out that if they stay with the business, they ultimately will be the owners. This doesn't mean that they are happy about the pay level or that they view their present needs as not important.

This phenomenon is exemplified by Gabe and his daughter Gloria. Gabe is the founding FBL of a clothing manufacturing company, and Gloria has been working for the company for four years. Gloria came into his office one day, out of the blue, to inform Gabe that she was frustrated with not being compensated based on the results of her work. She said it was not fair that the other two division heads, who run much smaller and less significant departments, had bonus incentive programs and she did not. Gabe explained to Gloria that she didn't have the same incentive program because "one day you are going to own part of the company and that should be *enough* incentive." Gloria responded that she didn't want to be compensated "based on some notion of the future," as she put it. She wanted to be compensated based on her current job performance. Gabe responded, again, that "the bigger prize of ownership later on should be a big enough incentive." However, eventually, he did agree to create a performance incentive compensation program for her that would reward her with a bonus based on objective performance results.

Some FMEs are willing to take less compensation than what is appropriate to the industry based on position and performance because of the potential of significant ownership sometime in the future. They are often willing to sacrifice current compensation for their dream of ownership, and they find it very hard to be assertive about underpayment with their parents when future ownership potential exists. However, their patience with being underpaid can, over time, wear thin and cause underlying resentment to build up. Steve Wolf, a TAB facilitator-coach in New Jersey, personally experienced this problem of underpaid compensation when he was working in his family's business: "Since it was understood that I would eventually own the family candy business, the only times I received raises from my father was when I got married and when I had my two children. Other than that, the pay stayed the same because some day it was all going to be mine!"

Some FBLs underpay FMEs who have had experience making much more money at other employment, particularly if the employment was with a major size company. One FBL wanted to bring his daughter into his family business, which had 50 or so employees. His daughter was making over $100,000 per year as a senior-level manager with a major company. The FBL offered her much less than she was getting in her current management position because he felt that his business could only partially take advantage of her work experience and also because he felt that "public companies overpay their management." So in his reasoning, it did not make sense to match the higher pay she was receiving elsewhere. But his daughter wanted her compensation to be no less than she was currently making.

Several months went by, and she decided to enter her father's business after all at a compensation level more in line with, but less than, what she was making at her current position. She accepted the decrease in pay because she had dreams of someday owning part of the family business. But even years later, she would periodically joke about her father's cheapness in paying her.

Sometimes FBLs face a conundrum when dealing with FMEs who may deserve more and are underpaid in comparison to the going market rate for their positions mostly because the family business cannot afford to pay the going rate. The FBL of one manufacturing business said that he was totally surprised when John, his extremely qualified son, informed him that he felt that he and his brother were underpaid. The father then engaged an independent HR consultant to compare the sons' compensation with the market value compensation nonfamily members were paid in the area to do the same jobs. The consultant found that the sons were being paid less. Unfortunately, the problem was not resolved well because the father felt the business could not pay the market rates for compensating the sons, and he made no adjustments. The result was that John, the extremely qualified son of the founder, left the business because he had high aspirations for his earnings and it was clear to him that the earnings he desired would not be attainable within the family business compensation policy. Interestingly, John later became very successful with his own business that was not in the same field as the family business.

Before leaving this topic of underpayment, it is interesting that sometimes FMEs feel that they deserve more and that they are being underpaid when actually they are being overpaid. One reason this happens is that these FMEs do not consider how much nonsalary compensation they may be earning in the way of perks and other benefits that they would not get if they were not FMEs.

One FBL, Tom, heard constant complaining from his son because he felt he was being underpaid. The complaining stopped when Tom engaged an HR expert to provide the son with the market value of the position the son held. The HR expert based the analysis on the market compensation range, including the value of fringes, for the son's level job in the St. Louis metropolitan area for comparably sized companies in the same general industry. The result of the analysis was that there was an overcompensation issue even though his son had thought that he was underpaid. The HR study neutralized the situation before it got out of hand. Nothing puts a stop to out-of-line emotions quite like the facts, especially when presented by a neutral third party.

When there has been a history of overpayment compensation to family members in the past and the company is doing well, you can't suddenly lower compensation to match the prevailing market rates without destroying the morale of the FMEs. A major culture shock will negatively ripple throughout the business and nonbusiness dynamics of the family.

Reason 6. Bonus Incentive Compensation for Nonowner FMEs

One of the biggest compensation challenges FBLs face is with FMEs who do not have an ownership distribution incentive. These FMEs also have less fear of termination than non-FMEs if they don't produce. The higher up the FME without ownership is on the job ladder, the more important it is to have FME incentive programs that are based on the family business results as a whole. This type of incentive has proven to be an outstanding tool for achieving both business profit and FME compensation objectives. It is important to distinguish the base pay of such FMEs from bonus incentive compensation that is based on productivity. In one situation, a manufacturer did not want to turn over any amount of ownership to his two sons who worked in key positions in the business. Instead, he created a bonus formula that called for his sons to receive 10 percent of the increase in profits annually of the family business from the respective years that each of them started in their respective key executive positions in the business.

Some family businesses create a bonus pool in which designated top-level FME and non-FME executives share in a bonus based on some incremental level of company profits. However, for this bonus pool approach to be meaningful as an incentive, an "open-book" management approach is required. All who participate in the program must have the information needed to decide whether there is a manipulation of the calculation used to determine the amount going into the pool. An open-book management approach does not require you to share the compensation of specific employees.

One FBL told me that he does not need to conduct compensation reviews with his FMEs that include a discussion of incentives because "they are family and understand why they are being compensated the way they are compensated." He is missing an opportunity to use the incentives to motivate FMEs to higher productivity. For any FME reward program to be effective, there needs to be scheduled compensation reviews with the FMEs.

If the positions of the FMEs are middle management or lower, it is usually better to have their compensation plan include incentives tied to achieving personal performance objectives rather than tied to the company's performance. Joe, the founder of a building materials distribution company, created an incentive program for his midlevel sales FMEs who had no ownership interest. Joe put a cap on the bonuses for these FMEs such that their bonuses were based on their sales results but they could not exceed a certain percentage of the FMEs' base salaries. This cap actually had a negative impact because the FMEs were aware when the maximum was being reached. The FMEs knew when they were capped out on the current year, so they delayed sales until the next year to ensure their bonuses.

Reason 7. Excessive FBL Compensation

While the focus of this chapter has been primarily on compensation matters involving FMEs, the compensation of the FBL family member is not one that goes without its own set of resentments. The founder of a paper company left his business equally to his son Henry and his daughter, but he left all of the voting control to the son. Henry worked full-time in the business as the FBL, but his sister did not work full-time in the business. As the results of the company increased under Henry's leadership, he arbitrarily increased his compensation but not his sister's even though her dividends increased each year. His sister became more vocal about her resentment. She complained to other family members about the compensation matter, and it became very damaging as viewed by those family members, ultimately disrupting the family harmony as well as Henry's teamwork with his sister at the business. The complaints did not stop until Henry agreed to peg his compensation to local fair market compensation for his position based on similar size companies with comparable profits. Henry found the more objective compensation policy resulted in dramatic improvements in reduced friction with family members and teamwork with his sister at work. It also reduced the possibility of legal action for claims of unfair compensation from his sister.

Sometimes the relationship of the compensation level of the FMEs to that of the FBL is that the FBL's compensation is several times larger than the FMEs', which brings about resentment from the FMEs. Roberto was the FBL of a meat processing business, which also employed his son and daughter. Three years earlier, Roberto had made his son and daughter Catherine president and COO, respectively, of the two main divisions of the company.

The two siblings, both in their early thirties, worked hard and were not filling these titles in name only, as is sometimes the case in family businesses. They were the leaders of their respective divisions within the company, and both divisions prospered under their leadership.

Roberto had for many years drawn a salary from the business that was three and a half times as much as his children's FME salaries. Roberto's daughter, Catherine, and her brother each received a base salary of $250,000 a year from the business, but Roberto drew a base salary of $650,000 a year. His son and daughter felt that their father's level of pay resulted in less money being available for the two of them, but they did not complain. Then, Roberto decided at age 55 to become a long-distance CEO of the family business he had founded. Acting on his dream to live in a golf resort community in Arizona, he sold his home in California, which was a couple of miles from the business headquarters. After he moved away, the siblings had only quarterly in-person visits and periodic telephone and e-mail communications with Roberto. These quarterly visits were, in the view of his children, very disruptive and were a minor source of irritation to them and to non-FME personnel. What irritated them more, however, was their father's compensation of $650,000 a year, which was the same as he had earned when he was active in the business every day and which the siblings considered excessive given Roberto's absence.

Catherine explained to her TAB board that since she and her brother had joined the family business, the company's sales had tripled and its profits were up sevenfold. "It wouldn't have happened without our efforts," Catherine said with a sardonic laugh, "so as you can imagine, I'm a bit resentful that Dad's still taking the same amount of money from the business—even though he's no longer regularly involved in it."

Catherine was asked if she and her brother had discussed how they felt with their father. She said they had not and explained that past discussions with him about compensation had been extremely awkward. One of her fellow board members, Clayton, said, "I can see you're frustrated, and I think you and your brother need to discuss this with your father, but let me give you a few questions to think about before you talk to him. Would you say your dad took substantial risks to start and get the business on its feet: financial, emotional, familial, and otherwise? Did he spend the kind of energy, focus, and dedication that are needed by a founder for a business to spring to life?" Catherine nodded her head affirmatively. Clayton then continued, "Am I correct in saying that if your father hadn't taken those risks and spent the kind of energy, focus, and dedication that he did, the business would not exist?" Catherine again nodded her head affirmatively. Clayton concluded with a final question: "Do you feel you'd be compensated the same $250,000 a year and enjoying your lifestyle if your dad hadn't taken those risks?" Catherine mulled this over and said, "No, I guess I wouldn't."

Clayton smiled kindly at her, and Catherine left the meeting with a better feeling. She was more in touch with the fact that her father was entitled to live the good life he had brought about and that even with his generous compensation, she was still enjoying a very good material life. Sometimes it just takes someone not beholden to you to remind you of things that you know deep down but do not want to face.

Catherine and her brother did talk eventually to Roberto. Roberto explained his viewpoint that his compensation was a fair return on ownership. But, surprisingly to them, shortly thereafter he changed his compensation to receive 50 percent of his full-time compensation.

Discussions between FMEs and the FBL concerning the FBL's compensation can be extremely awkward. FMEs' resentment often festers because they are hesitant to complain about the compensation of FBLs, who typically have a powerful presence in their lives. Sometimes the resentment is based on assumptions that are not correct. Ralph, who owns a textile manufacturing business, has an FME son, Benny, who informed him over drinks during a business trip that he found Ralph's considerable compensation to be unfair and he resented the money his dad took from the business. Ralph had been totally unaware of the resentment his son had been hiding. Like some FBLs, Ralph had never openly discussed or showed Benny the financials of the business. Ralph's reaction to his son's comments was to show the financials to his son including details of exactly how much he and others were making. Benny was shocked when he learned his father was being compensated much less than he had assumed. Benny admitted, "I just assumed you were taking a fortune out of the business because you are always giving fantastic gifts to Mom and you have always been incredibly generous to charities."

Conclusion

The sometimes uncomfortable fact is that FME compensation tends to follow a different set of rules than does non-FME compensation. Quite simply, compensation of family members is much less likely to be based on any *objective criteria*. This can make compensation discussions difficult to conduct as emotions enter the picture. When family compensation issues and conflicts are not clear and based on some logic, the most common result is family disharmony. As the business proceeds from one generation to the next, succeeding generations tend to handle FME compensation issues in a progressively more objective, professional manner. As a family business progresses into later stages, the founder's *early informal* compensation structure naturally tends to morph into an *increasingly more formal* structure.

   The sooner the FBL takes control of creating objective standards for dealing with compensation issues, the more likely it is the businesses will survive and flourish into succeeding generations of leadership. It is best to put the policy into writing. For many FMEs, as Kevin Armstrong, a TAB facilitator-coach in Vancouver, Canada, says, "If it isn't in writing, it doesn't exist." The more your written policy includes objective compensation practices, the less likely it is that family conflicts resulting from gray-area issues will occur. A clearly stated compensation policy often prevents conflict and is the best way to break through the emotional barriers that commonly come into play when discussing compensation. Compensation challenges are particularly common when there are multiple siblings and one or more of the siblings do *not* work for the family business. Making certain everyone has the facts about compensation will shut down some of the conjecture and help keep family relationships healthy.

Now that you understand the seven most common reasons conflicts over compensation arise and have learned how to keep the conflicts at bay, you are ready for the fourth element in the formula, Selecting the Family-Member Successor.

Checklist for Compensating Family-Member Employees

- FME compensation is typically based on subjective rather than objective criteria. This opens the door for many levels of conflict.
- A clear, deliberate, and consistent FME compensation policy should be written, distributed, and discussed with all FMEs so that there is no question as to what the policy contains.
- FMEs may not like the compensation policy, but they must understand how the FBL determines compensation—that is, what is "fair" in the mind of the FBL.
- Perks and company benefits other than salary play an important role in tabulating overall compensation, but they are often underappreciated by FMEs.

- Investor family members who are not active in the business should be given a copy of the compensation policy if the FBL wishes to avoid conflict from these family members.
- FMEs who perceive their compensation as being less than they are due need to discuss this with the FBL, even though this is sometimes very hard to do especially when the carrot of future ownership exists.

CHAPTER 4

THE FOURTH ELEMENT
Selecting the Family-Member Successor

I'm really into horses at this stage in my life, and it has occurred to me that creating a business is much like working with a new horse. You start with instability. With a lot of time and energy and care, you can calm that new horse. It also takes a lot of indefinable intuition. You'll never bring stability to a horse you rail against or harm; rather, you need to find out how the two of you can harmoniously function together. You'll fall on your butt a bunch of times in the beginning, but soon you'll find that you and your horse are riding calmly, smoothly, and confidently. You and your horse find that sense of oneness. Then one day, when sitting in your saddle, you experience beauty that you can't experience by any other means, and you think to yourself that the aggravation was worth it—much like the day you realize your business has made it over the hump and it really is going to meet your dreams.

A few years, maybe a decade, of working with this animal, and then comes the joy of getting to hoist your son, daughter, or grandkids on top of this horse. Watch as they first feel uncertain, smile nervously at you, and then look to you for your confidence. It takes a lot of trust all around to accomplish this: you have to trust your horse, and the horse has to trust the child, and then you must trust your child. Such is the experience of watching your FME successor take over the family business—turning over control of your hard-earned business to your family member's future, a future filled with promise, a future for which you built the foundation. Passing on your legacy is one of the greatest privileges of being an FBL.

Businesses are generally started by entrepreneurs, like me, with a passion for a certain industry. In the excitement and instability of the early years, few FBLs give any significant thought as to the potential future successor roles in the family business. Then, as equilibrium comes about, the founder will usually start to look among his or her children or other family members for the one whom he or she can imagine as the future leader. The founder sees a child or other family member in a new light and envisions that family member joining the business. Or perhaps, a family member expresses an interest in joining the business and sparks thought on the part of the FBL. And so, with the seeds of succession being planted, the business begins the journey from generation to generation.

You cannot run your business from the grave. Without a chosen successor and a development plan for the selected family member in place, your business is likely going to die with you. It could also become an insurmountable burden to the family members left behind. However, you can put the steps in place so that your business will have a much greater chance of continuing to successfully run under the leadership of your chosen successor long after your own batteries have run down.

Choosing the right successor often means charting a plan that allows for careful navigations around obstacles such as the expectations and emotions of other family members while still achieving the end results you desire. And in order for your "crew" to navigate successfully, you've got to give them the coordinates. You have to communicate your successor selection wishes and your plans in a way that will help alleviate bad feelings and potential family conflict.

There are 11 common obstacles that tend to provide challenges to the majority of FBLs around the issue of successors. I will discuss each of these obstacles in this chapter and methods for avoiding or getting around them.

Obstacle 1. Procrastination

"What do you mean I can't run the business forever?" As silly as the statement may sound, it just happens to be the mindset of far too many FBLs. It is illogical for an FBL not to have any successor chosen, yet many FBLs hold on to the day-to-day leadership role in their family businesses right up to the moment they take their final breath. They postpone, or entirely ignore, picking a successor until it is too late. Some FBLs say that they are just too overwhelmed with their day-to-day work to put aside the time needed to concentrate on this crucial issue. I knew one FBL who dodged the issue of announcing a successor completely by tapping his head and saying, "Don't worry; I've got my successor picked out right up here in my noggin."

Some people know they must make out a will but avoid doing so out of an unnamed fear, out of superstition, or the fear that thinking about such demands will jinx things. These are the same thoughts and feelings that stop many from designating a successor to the company. Many FBLs who procrastinate on picking a successor explain it away by saying, "I'm not going anywhere; there's plenty of time for succession planning." The fact is that none of us knows how long we will be around.

Most family business owners have not yet chosen a family-member successor and have no written plan for what their family should do with the business if anything happens to them. The excuse of being "too busy" is only one of many excuses that I have heard from FBLs who don't want to discuss selecting a successor. It's rarely actually about not having the time to deal with the situation and usually about procrastination. The key to overcoming the desire to procrastinate in selecting a successor is clearly identifying the reasons. You simply can't fight, or push past, an unknown.

One of the reasons for procrastination is a certain fear when it comes to gazing into the crystal ball and looking toward a time when we will be considerably older. It's as if doing so will somehow lure the inevitable and unwanted to creep in a little faster. When you are young and working hard at growing a business, it can seem almost taboo to stop and plan for a future time when you will be stepping down from running the very thing you are building. One FBL said that she feared appointing a successor because it would bring up and expose her fear of death. But these fears must be overcome because the best time for creating a written succession plan is well before you imagine you might need it.

Obstacle 2. Lack of Objectivity

There are critical questions every FBL considering a successor must answer, but sometimes the nearest answers are not realistic. The FBL of an electronics company wanted to commit his focus to religious activities, and he anointed his son, who at the time was in his midtwenties, to run the family business. He viewed his son's leadership through rose-colored glasses. The father turned over most of the FBL duties to the "great" leadership of the son. The business declared bankruptcy in little more than three years. Losing the family business was hard on the entire family, most of who were upset with the father's selection of his son as the FBL. It was also hard on the son because once a son has damaged a family business, it makes it really difficult to sit down and have that Thanksgiving dinner with all of those who had been dependent on the business for their support.

It is important to select only the most qualified successor. Nothing leads to a company's failing faster than the installation of a new, unqualified FBL. Yet family-member successors are often picked for subjective family reasons. As a result, many successors are put in a position to fail because they do not have the passion, aptitude, and leadership personality to be effective FBLs. It is not fair to put a son, daughter, or other relative in the FBL position if he or she does not have the required traits.

While the FBL often enjoys training a son or daughter to one day carry the family scepter, his or her expectations can slip outside the boundaries of reality. As you can imagine, if an FBL has happily had his or her eye on a potential successor since the child was in diapers, it can be difficult to see clearly whether as an adult this person is the right successor. Ali, with three of his children in his business, picked his middle son to be the future leader of the business because he, like Ali, had a great selling ability, and that was a key to the success of the business. The problem was that the son was disorganized and terrible at delegating, so he became overwhelmed as president. The company did poorly under his leadership, and it did not turn around into profits again until his older sister, without natural sales ability, took over.

One thing to remember is that the successor does not have to be a clone of the current FBL to be successful. The new leader will almost always look at the business from a new perspective and a different management style. Yet FBLs often look for candidates who remind them of themselves. Instead, they should pick a successor by starting with identifying the objective factors that are needed for someone to effectively run the business as the successor. Do not allow yourself to fall victim to making a poor successor choice based solely on emotional reasons tied to family pressure, regardless of how deeply you love your family members.

Obstacle 3. Birthright

You, as the FBL, are doing no one a favor by giving a family member the company leadership merely because of birthright. This "birthright" viewpoint is very much related to certain cultures. Jie, who was born in Asia, owned a family business with over 100 employees. Jie's view was that the first son is always "golden." He felt obliged by family tradition and expectations to turn the business over to his eldest son. My question to him was, "Do you know if your son passionately wants the job?" After discussing the succession selection with his son, Jie found out that his son's dream had always been to be an international traveling journalist. He lacked any real passion for the job. He had stepped into line and started learning the business because he felt it was his family duty to do so and because he didn't want to let his father down. In spite of knowing this, Jie selected his son as successor, and the son dutifully became the FBL. The company failed to grow under his son's leadership mostly because his heart just wasn't in it. It was a no-win situation. Within a few years, to resuscitate the company, Jie had to step back into the business well after he had retired. The son carried enormous guilt at not having succeeded in his father's eyes, and everyone involved was miserable.

There are also many situations in which a child thinks he or she has the innate right to be the leader of the family business based solely on age or birth position within the family. This can put a lot of pressure on an FBL who is torn between wanting to be a good business owner and a loving parent. So much pressure, in fact, that the FBL sometimes goes against his or her better judgment and selects the successor who makes the family situation more peaceful than would choosing the best person for the job.

A 70-year-old FBL, who had both his son and son-in-law working in the business, admitted he had never spoken to either of the men about the possibility of stepping in and taking over, and he had not groomed either of them appropriately for the job. He said that he was still working strong at age 70 and so he had no desire to appoint a successor any time soon. I knew by observing his body language that his words were a cover for the real truth. I pushed on, asking a few simple questions that resulted in the FBL's admitting that his son-in-law was, in his mind, the more qualified candidate for the job of successor but that his son had expressed a sense of hereditary ownership over the position. I learned that the FBL's wife had also made it abundantly clear on numerous occasions that she fully expected their son to one day take over the business "because qualified or not, he's our son." He discussed the high level of pressure surrounding the potential conflict when parents have disagreements about which child should succeed the FBL.

You can understand why the topic of succession planning was a loaded hot potato for him—one from which he did his best to steer clear. It was easiest for the FBL to avoid the potential complications from his wife and son relating to the "blood versus water" issue. He is older and still around, and he keeps his fingers crossed that his own good health, as well as the health of his business, will continue to hold out for a long time so that he can continue to avoid addressing the issue of the peril in the future of his business because at age 70, he continues to shy away from picking a successor.

If you want your business to continue to thrive, not to mention sustain family members, you are going to need a successor who is both willing and capable to take control of the business. That person may not turn out to be your first-born child. And although you may feel like you are letting a child down in not appointing him or her as successor, think how much worse the situation would be if you did and the child failed as the leader and lost the business, leaving your family in financial peril. It's far better to find the right successor and make up any disappointment to your child in another way. Before jumping to the conclusion that your son or daughter is, by his or her birthright, the rightful successor, take some time out to explore the idea and make sure he or she is the right successor.

Obstacle 4. Poor Communications

The golden rule of succession is to always clearly communicate your succession plans with the selected party earlier rather than later and be sensitive to how other family members may react. One FBL retailer spoke of his desire for his daughter to be his successor with real zeal, and he was more than excited about getting his long-held plan onto paper. When I asked the FBL how his daughter felt about all of this, he responded by saying that he had never actually discussed it with her but he was sure it was what his daughter wanted as well. I suggested he go to his daughter's home that very night and find out her true feelings. The following day I received a call from the FBL, and he was a far less spirited man. It seems his daughter's immediate response to the suggestion that she take over the company was, "Are you kidding? Why would I ever want to do that?" Her feelings came as quite a shock to her dad. He learned that her future plans in no way included taking over the business. Instead, she had plans for graduate school and a degree in education.

A survey of TAB board members showed that at the time they joined TAB, only 60 percent of all the FBLs who said that they had potential successors in mind had notified and confirmed the interest of their intended successors in being the future leaders of their businesses. The remaining 40 percent said that they assumed their chosen successors wanted to become the successors. Succession selection is definitely not a place where any FBL wants to take a chance with a risky hand. You may find that your chosen successor has plans for the future that are inconsistent with yours. The magnitude of things that can go wrong is just too overwhelming to leave succession up to the assumption that someone wants the job.

The flip side of this challenge is that it may not always be obvious to an FBL that someone has a sincere interest in being the successor. The FBL must be proactive to find out who among the qualified candidates may passionately want the job. John Keener, who is a TAB facilitator-coach in the St. Louis, Missouri, area, coached a TAB member, Bill, who assumed his daughter, who was extremely capable of taking on the leadership role, would not be interested in the job. She was involved part-time in the business, but she also had a family. Bill thought she wanted to be more of a stay-at-home mom, and he told John that, while it broke his heart to do so, it was time to start looking into selling the business to an outside party because he had no family-member successor. At John's urging, Bill held off on starting plans to sell the business until he held a family meeting with all his children to discuss the future of the business. Much to Bill's surprise and delight, he learned his daughter was passionately interested in taking over the business. She had never spoken up about it as she had assumed her father knew how strongly she loved the business. Subsequently, instead of starting to develop a plan to sell the business, Bill began a succession plan to keep the company in the family with his daughter as the designated successor, and he began to gradually transition the leadership responsibilities to her.

Your selection decision will be received better by other family members if it is backed up with the analysis of an objective third party. Once you have made a succession decision, let your family know about it in a manner that addresses and eases any jealousy or unhappiness your decision may create among other family members. Avoiding or minimizing family discord takes preparation before the decision is announced.

A second-generation metal fabricating business was equally owned 51 percent by a sister and 49 percent by her two brothers. Each sibling had grown children who were actively involved in the family business. After much consideration, the FBL decided that her own son was the best candidate to succeed her. Her son was eager for the job and more than capable of doing it from an aptitude standpoint, but he was more than 10 years younger than his cousins. The FBL knew her brothers had aspirations to see their own children in the successor role. One night the FBL went out for dinner with her son, and she used the occasion to tell him that he was next in line.

The next morning her son let the word out to his planning team, which included his brother and sister. The selection was out all over the business and among all the family members almost before anyone had even finished their first cup of coffee. The FBL's brothers were, of course, disappointed that the successor would not be any of their children, but they were boiling mad that the FBL had failed to inform them first, especially because they all worked in the family business together. The situation grew into a huge rift that eventually separated what had been an extremely close extended family. When the FBL did not get an invitation from her brother to Christmas dinner, she knew she had a real problem on her hands, a problem she had to fix. She called a family meeting during which she explained, in an unemotional and unbiased way, her reasons behind the successor decision. The meeting helped, but her relationship with her siblings is still strained.

Obstacle 5. Lack of Needed Passion

At age 60, Roy was thinking that in five years he'd like to retire. He wanted his son Ethan, who was in charge of design and product quality control, to take over his business, which manufactured products in China and imported them to the United States. He planned for Ethan, then 38 years old, to spend the next two years learning the ropes of the other parts of the business. This way

Ethan could be fully prepared to take over the company leadership duties before Roy retired. Fine and good, right? Wrong, because Roy, like so many other FBLs, had never discussed his succession plans with Ethan. He figured, "Hell, it's such a great opportunity; there's no way Ethan will turn it down!" When Roy matter-of-factly mentioned his plans to Ethan, Ethan stared at him blankly. "But, Dad, that's not what I'm planning on doing. I'm really thinking of taking a position off the coast of Belize; I just want to study coral reef habitats. That wasn't just fun volunteer work I was doing with Save the Reef; I want to make it my full-time job." Roy, after getting over his shock, ultimately convinced a nephew in his midtwenties to come to work at the business with the hope that in 10 years, the nephew could take over the business. Needless to say, Roy had to make a major change in the timing of his retirement.

The best successor candidates will have the qualifications to PAVE their way to success. The P in PAVE that you should look for in your successor candidates refers to "Passion for the business." Communicate exactly what succession will entail, including any sacrifices or commitments the intended successor will be required to make. Not everyone is able or willing to make this kind of sacrifice and commitment.

Often the FBL is unable to recognize whether or not the child has a real passion for the business. I have a friend who used to work on fishing boats on the East Coast. One summer she worked for a very young captain, Keith, who coincidentally had one of the most successful charter boats in the harbor. While he often was given a good ribbing by the older captains for being so young, Keith was also respected by them for his hard work and dedication to the very difficult job of making a living at fishing.

Keith's father contacted him and said that he was ready to discuss with Keith the details of how he would be turning the leadership of the family's very successful oil venture over to him. The twist of course was that Keith wanted no part of the family business; all he had wanted his whole life was to sail and fish. His younger brother, Joe, however, really wanted the job. He loved the family business and all of its inner workings, and he was good at it too. Despite Joe's passion and his aptitude for the family business, his father wanted to turn the reigns over only to Keith. In their family, Dad's word was law. But Keith fought it anyway, and they went back and forth negotiating. Keith made a deal with his father: Keith would continue to fish for three seasons as long as he came back to the family company and drove an oil truck during the winter. If, after three seasons, he could prove the fishing boat could make a specified level of income, which they agreed was needed to maintain a decent standard of living, he would be *released* from the role of successor and his father would turn the family business over to his brother, Joe.

Keith never worked harder in his life as he tried to meet his father's challenge. But while his boat caught a lot of fish, the business failed to come up to a level of profit that was anywhere near where Keith needed it to be to enable him to get out of a life he did not want. That winter, the boat was hauled out of the water and put up on blocks with a for sale sign in the wheelhouse window. Keith packed up his rods and reels and resigned himself to a winter of driving an oil truck, learning the business that would one day be his from the bottom up. His father cheerfully and continually liked to remind Keith how lucky he was to be the "chosen one." It's sad that Keith could not stand up to his dad and that his dad did not recognize and understand the passion Joe had for the business. Keith is not now and will never be happy running the family business. The business is doing okay, but Keith will never give the FBL position the justice it deserves. Keith kept his word not because of any threat such as that his father would disown him or treat him as if he were no longer part of the family. Instead, the source of the pressure, as is true of many families, was that the family culture was to follow the wishes of the father.

I hear stories like this all the time, and they make me distraught. Every successful family business I have worked with had someone with the passion and care that went into growing it. It is important that the successor share a similar excitement for the family business and literally love the business you are in. Wise FBLs know that pressuring a child or other family member to be part of the succession plan when they do not feel the passion is always a bad decision. Without passion for the family business and for the FBL position, the selected successor running the business will underachieve or even fail regardless of his or her ability. Take the steps to identify the most qualified family member who has the passion to be the future leader of your company, and the results will be a lot better for everyone involved.

Obstacle 6. Lack of an FME Candidate Who Possesses Most of the Needed Aptitudes

Sometimes one family member naturally rises from the pack and so easily flows into the successor position! Other times it is not as clear. What a difficult decision it is to pick out who among your children is the one with the most aptitude to handle the biggest job in the family business. This calls to mind being asked that question that is asked by many a young child, "Which of us do you [Mommy or Daddy] love better?" It takes a lot of tact and sensitivity to make such an emotion-fueled decision.

When I refer to the things that PAVE the way to success for a successor, the A in PAVE is the "Aptitude to be the future business leader." Note that I mention this after discussing passion. The reason is that regardless of ability, a person will not be a great leader of your business without the needed passion for running the business.

Which of the potential successors has the strongest aptitude to be the future leader of your business? An FBL cannot make this decision based solely on how well the FMEs are handling their current responsibilities. The role of the CEO-president is unique and requires an entirely different set of skills, behaviors, and attitudes from that of any other position. Certainly, different types of businesses will require their FBLs to have different types of education or sets of skills. The FBL will need certain types of technical knowledge and proven overall business experience specific to his or her field if he or she is to properly tackle the business situations that are bound to arise. Technical abilities alone, however, are not enough to make an effective FBL. There are other aptitudes he or she will need to have specific to the business. Identify those aptitude requirements that successor candidates must have to be considered for the job. Ask yourself which if any of the potential successors have an overall strong aptitude to think quickly, to think "on their feet," and to solve problems in creative ways.

One business owner wanted his retail chain to stay in the family. This FBL felt that his two sons, who worked in the business, lacked the aptitude needed to lead the business. He did, however, have a very bright daughter who worked out of state for a much larger retail chain. The FBL visited his daughter and discussed his desire to make her his successor. His daughter expressed her love of the business and an interest in running the family business. She planned to eventually join the family business, but she stated that she wanted to live in New York for at least a few more years before going home to work in the family business. After visiting his daughter, the FBL stipulated in his estate planning that, in the event of his death or incapacitation, his heirs would hire an interim COO to run the company while his daughter learned the business. He put his plan in a written format and then got together with his family, his sons, and everyone else who would be touched by the plan, to review the written plan. He explained that he felt that his daughter would have the best aptitude to lead the business after she obtained the needed experience. His sons expressed their disappointment and said that they felt they were being overlooked. But they both admitted that they had always known their sister was "the one" with the most abilities. Ultimately, they were happy to stay in their high-paid positions in which they were already working.

When the FBL died unexpectedly a few years later, his plan was brought into action. An executive, at that time retired, with experience in running retail chains was selected to take over the business as CEO for a five-year period while the FBL's daughter started working in the business and training to be the future CEO. The plan worked, and the company survived and prospered due to the owner's plan.

Obstacle 7. Lack of the Needed Vision of the Big Picture Potential

In Mississippi, the FBL of a small spa manufacturing company announced, to his over 300 employees, that after considering several candidates, he had chosen his highly educated and very intelligent daughter to take over as president and CEO. Within a year of the announcement three non-FME long-term department managers of the company, without any prior discussions with the FBL, up and quit the company, saying that they were quitting because of the daughter's promotion, which had put the company into a weakened state. Shaken, the FBL took the marketing manager out for lunch, and he asked her why she had resigned. Her answer was, "Your daughter is great at implementing things, but she doesn't have the vision to make this company what it can be, or to even see what is needed to keep it competitive." She and the other two managers had decided to go to companies that they thought had better futures and therefore more security for them.

When I refer to the things that PAVE the way to success for a successor, the V in PAVE refers to the "Vision of the Big

Picture Potential for the family business." Your successor should be able to bring about a strategic rejuvenation or reinvention of the business as it moves from one generation to the next. Your successor needs the vision to see the adaptations and changes the business will inevitably need to make to stay competitive and grow. Business information is increasing at such a fast rate that every business is vulnerable to new and better competitors. This means that you have to keep reinventing your business or else you may lose it. To continually keep reinventing, it's really important that the successor have a Vision of the Big Picture Potential of your business.

If you have multiple possibly qualified successor candidates, meet with each candidate individually in an environment that promotes open dialogue. Learn how he or she would make strategic decisions to move the business forward. Ask about long-range strategies for advancing the company, and assess whether the candidate's ideas and plans are in tune with your own. Find out if he or she has a belief in the company's mission. Make sure, if you have a vision for the future of the company, that your intended successor is in agreement with seeing that vision through. Nothing is more painful then handing over your life blood just to watch it be swiftly changed beyond recognition.

Many FBLs have their chosen successor agree to carry through the FBL's Company Vision for the family business. This type of agreement does not guarantee compliance, but it does set the expectations for the involved parties. With an understanding in place of the FBL's long-range dreams of the family business, there can be a strong and cooperative relationship between the current FBL and the future FBL while they work in the business together.

Some FBLs with multiple potentially qualified successors want to see who shows the best Big Picture Vision ability. The FBL of a distribution business created a plan whereby he transitioned equal ownership of stock in the family business holding company to each of his six children, although the stock transferred was nonvoting stock in the holding company. He kept only 1 percent of the stock for himself, but it was the only voting stock. He did this without appointing a clear successor to the holding company that owned the stock of several subsidiary businesses. Each of the six children was put in charge of one of the subsidiary businesses.

The father did nothing to discourage competition, and, in fact, he informed his kids that he would not appoint an overall COO until one of them proved, above and beyond all doubt, that he or she truly deserved the job. It would be an understatement to say that this approach created a severe strain on the relationships between the six siblings. The situation was resolved only when one of the siblings, the son who was in charge of the largest subsidiary, came up with ideas for a strategic plan that, if it worked, could move the family business into a much greater level of success. The father was so pleased with these Big Picture Vision ideas of his son that he appointed the son as COO of the holding company.

Obstacle 8. Lack of an Empathetic Personality Match

Is the successor candidate a natural leader? It is important for the successor to have the kind of natural behavior that is viewed as "presidential" in the eyes of employees, both FMEs and non-FMEs. There are critical leadership behaviors that not everyone possesses, regardless of intelligence or experience. The FBL's job in picking the successor is to look at whether the candidates have the needed behavioral or personality "goods." The E in PAVE refers to the "Empathetic personality match with the leadership personality needed to effectively lead the business." What kind of personality or behavioral type is needed to lead your business effectively? Be realistic when performing an assessment of your successor's leadership personality. Is the natural personality or behavior of the candidate that of a leader? Or does the candidate have to work at and adapt to the needed personality style to lead your business?

There is a mental and psychological health danger to a successor who takes charge of a business while lacking the natural personality style or behavioral style needed to be an effective leader. The stress can be huge and can become magnified if good results with the business do not take place and the successor feels that he or she is letting down the family. Are your successor candidate's self-image and self-confidence strong enough to stand up to the challenges of being an FBL? Your next leader needs the confidence to not buckle under the pressure of having many people looking for them to fail or actually wanting them to fail. This group will often include some of the people from whom the successor will need support. One of the most common challenges for any successor is overcoming the resentment that family members (especially those passed over for the position), non-FME executives, and clients and customers feel when a family member is anointed as the future leader of the company. Properly communicating your reasons for your successor decision will help alleviate bad feelings and potential family conflict.

Obstacle 9. Failure to Use Objective Evaluation Resources and Tools

When announcing succession plans, FBLs often face family jealousy, anger, distrust, and feelings of abandonment. One way to be on the offensive in proactively justifying your decision is to bring in outside evaluators to supply reasonably objective assessments of the candidates. Luckily, the behaviors the successor will need to have can be identified in candidates using a fairly simple computerized personality assessment. There are many independent parties trained to conduct personality assessments, including some very effective but inexpensive computerized surveys that allow you to assess the personality factors needed in a leader. Professionals licensed and trained to use these products are easily found on the Web by searching under the term "personality surveys."

Harlan Oelklaus, a TAB facilitator-coach in Austin, Texas, suggests that if your succession decision is among multiple candidates, the first step is, of course, for you to speak with all the qualified candidates to find out if they are even interested in the number 1 position. Then engage an objective third party to assess the needs of the company, both now and in the future, and to compare those needs to the strengths of each of the successor candidates. "It's best to use an independent party to conduct evaluations of potential successor family members," says Harlan. "These evaluations sometimes result in revealing information that can lead you to look closer at one candidate while weeding out others from consideration. I've witnessed FMEs who boldly assumed feelings of entitlement despite lacking the education or ability to run the business."

With the support of evaluations by independent parties, you can, at the time of announcing your decision, show that you tried to treat your children and family members fairly, if not equally. Having clear test results that were produced by an independent party doing the evaluation and that indicate the best person for the job can help the FBL make a decision and can help reduce the amount of tension among the candidates. Such a recommendation often helps get the support of other family members who have had different ideas on how the selection process should have proceeded and what the results should have been. When the FBL makes a choice based on actual data and recommendations from a party trained in making such assessments, there will be less suspicion that favoritism is at hand. Let your candidates see the results of the testing so that they better understand the criteria upon which your decision was made. It becomes a whole lot more difficult to argue in the face of actual facts.

Obstacle 10. Fear That When One of the Candidates Is Chosen, Others May Leave or Lose Interest

One commonly used excuse given by FBLs for their delay in picking a successor is, "I have several children in the business, and I don't want to offend the ones who will not be selected." My response to this concern about causing family waves is yes, delaying a selection decision will mean avoiding family conflicts for you, but it also means deeper conflicts for others down the road. Not having a successor pick rarely leads to anything other than family trouble.

Sometimes there is more than one candidate with equally outstanding successor qualifications, and this poses a big challenge to keeping the relative not selected in the process. It is not uncommon when one of the equally qualified FME candidates is chosen, for others to leave. Selecting a successor in a family business is no easy undertaking. It becomes especially difficult if several qualified siblings are in the running to be the new leader and the parents have treated their children equally all of their lives. The FBL is burdened with making a decision that may be interpreted by some family members as saying one child is better than the other child, and that makes it very difficult.

One FBL had three children, two sons and one stepson, working in the business. Each child wanted the successor position, and the FBL was concerned that the two not selected would leave when the selection was made. He requested that each of them take general intelligence tests and also complete a behavioral survey. After having them tested, he met with each child to discuss his or her passion for the job and to gain greater perspective on how each would proceed if given the FBL position. The FBL then met with a coach to discuss the results of the tests, surveys, and discussions to help him objectively review his choices in order to make a wise succession decision. The FBL ended up naming his stepson as successor, and he was able to keep his biological sons in the family business by promoting each to more important roles in areas that interested them. His successor choice made good business sense, and he handled it in a way that made good family relations sense. Furthermore, his approach also prevented the other FMEs from leaving the family business.

An approach used by many for situations involving equally qualified candidates is to have co-CEOs or copresidents. One family business that manages apartment buildings and leases apartments is owned by the two founding brothers. They were concerned that if they appointed one of their FMEs, the other would leave. So the brothers appointed the daughter of one of the brothers and the son of the other brother as copresidents. At first, there was a lot of inefficiency with the copresident approach. As the daughter commented, "We waste so much time arguing about some small matter, such as whether we should spend $2,500 to send someone on a trip." The cosuccessor approach can be made more effective and efficient by developing clear and separate lines of responsibility. The daughter copresident, who has no engineering experience, is now in charge of functions such as accounting, legal, apartment leasing, and getting new clients. The son copresident, who has an engineering degree, is in charge of all engineering- and operations-related responsibilities. If there is a deadlock between the two, a neutral outside party designated by the fathers acts as a tiebreaker. The cousins work well together.

Many family businesses with relatives having equal ownership have developed a format in which one of them is the top leader, but with restrictions. This often works out extremely well. For example, in one family business, the relative who is president of the business can make decisions that involve up to $5,000 in expenditure. Beyond that, he needs to get the agreement of his two brothers. Likewise, he can fire any employee of the company, other than his brothers, excluding any of the top managers unless he has the agreement of his brothers.

Succession decisions nearly always mean change to the status quo, and change is viewed by many people as a threat to the happiness and well-being to which they are accustomed. This can be especially problematic when dealing with family members who may have held a hope that they, or a family member close to them such as a son or daughter, might one day be given the succession position. A fear can develop on the part of family members who are not the anointed successors that they will have to let go of certain things they enjoy doing within the business to accommodate the succession plan. This fear can spread so far that it results in capable and hardworking family members checking out of the family business.

The FBL of one family manufacturing business informed his youngest son FME at a breakfast that his brother would be his successor. The younger brother heatedly let his father know he believed that the father was making a mistake and that he was better qualified for the job. The strife created by this situation affected many aspects of the FBL's family and work life. His youngest son stopped talking to him, except as needed at work. The two sons were constantly at odds with each other, and even the FBL's wife, who favored their youngest son, was rallying against his decision.

After a few months of turmoil, the FBL called a family meeting with his sons and wife to explain why he felt it was best to pick the older brother for the successor job. He reviewed the aptitude tests, behavior surveys, and written SWOT analysis results for each of the brothers that he had used to help him decide which son was more qualified to be the future FBL. He discussed the reasons for his decision as he saw them. The FBL discussed the benefits of the younger son staying in the family business, including ownership benefits, which he felt outweighed the problems of the older sibling being the future president. At the same meeting, the FBL presented a new role within the company with increased responsibility to the younger son, a role that was far better suited to his sales strengths and interests. At the end of the meeting, he told his youngest son, "You have to accept and embrace my decision, or you should make plans, over a reasonable time, to leave the business." The younger son did accept the situation, and he became a positive force in helping his brother when it was time for him to take over the operations of the business.

The announcement of a new successor can be made more palatable to other family members involved in the business, particularly the other candidates with outstanding successor qualifications, if they see a leadership development plan for those not chosen that includes increased perks and incentives for them. Granted, it can take a dash of skill, more than a pinch of care, and quite a bit of finesse to make those who were passed over feel wanted enough to stay in the family business. However, if you want to keep good family members working in the business, it's well worth the effort. You can walk the family tightrope without falling, even when it comes to announcing your plans for succession.

Obstacle 11. Lack of a Qualified and Interested FME Successor

It often happens that there is no family-member candidate who is both qualified and interested in being the future FBL. A survey of TAB members indicated that less than 50 percent felt they had an FME who was both capable of being trained to effectively run the business and interested in being the future leader. Some had children who might in the future be capable of being trained to run the business effectively but were too young for the FME to know if they even had any interest in the business. It's not unusual for a family business to have no one who is both up to the job of being a successful successor and interested in being the successor. If an FME is not, in your opinion, destined to be the successor, that information should be shared with the FME sooner rather than later. Without a qualified successor, many family business owners provide for the event of their demise or a disability that would prevent them from running their businesses by selecting a current non-FME or someone outside the business to serve as an interim successor while the business is listed to be sold.

During the years prior to Jason's joining TAB, I had chosen a non-FME executive officer of TAB to be my interim successor in the event of my demise or my having a disability that would prevent me from running the business. The executive understood that in the event of my death or disability, he would be the interim successor only until the company was sold. My daughter, Lynette, was designated as controlling the voting stock of the company. She knew that she should take the needed steps to sell the business. This plan changed, as I mentioned before, when Jason joined TAB and was designated as my successor. Watching Jason develop into an outstanding leader of the business I created fills me with pride. But it took looking outside the box for me to pick the right successor.

Conclusion

The FBL of an engineering firm told me once that "one of the challenges of maintaining a successful family company is to keep the blessing of the business from becoming the curse of the family." Having a trained adequate successor can help the family business continue as a blessing for the family. Picking a successor can be a process filled with the spirit of joy and giving. On the other hand, for many, the succession selection can be an intimidating process. Preparation and communication mixed with a positive attitude will make the process much easier.

Many FBLs, whether consciously or not, prefer to stay in a "safe" place where they convince themselves that their health is just fine and that they are going to hold the FBL position for many years to come. Recognizing the potential of health issues and threats to life or mental acuity that may be in the twists and turns that the road ahead holds are just not things about which most people want to think.

Designating a future FBL is, by definition, not treating children or other family members equally if more than one of them wants to be the successor. The one who is selected to control the family business in the future may, at first, appear to be the only winner. However, the real winners are all the family members who will benefit from a controlled transition with the best candidate to become the FBL as the selected successor.

This chapter has shown you who and what to look for and how, once you find the right successor, to put the selection in place without upsetting the family apple cart. But succession doesn't stop with the selection. This is why the next chapter in our family business journey involves grooming the successor. The steps you need to take to maximize the development and grooming of the successor are covered in Chapter 5, "Grooming the Family-Member Successor."

Checklist for Selecting the Family-Member Successor

- One reason so many family businesses don't make it past the first generation is the FBL's failure to appoint a successor and create a workable transition plan.
- A successor must possess the Passion, the Aptitude, a Vision of the Big Picture Potential, and an Empathetic personality match if he or she is to PAVE the way to successor success.
- Gaining the help of outside, objective personality evaluations is an exceptional tool to aid in the succession choice.
- FBLs should not give up if there appears to be no viable FME candidate. It may require looking outside the box and

opening up the idea of succession to more family members to uncover an unknown interest.

- FBLs should not be misled into choosing a child or family member because his or her heritage puts him or her "in line for the job." The continued success of the family business is critical to everyone's happiness and well-being.
- FBLs need to choose a successor and communicate the choice in a way that gets the greatest buy-in from FMEs and non-FMEs and preserves the peace and harmony within the family.
- FBLs should follow the golden rule of succession and make sure the successor they choose actually wants the job!
- A caretaker–interim COO can bridge the gap if the chosen successor is not ready to take the reins.

CHAPTER 5

THE FIFTH ELEMENT
Grooming the Family-Member Successor

The grooming of a successor to lead your family business successfully requires all the preparation needed for any privately owned business and more because it is a family business. Your successor needs to be developed and prepared to become a future FBL, which is a complex job that affects both the results of the business and the success of many family relationships.

It is extremely important to have a strong succession grooming plan in place that prepares the successor to handle these issues. The sudden flare-up of issues for a successor who does not have the needed experience or training to handle them is a leading cause of why later generations often experience a level of success that is significantly less than it was under the FBL of the previous generation.

Some FBLs select a successor and then say, "Whew—I've got that covered." In many cases, *leadership development* of the appointed successor does not take place, which is unfortunate because such development would prepare the successor for the transfer of business leadership. The lack of this type of development is a major reason that, according to the Family Business Institute, only 30 percent of all family-owned businesses survive into the second generation, only 12 percent are viable into the third generation, and an extremely small number—just 3 percent—of all family businesses operate at the fourth generation and beyond. With the odds stacked heavily against the next generation succeeding in running the family business, it's important to arm yourself with the tools you need to effectively groom your chosen successor.

Grooming and eventually turning over leadership of the business to a family member is a very different and more emotional undertaking than a succession plan for an unrelated person taking over a nonfamily business. Developing a family-member successor requires more patience, more investment of your time, and possibly more business resources than would a plan to develop a non-FME successor. Let's look at eight common roadblocks to properly grooming an FME successor and learn how to map the way so you steer clear of these pitfalls to succession success.

Succession Roadblock 1. Not Transferring the Wisdom of the FBL

In one of my favorite episodes of *Everybody Loves Raymond,* Raymond's mother, Marie, refuses to give his wife, Debra, a key ingredient for making Raymond's favorite meatballs. Marie withholds the key ingredient because she can't bear to share her "power" over her family with Debra. She cannot handle losing her role as the reigning queen cook of the family. Some FBLs knowingly or inadvertently withhold key information from their successors. They do not want to thwart their successor's efforts as Marie did, but they may not want to let go of some aspects of their key position.

What is the best way to transfer to your successor that wisdom which you have acquired from experiences you have faced as the

FBL, both good and bad? Your choice of the methods you will use to help you transfer your wisdom to your successor will depend, in part, on how you like to interact with your family members. For many, the right methods include scheduled times, such as weekly luncheons with your successor, to review progress and explain your views on what is happening or should be happening. Without these scheduled meetings, the development of your successor will be much slower and your successor may not be ready when he or she needs to be.

One FBL owned a bakery chain with three locations. Each of his sons managed one of the stores. He told his sons that they were the future successors of the business. When I discussed with the FBL his need for a plan so that each son would have at least some minimum level of business knowledge about the finances, merchandising, and other key areas of running the business, the father, apparently refusing to accept that he would not always be in charge, responded that he was too busy running his company to make time for such a plan. Several years later he took vital information needed to run the business to his grave. His sons had no knowledge about such things as what to pay for supplies or the personal cost of the business, but they had to jump in and start running it. None of them had ever seen many of the key legal, financial, and operational records of the company, let alone discussed them with their father. They could not even find where the FBL had kept the company tax return records and other vital information for previous years. The lack of available information caused the company's existence to be "touch and go" for a few years while the sons learned about the areas of the business that the father did not teach them.

During the time that Jason was being groomed for the president position, he and I scheduled weekly update and review luncheons, during which we discussed any items either of us thought were important. I found this to be a very enjoyable and invaluable time to transfer wisdom and to review his progress. The weekly meetings were conducted with the help of a written agenda that was prepared before the meetings. Sometimes, I pointed out to him areas where I felt things might be done differently and why I thought so. We were able to make many course changes as they were needed. We still have many working meals together, although they typically no longer have agendas.

Another benefit of scheduling regular update and review meetings with your successor is that these discussions will strengthen the successor's interest in learning from you while also boosting his or her confidence. To make the best use of the update and review meetings, allow your successor to question and challenge the development plan and the inner workings of the company. The successor will definitely glean a good deal of knowledge from being allowed to do so, and you might just learn something too. Be conscious of establishing and managing expectations of the successor during the update and review meetings. Start the meetings by focusing on things that have gone well. It is important to recognize good performance before discussing things that the successor might do differently. You may be faced with a successor who feels unfairly evaluated and may respond with such behaviors as defensiveness and sensitivity to your comments at the regularly scheduled weekly meetings.

It's your job to help your successor develop accountability, and you can't do that without pointing out things that may have been done differently. Hopefully your successor will also understand that the advice shared is not being given as a way to put him or her "down" but rather to enable you to have a strong positive impact on making the succession happen sooner. For your advice to be embraced, you need to switch hats at some time during the day and put on the mentoring hat. Mentoring your successor requires you to be available to answer questions or give advice to your successor. During Jason's first few years at TAB, I called several times a day to ask him if he had any questions or anything he wanted to discuss. Some of the time he did, and we had long discussions. Other times, the answer was "Thanks for calling, but I have nothing that needs to be discussed." Once you get used to it, mentoring a successor will enrich the lives of both you and your successor while bringing great results to your family business.

Don't limit sharing your wisdom only in formally structured meetings. The informal times spent "talking shop" make the development process interesting and valuable for the family-member successor. Talking shop often makes the difference between success and failure when the successor needs to assume the role of FBL earlier than expected. One family-owned and run metal fabricating company had just celebrated 25 years of continuous operation when sadly, the founder, Wolfgang, died. Luckily, Wolfgang had been grooming his daughter, Ingrid, since she was a child. She heard shop talk between her grandfather and father while she was growing up. This informal exposure to her family's business continued when she started working in the office of the factory after school and on weekends. All the while, Ingrid listened while her dad discussed contracts and engineering drawings at job-site trailers. Together, when they rode home, they talked shop. Her father was grooming her by sharing his experience.

After getting her college degree at 22, Ingrid began working at the family business full-time working side by side with her father at corporate headquarters. She spent as much time as she could with her dad. They talked at the office and when not at the office, with her father freely sharing his wisdom. Ingrid was happy to work beside her father while he shared his experience and wisdom. It was a positive experience for both of them. One day a month, they would go to lunch and use the time to identify such things as where the company had challenges and opportunities and where it might need additional help. Her father was clearly a mentor, and he hoped she would one day succeed him. He just did not expect it to happen until later in his life. Ingrid took over the family business when she was just 27, right after her father died unexpectedly of a heart attack. She credits her easy transition into leading the family business to the mentoring from her father who so joyfully shared his wisdom with her. The obvious advantage of Ingrid's childhood involvement in the business, along with her many adult years working full-time in the business with clients and engineers, made her transition to FBL feel seamless for her. In reflecting on her transition, Ingrid noted that she did not have any major problems taking over the business because her dad talked shop with her for so many years, giving her an insight into the job that no formal education could have replaced.

Jason and I often talk business during off-the-clock family time, and it's the same with most FBLs I know with their intended successors. Some of our best course changes got their start during these informal discussions. The time I spent transferring knowledge to Jason is time that I continue to cherish. Enormous psychological reward and real joy come to me from watching Jason approach business challenges using some experience I have shared with him during our shop talks. Best of all, that gift continues to give and expand as Jason and I work together toward growing TAB to its potential.

The transfer of knowledge to your kids and grandkids by talking shop can start while they are very young. As previously mentioned, while growing up, I was fortunate to hear business discussions between my father and uncle. It was difficult for them, at times, to refrain from discussing the business at meals with other family members present. My father shared some business challenges and achievements with me from my earliest years. Bottom line: if you love what you do, you will have a desire to discuss it. These types of discussions nurtured my understanding of business in an amount that is hard to measure but significant in impact.

It should not surprise you that I have talked shop with my children and grandchildren since they were very young. I always keep a keen eye out for their interest level. The first time I remember my grandson Jake (Jason and Lynette's son) showing an interest in TAB was just after we had celebrated his fourth birthday. I was taking a walk with Jake, my daughter Lynette, and some of our horses and dogs, while Lynette and I were discussing a TAB challenge. Jake jumped right into our conversation. Upon noticing Jake's interest, I asked him what his thoughts were about handling the challenge. I was amazed and, I admit, also quite pleased, that my four-year-old grandson found our business "game" amusing enough to want to play along and share his advice. Jake then fell into one of those moments when, within the innocent smile on a child's face, there is reflected a level of pride and connection that pleased both of us. After Jake gave us his opinion on the situation, he marched off to catch up with one of the dogs, and the business small talk was over for the moment.

I know how tempting it is to snatch our fledglings from the nest and push them into the business. I have no intention of doing that. However, Jason and I will continue discussing TAB with my other grandchildren who show an interest in business discussions as long as doing so does not hinder the many wonderful experiences of childhood. In the meantime, I am sharing with them my business experience that is unique to those raised in a family business.

Succession Roadblock 2. Not Having a Successor Development Plan

Think of Prince Charles who has trained his whole life to be king but, according to some, feels frustrated and may have low self-esteem because his mother, the Queen, seems intent to hold onto the job till she dies. By the time she dies, he may then be of retirement age. There has to come a time when a major portion of the power shifts or there will be frustration.

To avoid frustration, you should have a clear plan (Successor Development Plan) that shows when you expect the successor to be ready to assume the responsibility of COO, if you expect to continue in some way with the business, and the final responsibility in the event that you exit the business, whether voluntarily by retirement or involuntarily by death or disability.

Develop your successor gradually with phases for his or her assuming the different responsibilities stated in the Successor Development Plan. As your successor is able to assume more of the leadership role, the plan will act as a barrier to potential dangers that may face the business during the development period. Your Successor Development Plan should include scheduling the gradual transfer of the responsibilities and authority in different areas of the business with the objective of giving some control and then adding more authority step by step as your successor demonstrates results.

For the sake of your family, and the continued success of the business, don't stretch out the grooming of your successor without establishing a clear time in which at least the COO responsibility will have been transferred to him or her. Successors are more likely to grow impatient and angry if they have no timeline for increased responsibility. While some successors will have the patience to wait many years to take over the day-to-day operations of the business, many other appointed successors have left their family businesses to pursue outside opportunities. They left because they got tired of waiting for their "turn" and decided to look elsewhere for new and challenging opportunities. Even chosen successors with a lot of patience can run out of patience. When a successor leaves the family business, it not only leaves the FBL without a trained successor but it also, in many cases, destroys the FBL's ability to keep the business in the family.

This timing issue of when your successor is ready is a delicate tightrope act when you feel that your successor is not ready, but he or she wants to move into the leadership role without further delay. Don, the owner of an appliance service and repair business, faced this challenge. He had two sons working in the business, and when

Don reached 60, he named the elder son as his successor. He told everyone in the family that he intended to retire when he turned 70. After a couple of years of being groomed for the successor position, the elder son felt he knew enough and could do a better job managing the business than his dad. Instead of sitting down and discussing things with his dad, his son constantly complained to his mother, his brother FME, and the other employees in the business about what his father was doing wrong. He made it clear to all of them that he felt that he could do a better job running the family business. It did not take long for his griping to get back to Don, who did not feel his son was ready to take over the reins. He saw many areas in which his son needed to develop before assuming full control of the business. Don's wife, eager to have her husband retire sooner rather than later, urged her husband to take the son's words to heart and hand over the running of the family business. Don wanted to make his family happy, so against his better judgment, he let his son take over. His son made some terrible mistakes, which within a few years destroyed what had been a very successful business. Consequently, both sons were left without a family business source of income, and Don's life work was destroyed forever.

Family pressure to move someone to the next step before the successor is ready can complicate the process of developing a successor. Having a Successor Development Plan with benchmarks in place will help you bypass this concern. Successors with overeager expectations and wants can be retained in the business by providing a plan that shows them what has to be achieved before they move on to the next level of responsibility.

The "right" timing of the phases of succession development boils down to choosing the rate for turning over responsibility that suits both the needs of the FBL and the successor. There may be major disagreements about the succession timetable between you and your successor due to your successor's eagerness to gain more authority and responsibility for operating the business and your feeling that your successor is not yet ready to fly solo. This situation is particularly common when the successor has worked in the business for a long time and is already familiar with many aspects of the business.

Another potential problem is when your successor is not ready to move on to the next phase of responsibility because he or she is taking longer to learn the ropes than either of you originally expected. The timing may have to be delayed for your successor to succeed with the current phase of responsibility. As Bruce Healy, a TAB facilitator-coach in Calgary, Alberta, says, "One of the keys to turning over the COO or general manager function to a relative is that the FBL must be fully committed in advance to giving the revised structure a full chance to work. If not, the turnover will likely fail."

The Successor Development Plan for Jason called for him to take over as president of TAB within 24 to 36 months of his starting full-time employment with TAB. Keep in mind the years of business responsibility that he already had prior to joining TAB, which I have mentioned before. Together, we developed the Successor Development Plan that allowed Jason to develop his skills and get the experience required to successfully take on the president's role. It involved a phased transition of all the president functions to Jason over the three-year period, with Jason assuming different responsibilities within stated phased time frames.

Because Jason had worked for a major accounting firm, our plan called for him to initially focus on the financial responsibilities. Once Jason achieved a comfort level and attained certain benchmarks in those areas, the next stage of the plan called for the marketing and sales departments to report directly to him. Jason's greater responsibility and authority for franchise sales included measurable sales benchmarks that, when achieved for a period of one year, would result in Jason taking on more areas of responsibility. When Jason achieved those benchmarks, his responsibility for the sales staff was transferred to another executive, who then reported to him. Jason then headed up operations for the company, which allowed him to gain important management experience and profit and loss responsibilities for the business. As Jason was ready to assume additional responsibilities, the reporting lines of our company's organizational chart were shown to reflect the changes in additional departments reporting to him.

Family businesses that fail during successions don't plan to fail—they just fail to create and use a plan to develop their family-member successors. Those who create Successor Development Plans with a clearly scheduled, phase-by-phase path to the president's role are likely to find their successors more fulfilled, enjoying better family relationships, and achieving greater business success.

Start creating your Successor Development Plan with your successor as soon as he or she is selected. If you procrastinate on creating a Successor Development Plan, a day may come when you or your heirs realize that you waited too long. That day may be one in which you are unable to help with the training because of incapacity or because you are no longer breathing.

Once your Succession Development Plan is put into action, you need to stay on top of it and monitor closely whether or not the plan is working, including the timing for the successor assuming more responsibility. This means keeping the wheels moving forward while making frequent progress checks. Vigilantly keep aware of the progress while looking for potential blowouts or critical factors that get lost or overlooked and need to be pointed out to your successor. If, according to the plan's time frame, your successor is not making adequate progress, or progress is taking place faster than anticipated, course changes will be needed to better reflect the reality of what's happening.

Succession Roadblock 3. Having Difficulty Giving Up Control

Developing a successor to a point where you can feel safe about passing the torch to him or her requires letting go of some of the control. This will go a lot easier for you if you embrace rather than fight the loss of control. Believe me, I know personally that this is not an easy thing to do. Remember, a successor will rarely reach the desired level of preparation your business needs if you operate your business in a way that leaves the business completely dependent on you.

Many FBLs have trouble successfully delegating any significant level of control. This is because they feel comfortable only when they control every aspect of their business, and they lose this comfort level if they delegate authority to a successor. They are so hands-on that they create a leadership gap that leaves their successor unprepared for the challenges ahead. Is it any wonder that so many family business successors with this type of FBL, even those successors who have outstanding natural aptitude, do not perform adequately after assuming the leadership role?

Ask yourself if handing over responsibility for key parts of your business to your successor presents a major psychological roadblock. If the answer is yes, the high D for dominance in your natural personality, which has made you such a driving force in making your business succeed, creates a sizable obstacle resulting in your stubbornly holding on to too much control. You must fight your natural controlling behavior and hand over both the responsibility and authority for key parts of your business. You need to take whatever steps will work for you to make this happen.

For many of you, your business is much more than your livelihood. It is your lifeblood. I have heard many family business owners make verbal reference to having a relationship with their businesses that is so strong that some even go so far as to refer to their business as "my baby." Of course, it is difficult to turn over something we love to someone else. The key to fighting your controlling nature is to view turning over some of the control as protecting your baby. If you don't let some control go, it will slow down or even destroy the development of a successor, who may become needed by your business, your baby, to be safe.

One FBL, Charlie, has a daughter with the aptitude and behavioral style that easily positions her for one day taking over the business. She fulfills an important role as director of the company's IT department and loves the operational aspects of the business. However, Charlie resented it when she suggested setting up procedures and systems for reorganizing other areas of the business to improve the performance of the company and speed its growth. Like many FBLs, he had a high level of dominance in his personality, and he was very uncomfortable with anything that challenged his control of the business. Charlie was the biggest obstacle standing in the way of the next stage of growth.

Getting past his need for control wasn't easy. His daughter appealed to his fatherly love to try to get him to see how important it was to allow her to become everything she was capable of becoming. Unfortunately, this didn't work. So finally, after 15 years with the company, his daughter told Charlie that she was thinking of leaving the family business. She explained her belief that her father's control issues would never allow her to assume the day-to-day responsibility as executive vice president and COO of the company. Only after he understood and recognized the seriousness of his daughter's concerns did he allow her to get involved in those other areas that interested her. Promoting her to executive vice president and COO of the business and letting her thrive in this position had another benefit to Charlie. It allowed Charlie to free up his time to better focus on developing new business. No longer a slave to the day-to-day operations, he was able to take advantage of the special status that founders have for getting in the door and gaining an audience with the real decision makers of other companies.

Handing over the baton gracefully and without reluctance is a lot more challenging when you are only semiretiring as opposed to fully retiring and not remaining active to any degree in the business. You can't live a semiretired lifestyle and still have the same level of day-to-day control. However, you can maintain the

CEO position within your company, as many FBLs do, and still give up day-to-day charge of the business. You can do this without having to relinquish all control to groom your successor.

To succeed, your successor must be given room to establish his or her own personal leadership style and personality. Your successor will never be just like you. Your successor will have Strengths and Weaknesses that may match or surpass yours as well as Opportunities or Threats to their success that are greater than what you have. It's interesting to see how many FBLs have difficulty accepting that their successors are as good, or better, than they are in certain areas, even though these are the reasons they chose the successors in the first place. For some, even a much-loved family member can be a threat. This has led many FBLs to cling to control. It seems that it is not easy for them to give up their "baby," even if they are giving it up to their baby.

For other FBLs, giving up control of the business is threatening because of their fear of feeling useless. No one looks forward to getting old. Holding on to full control of the business can provide a false sense of vitality that can almost fool you into feeling invincible. But you have to face the fact you won't live forever. You can't take the business with you, so you must come to terms with giving up day-to-day control. I'm not saying it is going to be easy, especially if you have grown the business from its conception.

Anna, a woman in her fifties, is the FBL of a family-owned advertising agency. She once recounted how her life changed dramatically when she was in her early thirties. Her father died suddenly in a car accident and she was left with the responsibility of becoming an FBL. Until that time, she had been working for another company in a different city. Her father's death brought her unimaginable heartache. At the same time she was trying to come to terms with her loss of him, she had to run a company that was left to her without her being trained to be the successor. Faced with her new responsibilities, Anna immersed herself in the family business and somehow led it through a few rough years after her father's death.

At the time she related her story, she had a grown son, whom she had designated as her successor. However, when asked how she was grooming him, Anna admitted that she had neglected to develop a plan to train her son for the leadership position he one day would take. I wondered how she could risk exposing her son to a situation similar to the one she had to endure. Anna was able to admit that she was afraid to start turning over *any* control. She was afraid that the more responsibility she handed over to her son, the less important she would become. This meant a lot to her since so much of her identity was tied up in being the leader of the business. It was more than a bit scary for her to think about a future without controlling her business. Anna sought help with a psychologist who helped her understand that leading her business was only one part of who she is and that there were pitfalls in Anna's identifying herself only with her business accomplishments. When it all sank in, she was able to move forward in grooming her son.

The thing about control is that, for many business owners, it seems so utterly appealing to hold on; that is, until you finally let it go. Then you wonder why you waited so long! I urge you to embrace the experience and joy of watching someone you love behind the controls of the machine you built. Get past the fear of letting go and start taking the steps toward embracing it. Once you get used to having a looser grip on the wheel, you are going to like, and maybe even love, the feel of it most of the time.

Succession Roadblock 4. Not Involving the Successor in the Company's Strategic Planning

Despite its importance, strategic planning is a greatly underutilized tool in the family business. Just a little over half (54 percent) of the firms responding to Laird Norton Tyee Family Business Survey in 2007 said they had a written plan. But strategic planning is extremely important not only for increasing the success of your business but also for ensuring the preparedness of your successor to take over. At TAB, we use a process called "Strategic Business Leadership" (SBL), which was designed specifically for privately owned businesses including family businesses. SBL is a five-step process that makes strategic planning easy to accomplish. SBL is effective because it also ties in the tactical and operational involvement of the FBL that is inevitable with family businesses.

Once your successor has been selected, he or she needs to be involved in all future steps of the formal strategic planning process for the family business if he or she is not already involved. Their strategic planning involvement should include attending weekly review meetings and annual reviews. Before your successor attends his or her first Strategic Planning Meeting, he or she needs to know the strategic direction of the company. Under the SBL process, this discussion starts with the written Company Vision Statement for the desired future of the family business. The Company Vision Statement outlines where the family business is hopefully heading. Without this knowledge, any training you provide your successor will lack purpose because your successor does not clearly know your destination for the business.

The successor needs a copy of the written Company SWOT Statements that identify the Strengths, Weaknesses, Opportunities, and Threats of the family business. The two of you should have discussions on each of the points in the SWOT Statements. Next, the successor needs to see the written company plans including the company's goals for the next few years of operation. Having working knowledge of how the strategic plans were developed will help your successor better understand the business. It will also help your successor learn how to nurture the plans for the business. SBL plans clearly map out the actions needed to make the strategies of the plans successful. They also provide benchmarks so it is easy to recognize if the company plans are progressing as desired or if course changes are required in order to reach success.

Before having your successor attend his or her first weekly Strategic Planning Review Meeting, which some companies call a "planning team meeting" or an "operations team meeting," provide your successor with up-to-date information about the business, including legal and operational information, a summary of the financial status of the business, a projection of its financial future, a legal and administrative profile giving information on the structure of the business, an operations report, a sales and marketing overview, a management systems information overview, and a human resources overview. (A summary list of these sources of information is shown as Exhibit B in the Appendix.) Educating your successor in these different business areas usually requires involvement of key executives in your company and sometimes outside professionals, such as your auditing firm or outside legal counsel. Sharing this family business information gives your successor a much better understanding of the business and jump starts their development into becoming an effective member of your planning team.

I brought Jason up to date on TAB's written SBL Statements almost from the moment he joined TAB. I asked him to participate in the strategic decision-making process, which made for an easier transition for him as he began to take over more of the control. I asked and encouraged him to identify changes he felt would have potential to make the company operate more smoothly and profitably. Not only did this allow Jason to see that he really could make a positive difference, it also went far in gaining, over a period of time, the buy-in of those non-FME executives who, when he was first brought in, had been questioning his value as the future successor. It was understandable that there was skepticism, at first, of a family member coming in as the future successor, when the person had never worked for the business. Instead of getting upset about this, I tried to keep in mind that, after all, TAB is the source of income for these non-FMEs, and this income source is on the line if the successor fails.

Succession Roadblock 5. Not Allowing the Successor to Make Mistakes

For your successor to grow, you have to let your successor spread his or her wings and fly. Think about the lesson learned from the Greek myth of Icarus. Wearing wings of wax and feathers fashioned by his father, Icarus takes to flight and freedom. Ignoring his father's warning to stay away from the sun, Icarus, smitten with the sensation of flying, soars too high. The sun melts the wax wings and Icarus dramatically plummets into the sea and meets his doom while his father helplessly watches. Applying the moral of the story to the business world, it is better to let your successor learn to fly when you can still reach out and help prevent a crash.

The pain of watching a family member, especially your child, fail because you gave the go-ahead to fly too soon is not something you want to experience. This makes handing over the business to a successor not fully prepared for flight a frightening possibility to face. Just like Icarus and his wax wings, if your successor, in his or her inexperience, gets too close to the sun, the business could easily suffer an irreversible meltdown.

As the parent or family member that built the business, watching the business crash and burn hurts on many levels. If you are like most FBLs, you love your company and want to see it thrive and grow, and this requires that your successor have adequate time and learning experiences to become a wise leader. One of the most difficult, if not excruciating, moments in developing a successor is when you see your successor making a decision that you believe is a mistake but you know that it will be best for grooming the successor if you step back, cool your heels, and watch it play out.

Jason once said to me, "Nobody in his right mind would have hired a 33-year-old with *no* franchise experience to be COO of a multi-million-dollar company." Yes, I made a family-impacted decision to put a 33-year-old in a key position, but it wasn't a decision I made lightly. As I advise all FBLs to do, I looked at a wide variety of aspects to determine if Jason was ready to assume substantial responsibility, as the maturity level and abilities among people differ so greatly. I was committed to closely mentoring him during the early years. I was also confident that while there would be some things that he would learn only by making mistakes, I was confident that Jason was the kind of person who doesn't repeat his mistakes. I said to myself that I would allow him to make mistakes. If I feared that his actions would impact too negatively on the company, I would try more proactively to change his mind by asking the right questions and getting facts that would result in Jason realizing that he needed to change his way of thinking. I believe that allowing a successor to make mistakes is needed to give a successor a true feel for the day-to-day weight and responsibility of having a key role in a family business. Not supporting decisions, even mistakes, undermines your successor's authority, confidence, and learning curve.

When you see a problem with the successor's path, you need to fight the desire to say, "We're not going to do that anymore." It is hard to let go and sit back when you see something happening with which you do not agree. Staying behind the line of advising and not crossing over into meddling is not easy when you believe, based on your years of experience, that your successor is taking the wrong path. You have to step back when you think your successor in development is going down the wrong path and try to let him or her see that the path he or she is following is going in the wrong direction.

Sometimes you have to go against your basic nature and hope that those decisions of your successor with which you disagree will work out better than you expect. Your successor can grow only when he or she does not feel pressured to make the same decisions you would probably make. It is not easy for most of us who are FBLs, but we can restrain ourselves if we keep in mind that developing our successors is more important than any *particular* project as long as a negative outcome from that *particular* project is not likely to hurt the business too much. There may come a time when the dollars involved become so significant that you need to get much more involved to change a decision that you feel is wrong.

It's a little easier for us to restrain our natural tendency to require our successors to make decisions that we like if we recall how it felt when we were left to clean up our own mistakes compared to how it felt when someone else did it for us. From which scenario did you learn the most? The greatest lessons always happen when you are allowed to make a mistake and then see it through by doing what was needed to correct it.

Succession Roadblock 6. The Successor Failing to Develop

The development of Jason as president of TAB has me secure in the knowledge that TAB will stay in the family at least into the next generation. But developing a successor does not always work out as well in many family businesses, regardless of how confident the FBL is in the ability of his or her chosen successor. Sometimes it just doesn't turn out the way the FBL would like. The most common reason is that the chosen successor does not have the talent that the FBL thought he or she had for the job.

This type of situation came up in conversation one time when I was sharing dessert with a friend while we were both on vacation in Key West. We were sitting in an outdoor café, the weather was sublime, the key lime pie delicious, and we were enjoying a catch-up type of conversation since we had not seen each other in some time. In other words, it had all the makings of a perfect afternoon. Then my friend received an unexpected call from his office, and his tone and mood went sour. Apparently something bad had happened at the office, and his son, whom he had been grooming as his successor since the boy was in his teens, had been unable to solve the problem. In fact, from what I could tell from the side of the conversation to which I was privy, the son, in trying to solve the problem, had made the situation even worse.

My friend worked his way through a long and involved call, while I ate my pie and tried to salvage the experience of the moment by enjoying the great view. When he finally hung up the phone, he emitted a great sigh that signaled to me we were in for one hell of a talk. He admitted this was not the first time his son had been unable to see the company through a crisis, and he was more and more certain each day that he had made an error in appointing his son as the successor. He reluctantly told me that he realized that he had made the succession choice believing his son could grow into the job but that he had to face the fact that his boy did not have the talent for the job that he thought he had.

I asked whether he had any other family member who might be better qualified as the future FBL. He responded that he had a younger cousin working in the same business but for another company who would be a brilliant successor and who was eager for the job. My friend said that he hadn't asked his cousin to join his company because he feared that selecting the cousin would destroy his relationship with his wife. My Florida friend felt cornered and compelled to walk a precarious family tightrope because of spousal pressure. The solution was having a family business coach meet with my friend and his spouse to discuss how the spouse's and their son's future would be more secure in the case of the demise or serious illness of my friend if my friend's cousin came into the business and began to be groomed to be the future FBL. They discussed why their son just did not have what was needed and also the fact that an offer of selling part ownership to the cousin would probably be needed to attract him to leave his job and join my friend's business. Reluctantly, the wife agreed, and things as of now seem to be working as hoped for in the business with the cousin still in training to become the future FBL.

Another common reason the chosen successor just doesn't develop the way you would like is because he or she has less passion for the job than you thought. Meyer, the owner of a retail operation, related how he had selected his son as his successor and had tried to "make a man of" his son and get him ready to assume the leadership of the family business. Meyer was confident in his son's ability but concerned about his son's lack of passion for the retail business. His son's development was not particularly good. His work effort, or rather the lack of it, became a major distraction to other employees. Meyer was often aggravated and frustrated about the situation. Six months into the succession development, Meyer found out about his son's dream of starting a high-tech business based on a particular type of Web site that he wanted to develop. He agreed to help his son start the high-tech business with a limited investment in his son's venture and to mentor the son. The son's work ethic in his new venture could be described as "workaholic." Six years later the family retail business was sold to a third party. It took a few years, but the son's new venture ultimately prospered.

It is not uncommon for an FBL who has known a relative for the relative's entire life to misread whether he or she has or can develop the emotional nature needed to be the future leader of the family business. David, who is the FBL of his business, was proud when his oldest son Bryon, who was 28 at the time, told David that he wanted to eventually succeed his father. David was a little concerned about Bryon's history of "blowing up" when someone—sometimes other employees or even customers—disagreed with him, but he chalked this up to Bryon's youth. When working with Bryon on his Successor Development Plan, David discussed his concern about Bryon having blown up at employees and even at customers. Bryon assured him that it would not happen again.

Sad to say, within the first six months of his being designated as the successor, Bryon blew up at three of the warehouse workers over small mistakes. David had many conversations with Bryon, but his behavior didn't change. Finally, David recommended to Bryon that he get professional help with his issues, and Bryon refused. David then sat down and said to Bryon, "Son, I have to resolve this issue of your outbursts, or I will never turn over leadership to you—and that's really not what I want. I want you to seek professional help at company expense." After a long silence, Bryon said, "I'll do what it takes to control my temper." Bryon received help from a professional who worked with him, over a long period of time, on his anger management problems. He worked on his temper and tried to eliminate or neutralize his outbursts. Bryon did improve; however, he never overcame this emotional weakness sufficiently to satisfy David. Two years after he had started to groom Bryon to be the leader of his business, David decided to change course, and he explained to Bryon that he felt more comfortable with his youngest son, who was 25 at the time, becoming the eventual successor. David did what he had to do for the good of the family, which was very dependent on the success of the family business. His relationship with Bryon, sadly, never got back to where it was before David changed course.

Your succession development needs to allow for a testing or trial period to determine if your successor has what it takes to become the future FBL. Be prepared to change course, as Meyer did, because you will not know if your selection turns out to be a good choice until you see how your successor handles an increasing amount of responsibility. When you pick and start training a successor, it does not mean that the die has been cast and the decision is set in stone.

Succession Roadblock 7. Not Using a Caretaker–Interim COO

It often happens that an FBL puts off his or her dreams of retirement or semiretirement because his or her successor is not ready to take over. The FBL does not want to elevate a current executive in the business to the presidency because he or she wants to leave the FBL position open for the chosen FME successor. This roadblock can be bypassed by bringing in an outsider who understands that his or her role is to hold down the fort until the successor is ready to take over and, in the meantime, to help develop the successor. The key is finding the right person for the role of caretaker.

The most qualified candidate to temporarily run your company may be a senior member of your management team who both understands the business and wants to run the company for a period of time while your appointed successor gets brought up to speed. Unfortunately, this type of temporary position being held by a current executive who wants and feels deserving of the long-term leadership role often has resulted in that individual resenting having to develop the family successor for the role that he or she feels should be his or hers. Ultimately this has sometimes resulted in the loss of the highly qualified current employee.

This is why engaging an outside executive to come in as the caretaker–interim COO while your family-member successor gets ready is nearly always a better choice than putting a current employee into that temporary leadership position. As Harold Apple, president of Vector Technologies, Inc., in Indianapolis, Indiana, has stated, "Professionals from CEOs to functional heads can be leased to fill a gap while a relative is gaining the requisite experiences to move up and run your company. The 'temporary' relationship of the leased employee can be a comfort to heirs while providing stability and leadership to the company."

To a large extent, engaging the right interim leader is dependent on the preparation and understanding you put in before the person is hired. Understand what motivates each candidate for the caretaker–interim COO position, and ask yourself if the role with your business can provide a job that will satisfy that motivation. The best caretaker–interim COO is often someone who has had success in leadership duties in the same or similar business field as yours but is currently retired and is dissatisfied with retirement. Sometimes there are good candidates who are available only because they were let go due to the closing of a division or some other factor that was outside his or her control.

The caretaker–interim COO must clearly understand your objectives and the ground rules of the engagement. He or she must fully accept that the ultimate control of the business will remain with the family ownership regardless of the title of the caretaker–interim COO. This will typically mean that you have the final say, but in the event of your death or incapacitation, someone in your family may retain final decision-making authority while the non-FME executive has day-to-day COO authorization. The caretaker–interim COO needs to know and be committed to achieving the goals in your Company Vision Statement and all the critical elements of your company plans and personal plans for the family business. This sometimes includes honoring unique objectives regarding the relationship between the FBL and his or her chosen family-member successor.

The pay scale for attracting the caretaker–interim COO is an especially important factor. It should be as competitive a compensation program as your company can afford with very generous perks based on company results and the results of the development of your successor. This is definitely one situation in which you are better off overpaying than underpaying. If you hire a caretaker–interim COO for significantly less than he or she feels the position is worth, it is highly likely that he or she will quickly become dissatisfied and leave the first time a position becomes available that pays more. One owner of a car dealership provided a big pay bonus for the caretaker–interim COO that was payable as soon as his son took over the top company leadership position from the caretaker–interim COO. Similar incentives can go a long way toward keeping a caretaker–interim COO in place until your successor is ready.

The terms of engagement or employment of a caretaker–interim COO should be in writing and include such things as what action is to be taken if the family-member successor proves unsuitable for succession or leaves for other reasons. It should recognize that the caretaker–interim COO is unlikely to maintain his or her position if the company needs to be sold, and it should provide for a specific bonus for the successful execution of the exit strategy. This will help motivate the caretaker–interim COO to perform effectively.

Succession Roadblock 8. Not Investing Enough Company Resources in the Successor's Training

Developing a family-member successor typically requires more commitment and investment from the business than developing a non-family-member successor. Maximizing your successor's growth potential usually takes more than just on-the-job training. This training or education comes with a price tag. Most successors, even if they have worked in the business for a significant time period, don't know what they don't know.

After considering many options, Jason and I chose the International Franchise Association (IFA) as the primary organization from which Jason could gain the most valuable outside business information to help him develop as the president of TAB. TAB pays the expenses for Jason to go to conferences of the IFA and become involved in its programs. TAB also paid for Jason to take a program offered by the IFA that resulted in him becoming a

Certified Franchise Executive (CFE). He learned about franchising methods used in the industry that he would not have been exposed to from anyone within the TAB organization. He now sits on the board of governors of the IFA. Jason took other programs that we felt would help his development that were not offered by the IFA, such as training with Target Training International (TTI), which resulted in Jason becoming a Certified Professional Behavioral Analyst. Being able to analyze behavior is an important skill needed to facilitate and coach TAB members.

For some of you, spending business funds to send your successor to outside training feels like money is being taken right out of your own pocket. However, allocating the successor's time and the company's money to outside business training may be one of the most important investments you can make in your successor's development and your company's future. Your question should not be whether your successor should attend select programs, seminars, and conventions. You need, instead, to ask yourself, "Which of the many options for outside training can help my successor best move forward, and what specialized education is the key to improving my successor's productivity and quality as a leader of our business?" Identify with your family-member successor what is missing in his or her experience or performance. An increasing number of business trade organizations, like the IFA, offer specialized online courses and even degree programs that may be just the programs your successor needs. Before your successor joins any organization, however, attend meetings of the associations, if you're allowed to do so, as a guest and see what they offer.

I believe strongly that it is important for your successor to join a peer board, like that offered by The Alternative Board. In this type of setting, your successor will be able to work with other leaders who run businesses, which will help him or her in running your family business more effectively and more competitively in the future. The value in our peer boards derives in part from the fact that the members are not in competition with each other. Peer board membership is one of the best ways for your successor to get advice and solutions for handling tomorrow's small business challenges because the advice is from leaders who are not locked into the traditional thinking patterns in your particular business field.

Some of the best benefits happen as a result of ideas gained during social times when the FME successor gets to talk shop with people running businesses in the same type of industry.

Conclusion

Being able to professionally nurture your successor so that he or she can become the best he or she can possibly be is one of the great privileges of being an FBL—one of the best win-wins there is. You are providing those you love with satisfying and challenging employment that greatly enhances both their work and life experiences. You are also protecting the future of a business that is so important to you and your family.

Jason's development as president of TAB has not only helped TAB bring financial benefit to our family but it has also become a wonderful part of our family relationship. My relationship with my son-in-law and my helping to groom him to become an outstanding president brings immeasurable enjoyment to my life. His development did not happen by selecting him as my successor FBL and then just letting the development take its own direction.

Selection is not enough. It is the rare case in which handing over the whole business in a hurry, with little successor development, succeeds without a lot of mistakes that are painful to the family business. Too many successors are not adequately developed at the time the FBL unexpectedly dies or experiences health issues that keep him or her from running the company. When an untrained successor is suddenly forced to step into the FBL's shoes, it leaves a tremendous burden on the successor. Getting your successor up and running is a delicate balancing act in which you need to move fast enough to keep your successor happy but not so fast that your successor lacks the experience to move to the next level of being able to run the business properly. I have mentioned roadblocks in this chapter that you may face in developing your successor, and I've shown how each of these roadblocks can be circumvented by using the methods I have described.

You do your family a disservice if you have no trained successor in place and, unexpectedly, there is a need for someone else to run your business. Take steps now to make sure your future successor is trained and ready when needed. If your successor has been adequately groomed, he or she will know how to solve most of the problems that can and probably will arise. Delaying the training and development of a successor creates a much greater potential for family business and relationship problems to occur at a later date.

Now, it's time to see how the family business's culture, the topic of Chapter 6, can be used to make your plans for your family business and family relationships happen.

Checklist for Grooming the Family-Member Successor

- Grooming a family-member successor requires you to make a deep commitment of time, money, and personal energy.
- Don't hold back key information regarding the business. Share key legal and operational information early on including a financial summary, legal and administrative profile, operations report, sales and marketing overview, management systems information, HR overview, and any other critical information.
- Put your Successor Development Plan in writing. If it isn't written down, it doesn't exist.

- Don't hold on to day-to-day control after your successor is ready to take the helm.
- As soon as you have chosen your successor, involve him or her in the company's strategic planning.
- Support your successor's decisions, and allow your successor to make mistakes that serve as valuable learning experiences.
- If your successor does not develop as you anticipate, be prepared to change course.
- Consider hiring a caretaker–interim COO if your successor is not yet ready to be the FBL.
- Guide your family-member successor to take full advantage of training sources available outside the family business, and be willing to use company resources to pay for training.

CHAPTER 6

THE SIXTH ELEMENT
Aligning the Culture of the Family Business with the Company Vision

In general, the culture of a family business is the amalgamation of the FBL's values, philosophies, business practices, communication styles, and written and unwritten codes of conduct. Put roomfuls of any people together in any business and you will have various levels of conduct that morphs into a culture. Now, add a lifetime of family history into the mix, and the potential for conflict from the family culture takes on a whole new level of intensity. Family politics and business politics overlap. Company culture takes on a different meaning in the context of a family business because you have all of the cultural dynamics that nonfamily businesses have meshed in with family dynamics.

A family business can have all of the great ideas in the world firmly in place, but if the inherent culture of the family members in the business is not aligned with the Company Vision for the business, then those ideas have little chance of moving the business to greater success. You have to navigate through and around the family's Cultural Potholes or fill in the potholes to sustain good relationships in both the family and the family business. A smooth journey without breaking the shocks requires extra attention and planning. This chapter identifies 12 of the most common Cultural Potholes for families that work together and the most effective ways to handle these issues.

Cultural Pothole 1. FMEs and Non-FMEs Interpreting Communications Differently

The communication challenges faced when working for and with relatives are unique. I can't begin to count the times I've heard of or seen FBLs or FMEs overreact to comments made by relatives in the business environment. This situation took place during a planning team meeting chaired by John, the father of two son FMEs. The younger son in the business felt slighted by something that his brother, Stan, said when discussing a business proposal. He vehemently responded, directing his comments to his father: "Why can't Stan just tell me what he wants done? Stan doesn't speak to me; he *yells* at me. My brother can be such an arrogant jerk. He interrupts every time I try to express my opinion." The younger brother would not have reacted the same way to the same comment from anyone else. His response was magnified because of all the resentment he's carried inside since his brother tried to flush his head down the toilet when they were six and seven years old.

According to a study out of the University of California, our messages are communicated 55 percent by facial expression, 38 percent by tone, and only 7 percent by content. While many FBLs fail to recognize how their facial expressions and tone affect their family communication culture, their FMEs usually notice these subtleties. Children pick up on a raised eyebrow or hands folded across the chest or any other negative expression they have seen their parents do at home—years before they ever saw them do it at work. A message accompanied by a good delivery stands a greater chance of being heard.

The nature of family relationships automatically brings in childhood baggage when it comes to how a family member receives communications. The tone and volume of the voice of a family member tends to have greater impact than that of a non-FME who is saying the same thing. Memories of being reprimanded as a child never fade. Speaking loudly and with a stern facial expression may cause the FME to subconsciously shut down in a way that would not happen with a non-FME. If you are not sensitive to these dynamics, your words may not be heard and your message may be lost with your FMEs.

As a child, Ann had been treated with unfailing kindness and tenderness by her mom, Bess, so she has a hard time handling it when her mom FBL gets frustrated and disappointed with her over a business decision. Ann takes the disappointment of her mom FBL with much more intensity than any other employee would. She acknowledges that "criticism from Mom stings far more than it would if it were delivered by anyone else." Ann explained that there are times when at the end of the day, she goes home feeling dejected because her mom couldn't be bothered to even look up from the computer when conveying a message to her or saying good-night. Family members who yell, who use condescending tones, or who speak in an arrogant manner to other family members at work are undercutting the efforts of those they treat this way to help build a successful venture. FMEs are often much more thin-skinned to criticism from a relative in the business because they bring their past into every interaction. These are the types of things that result in the FBL or an FME feeling communications among family members are mostly closed off in the business.

TAB facilitator-coach Jan E. Drzewiecki says, "Family communication styles are often bad because in a family business, family members are more likely to say what they think to each other than they would if they were an employee of an outside firm. Quite honestly, sometimes it doesn't differ too much from the way they spoke to each other when they were growing up."

This attitude does not always lead to the goal of communication, which is for the FME to hear the message, take the time to internalize it, and act on it.

A family business culture that accepts poorly executed communications among FMEs will cause resentments to build, which often carries into a palpable tension for family relationships outside of the business. Your expectations should be to have the type of communication culture between family members in the business that minimizes these resentments. Making these expectations become a cultural reality among your family members usually requires a proactive step on your part. Things work better in a business if there is a culture agreed to among family members in which everyone feels safe and comfortable in expressing their views in an open and honest manner.

This can be achieved by using the TABenos process, which I developed to help create safe communications cultures. *TABenos* is derived from the ancient Greek word *temenos*, which is translated as "sanctuary." It involves a series of exercises that minimizes the natural defenses people have to open communications, and it results in the participants agreeing to a set of guidelines that dictate how the individuals, in this case family members, within a group of people will communicate with each other. TABenos helps to soften the sting felt when criticism is delivered by a family member. In addition, it eliminates issues of tone, loudness, invalidation of ideas, and most other aspects of negative communication that hurt the company culture and destroy family relationships.

So now, let's look at how the TABenos process works. TABenos starts with a meeting that is usually limited to family members in the business, although some have allowed spouses of these family members to attend even though they do not work in the business. Before the first TABenos meeting, a facilitator who is a neutral party, someone outside of the family and not an employee of the family business, needs to be selected by the FBL to facilitate the meeting. The TABenos exercise will be effective only if the facilitator remains neutral. If the facilitator of the meeting has a stake in the results, his or her ability to maintain neutrality can be quite challenging. In addition, if the facilitator of the meeting has a position of authority, he or she cannot achieve the desired meeting dynamics because those dynamics are based on no family member holding any more weight at the meeting for his or her views than the other family members. The TABenos process requires that everyone's views at the meeting be treated equally, which generally means that an FBL cannot possibly facilitate a TABenos meeting.

The facilitator opens the meeting by explaining that the purpose of the meeting is to get communications issues out in the open and develop a family communications culture that provides safety, honesty, and openness for family members both inside and outside the office. The facilitator than goes over the meeting ground rules, which include such things as having participants agree to the principle that the words or terms expressed by the participants cannot be directed toward any person. For example, it would be unacceptable to say, "I need my brother to stop being sarcastic."

Now the facilitator is ready to call on each family member to respond to three TABenos exercise questions. The first exercise question asked is, "What does your communication protective armor or defenses look like?" "Interrupting" is an example of an answer. The second question asked is, "What actions taken by others cause you to put down that armor?" "No threats of reprisal" is an example of a response. The last question asked is, "What benefits will be gained as a result of feeling safe and being able to set aside our armor with other family members?" "Greater teamwork" is an example of a response to this question. Exhibit C in the Appendix gives a list of responses for each of the three questions that came from one TABenos meeting. As can be seen in Exhibit C, each family member gives his or her short responses to the questions, often with answers that are only one or two words.

The facilitator will write down the responses on a whiteboard or on some projection device that is easy for everyone to read, without identifying who gave the response. Then the facilitator will ask for a verbal commitment from everyone at the meeting to follow the TABenos culture when communicating with each other and to point out any future displays of armor or communications that cause the armor to appear. The TABenos commitments that participants make to each other at the meeting should be used when family members communicate with each other, whether one-on-one, at family-member meetings, or when there are non-FMEs within hearing distance.

The benefits from TABenos have been proven to go far beyond improving the working relationships between FMEs. Family members carry over the TABenos culture so they communicate much better among themselves and with other family members not employed in the business, even outside of the business arena. As the TABenos culture evolves among your FMEs, it will bring about the honesty, openness, and trust that should be part of the culture in every family business. Sometimes it takes time to build a safe TABenos family communications environment. As new communication patterns may form over the years and new family members might join the business, it is a good idea to periodically update the commitments to TABenos by going through the entire TABenos exercise again.

Cultural Pothole 2. Unclear Guidelines as to What Business Discussions Are Not Allowed

Some family businesses prohibit discussions, nonfinancial or financial, about the family business if anyone present is not employed by the business, even if they are family members.

But for most of us, it's okay to discuss most business matters in front of our immediate relatives who are not FMEs. In fact, it is often difficult to not talk about business with an FME when away from the office. Jason and I find it difficult to get away from talking about business when we are with each other and other family members. Jason and I have agreed, with the support of our spouses, that we will stop family business discussions under certain circumstances such as when a family member yells, "Enough TAB talk already!" We have also agreed to not talk about TAB during family-member celebrations, such as birthdays or anniversaries. Setting theses boundaries keeps the family peace and forces both of us to drop business and just enjoy family time.

What about sharing financial or strategic information with family members who are not employed in the business? In most family businesses, FMEs may share some types of information such as growth expectations or bigger picture strategic developments with a spouse or other family member who is not employed in the business or does not own any stock in the business. There are some types of information, such as certain types of financial information, that FMEs can share with those family members who have some ownership stakes in the business but not with those who do not have such stakes. Other family businesses take a hard position that FMEs must not repeat information to which they were privy just because they are family members, as is part of the Family Culture Statement of a third-generation landscaping company:

> Our family business culture calls for all family-member employees to keep the highest level of confidentiality since they may have access to information that cannot be arbitrarily revealed to others. If family members are in attendance at a family function, for example, a family dinner, they may hear discussions about the performance of the company or concerns about employees or customers.

Family members who are privy to this conversation must not repeat this information to which they were privy. They must use absolute discretion concerning matters learned by them only because they are family members.

Cultural Pothole 3. FBL's Unwillingness to Be Open to FMEs' Innovations

Barry, the younger son in the family's construction company, served as the head of the estimating division. His older brother was the director of sales. During a meeting of department heads, which was chaired by his father, Barry expressed his ideas about changing the commission structure used for the sales staff. When his father explained that Barry's plan would be a significant departure from the way sales commissions had been structured in the past, Barry responded by stating, "As your son, I think we should challenge the way we have done things in every part of the business." Barry's father didn't shut him out. Instead, he asked Barry's brother, "As the director of sales, what is your opinion?" The action taken by the father paved the way to a family culture that was open to nontraditional thinking and, at the same time, headed off a potential major conflict between the brothers since Barry's brother was in charge of the sales department. Unfortunately, not all FMEs want a culture that is as open to new ideas by FMEs.

Many parents raise their children telling them what to do, and these parents have a long history of not hearing their children's ideas as to how they would like to do things. TAB facilitator-coach Jan Drzewiecki shared with me her belief that "if there is dysfunctional behavior in the family, it tends to spill over from family life into business life." Jan further expanded on her belief by saying, "Many FBLs think their ideas are the only good ideas. As a result of finding that their ideas have fallen on deaf ears, family members employed in the business start to retreat from the creative thinking process. They get tired of being told 'no,' so they stop making suggestions. This ultimately hurts the growth and success of the family business."

The interdependence many FBLs feel in their roles as a business owner and their identity as "father" or "mother" are important psychological motivators. The great pleasure some FBLs take from providing for family members, sometimes called "patriarch/matriarch motivation," assumes patronage. But this also sometimes perpetuates a culture of not listening to the ideas of their children FMEs if they did not listen to their children's ideas when they were growing up. Many of the parent boss challenges of not being open to the ideas of children FMEs stem from these childhood interactions when the roles were clearly delineated between child and parent. The results of these interactions carry over into the more complex role when parents become the business bosses of their children. These difficulties can have far-reaching implications that can come between a parent boss and child FME and bring about a disruptive impact on the family business culture.

When a son or daughter joins the family business, all the emotions of the parent-child relationship are magnified by the added complication of having to work together in an environment controlled by the parent or parents. If the parent boss is not open to the ideas of the children FMEs, it leads to conflicts about authority and the son's or daughter's authority and participation in the company. These matters need to be proactively resolved with a culture of openness to nontraditional ideas before they become major problems.

My father always said he felt that one of his roles as a parent was to help prepare his children to fly with their own wings. In some ways it is easier to do this when a family business is not involved. The role of a parent who manages his or her child includes challenges not faced by a parent in nonbusiness life. Encouraging talented children to grow within the family business, while controlling their adventurous nature, requires openness to new ideas. Take care not to fall back on family baggage and discount or shut out a child's ideas. It sometimes is a fine balancing act for a parent. One of the common cultural differences among family businesses is the openness of the FBL to innovations suggested by FMEs when those ideas go against traditions.

In some family businesses, the culture is such that no family member questions or speaks up to the FBL until he or she is spoken to. All opinions are kept close to the chest, and a stiff upper lip is the desired personality trait. The business halls are quiet, and the décor is tastefully appointed but devoid of personality because that fits the values of the FBL. Four sons in one family business call their father "The King" because he is so unwelcoming to their ideas. At times, the problem grows into a confrontation in front of other employees. If this culture goes on too long, it can cause the children FMEs to be viewed as "losers" in the eyes of the other employees.

The problem is more likely to cause friction if the child FME is a strong manager, which makes the FBL more defensive and unwelcoming to ideas because he or she feels threatened. This is especially challenging when a child FME's responsibility overlaps into areas that the parent considers his or her personal turf. There will be less child employee and parent boss role relationship confusion if the child FME knows what is acceptable in the way of speaking up to the FBL. When a child FME wants to make major changes to how the family business is run, it can be particularly difficult for some FBLs to try the new ideas because they are not their ideas. "I can't get Dad to take my ideas seriously" is a frequent complaint. This is not an easy problem to solve, and for many family businesses it is a very delicate matter.

One of the most effective ways for you as a parent boss to overcome this cultural challenge is to establish a mentoring relationship with your daughter, son, daughter-in-law, or son-in-law. For many, a mentoring culture enriches their lives and businesses, and it brings great results to the family business, in part because the culture changes to one in which the ideas of FMEs are welcome. It's true that a mentoring culture is not a true democracy, but it can move the culture closer to being one in which every family member, regardless of position, can take part in business strategy discussions. They can humorously yell out their opinions and ideas, and they can express their disagreements. All FMEs know that they can discuss their ideas with the FBL and their ideas are welcome.

Cultural Pothole 4. Cultural Attitudes toward Female FMEs

Imagine a family business in which the father's rule is that no females are allowed in the business. While that is not common, it is common for the culture of a business led by a father to have more obstacles for daughters who want the opportunity to lead the family business to overcome than for sons. An example of this type of culture took place when one female family member, who for many years had been an executive in her family's business, was shocked to find out that her father, without her knowledge, was talking to her brother about joining the family business and becoming the successor. The brother had never worked for the business.

There has been progress in the area of the perceptions parents have of daughters in their businesses. However, in the culture of some family businesses, there would appear to still be significant barriers that daughters face. Many FBLs still talk about the great aptitude of their daughters and then go on to share their concern about their daughters' abilities to lead and handle the pressure. Some admit that they do not want their daughters to become the full-time family business leader because they'd rather see their daughters spend more time with their kids.

This cultural bias against female FMEs came across very clearly with one FBL's policy for check signing privileges. Hoyt signed the checks in the company unless he was absent or unable to do so for some other reason, in which case he had given his son the authorization to sign checks. His daughter, one of four regional store managers for the business, asked her father to allow her to sign the checks if he was traveling out of town. He turned her request down. Hoyt's daughter told him she felt his decision was made because she was a daughter and not a son and she said Hoyt's decision was sending a message to other employees that said, "I don't trust her so you don't have to trust her." Although check signing was only one example of her father's unequal treatment, she felt it was a symbol for others in the company that he did not hold his daughter in the same level of trust and value as his son.

Hoyt considered her point and realized his behavior might indicate a bias toward the son. He gave his daughter, in whom he had full trust, the right to sign checks up to $1,000 by herself and up to $10,000 with the cosignature of their attorney if he was out of town. He explained that at some point she would be able to sign checks without limitation, but he did not know when that would be. The solution brought about a situation in which both were comfortable. The signing rights problem had existed only because Hoyt had never looked close enough to see that he had a discriminatory cultural attitude toward his daughter FME because she was a female.

Cultural Pothole 5. FMEs Lending to or Borrowing from the Business

The family policy for lending money to the family business by family members or lending company funds to a family member is a culture element that can be particularly sensitive to family relationships. Many families view giving personal loans to their own family business as just something that is handled very informally with little if any documentation. Like many founders, there were times in the earlier years of TAB that I personally loaned money to TAB.

Things get more complicated when there is more than one family member with ownership in the business such as with Terry, who co-owns an export company with his son Roger. Terry lent $50,000 to the family company so that the company could set up a Web site with a new platform that would help attract and service more overseas interest in the company products. Terry had helped out with loans to the business many times in the past. There was a note signed by the company with a scheduled payoff in one year. When the year was up, the loan was not paid off because Roger felt that doing so would hurt the liquidity of the business. Terry complained that if the debt had been a note to a bank, it would have been called. Terry was upset and made it clear that he would no longer make any more personal loans to the company. He required the business get a new loan from a bank to repay the debt to him. This was a change in culture. In the future, when the company needed to borrow funds, the business would go to a bank.

In many families, anything and everything that connects with money issues will ripple throughout the family. Money going into the business from family members is only one of the money areas for which there is likely to be a culture among the family members. There is the opposite side of the money flow in which many family businesses have a culture that embraces family members borrowing from the company. If you want a culture that embraces the company lending money to FMEs, the rules for borrowing from the business should be clearly communicated to family members. Many family businesses have a culture that allows family members to borrow from the business for personal use only with a lien against their future earnings or their ownership in the business. Family members' needs and circumstances change, so it is important to spell out what can be drawn upon in a way that leaves no questions. This avoids arguments about favoritism and fairness. Who can borrow how much and under what circumstances are critical issues not just in the financial realm of a family-owned business but also in the arena of trust among family members.

One FBL commented that allowing the family business to lend money to children was, for his company, a formula for parent-child conflict. He added, "When you make a child a loan, you should assume you won't get it back. If you *are* paid back, consider yourself one of the lucky ones." The policy for allowing the family business to lend money to children in the business should be clear as to when it must be repaid and the consequences if it is not repaid on time.

Cultural Pothole 6. Sibling Rivalry

The roles of siblings in business are manyfold. They include the roles of being partners, friends, employees, shareholders, and executives. All these roles must be carefully explored and integrated in a way that keeps conflict to a minimum and keeps the focus on company objectives to a maximum. When a second child enters the family business, it's not uncommon for there to be family disharmony and divisiveness that did not exist before. In some cases, the root of the problem can be traced back to parents who encouraged competition between their children. This can lead to hard feelings between siblings when they have to work with each other in the family business.

Robert and Henry are brothers who were born only 17 months apart. They competed in everything since childhood. Their personalities were always different from each other. Robert, the older and more extroverted of the two, frequently got the two of them and their friends into minor scrapes with authorities. Henry, who was more sedate than his brother, was usually dragged along, which he bitterly resented. As they grew older, both boys began working for their father, Al, in his machine parts distribution business. Their ongoing rivalry continued into the business. For years, Al ignored their bickering when it reared its head at the workplace saying, "It's always been that way—they're brothers." The other employees didn't share his acceptance. Their bickering had a way of being contagious, leading to open bickering by other non-FMEs. It became part of the culture of the business.

Now move forward and picture a weekly meeting among Al, Henry, and Robert when the sons are in their thirties and no longer boys. By then, Robert was president of operations and sales and Henry was vice president of finance. During the meeting, there was a business disagreement over credit policies of the company that provoked an emotional reaction from both sons. Different information was given depending on which son was telling the story to Al. The dispute heated up when Henry accused his brother of artificially beefing up gross sales without proper regard to the credit problems being created. Al, realizing the problem was getting further away from being resolved as each of his sons dug in to each other, called the meeting to an end.

The next day, the three of them met for lunch. Al had finally "had it" with their bickering. He explained that the underlying reason for the dispute between the two sons was not really a business dispute; it was sibling rivalry and had to stop. He made it clear that the dispute was because they were competing, and it was time to work together and show other employees that all the executives are working together as a team. Al explained that if they wanted to continue working at the business, he needed each of them to give a commitment to his brother to work together for the Company Vision of the business. By bringing the sibling rivalry factor out in the open, Al helped increase harmony between his sons within his family-run business, and over the years this impacted in a positive way on all the employees in the business.

In a family business, you should head off any bad dynamic that starts to emerge between siblings as soon as the manifestations of it are observed—certainly you should do it a lot sooner than Al did. Sibling problems typically spring into existence early in life. As a parent, you may have been accepting it for decades, just as Al had been dealing with the rivalry of his two sons. If you continue to ignore it when your children join you in the business, the rivalry will create a culture of family members working against each other in the business. Siblings working together in a family business often need a clear message that their bad dynamics will not be tolerated in the business. They may need help in learning how to take a step back and develop a new approach to their multiple relationship roles inside and outside the family business.

You can help this situation by developing job descriptions and positions for the siblings that cut down on role confusion. It's wise to look for how siblings can support each other in areas where they may not be strong and use this information to better define their respective roles in the business.

Cultural Pothole 7. Split-Personality Culture

After one father sold the family business to his two sons, constant bickering started taking place between the two sons that caused the business to have two different camps, each working against the other with each having a vastly different company culture. Not surprisingly, the business soon fell into trouble. In the end, the family was forced to liquidate the company to fulfill tax obligations. The family was heartbroken; their mom, wives, and children felt that the two sons had let them down, and the fruits of their father's lifetime of labors were erased forever.

Family culture challenges in a business become further complicated when more than one family owns the business and the children from more than one family work in the business. The introduction of cousins into the mix introduces a new set of cousin relationship issues with the added dynamics of the different parental units involved. This can result in different sets of culture in the business among the FMEs, which some call a "split-personality culture."

In some companies in which relatives equally own the business, they literally rotate the title of president in order to avoid the problems associated with deciding on only one leader. One family alternates the top position each year between two brothers. They have done so every year for over 20 years, and it works for them. The company has grown significantly since the alternating ownership started, and the best part is that the brothers have remained on friendly terms. In other businesses where it is done, it has not worked out because the family business culture changes every time the president changes and those culture changes bring to the surface conflicting views about the values of the business among the employees.

Like it or not, when you have multiple FBLs and their children working in the same business, you have to be very careful about conflicting cultures forming in the business. In family businesses that are collectively owned by multiple families, the best way to keep cousin culture problems from festering into major disasters that involve more than one family is to address the problems as soon as you see them manifesting. It's vital to hold regularly scheduled meetings in which all family partner owners are present to discuss their children in the business. Discussions should take place among the parent partners regarding any FMEs that may be causing problems. Are there children FMEs who try to take unfair advantage of nepotism? These kinds of problems can be disastrous to developing a positive, unified culture if action is not taken. Confronting the problem of any child FME who is abusing his or her rights is always best done sooner rather than later.

Cultural Pothole 8. Work Ethic Expectations

One third-generation landscaping company experienced a problem with one of the sons of one of the three brothers who owned the business. He was assigned to work for various managers who each asked that he be transferred after a few months. The reason given was that he did not want to do the hard work since "his last name is on the company stationery." The following is an excerpt of the written statement sent out by the uncle president to all of the FMEs in the business. This statement was written not only to address the problem with the nephew but also to make it clear what cultural expectations for work ethics were expected from all of the FMEs:

> Having positions in the company is a privilege for family members, and this carries with it expectations of the highest level of ethics, personal accountability, leadership, and full focus on the family business. They must be constant role models for performance as family-member employees. Other employees will be looking at the example you set with the hours you work. This includes your overtime, vacation time, and work on the weekend.

Another situation involved a family manufacturing business. Ernest explained that before he joined his family's business, he knew his father worked long hours, usually six days a week. He also knew his father used to work long hours, usually six days a week, when he was the same age as Ernest. What he didn't realize until he joined the family business was that his "old-school" father would show up late in the afternoon and give him work to be completed that day that would take hours. There were times Ernest was frustrated because he felt that he could never finish what he had to do. Ernest eventually accepted that he was expected to work long hours, six days a week, as part of the price to pay for the future opportunity of leading the family business.

Another family business had challenges dealing with a sibling who had the ability to perform but, because of poor work ethics, was not performing satisfactorily as a production department supervisor. Juan, who owned the business, had reached the breaking point after his sibling had, once again, not met a shipping deadline committed to a key customer. Juan said that tolerating his brother's poor performance was not acceptable so he fired his brother, Eduardo. However, he had a great feeling of guilt, and as a result, he hired Eduardo back the next day. He explained that he felt confident Eduardo had gotten the point and would work harder and be more focused to improve his job performance. Have you ever heard of a person feeling guilty and hiring back a non-FME the next day? Probably not! It's much harder firing a relative, even when the relative's work ethic is unacceptable. But firing the relative and then rehiring Eduardo turned out to be the right solution. Prior to being fired, Eduardo had really never accepted the work ethic culture desired by Juan. Eduardo had viewed his brother, Juan, as a workaholic before he joined the family business, but he didn't realize that Juan expected him to work similar hours. Eduardo started complaining about the long hours, and the struggles between the siblings became extremely unpleasant. Before Eduardo came back to work at Juan's business, he finally accepted the fact that he would never again complain about the work hours. It took their man-to-man discussions to drive the message through to Eduardo that he either had to work somewhere else or buy into the work ethic culture desired by Juan. The special challenges involving siblings with the work ethic being dictated by the boss sibling in the work environment need to be addressed or the problems will carry over and be magnified in the family environment.

Many FBLs have the dream of one day reaching a point when it is possible to enjoy the fruits of their labor but still actively keep control of the business. My father referred to this as the time he could be working on his business, but not in it. For this to happen, the family business must grow to a point at which it is not dependent on the FBL's day-to-day involvement. If the company develops well and prospers, the FBL can take the time off that he or she could not take off as the COO of the business. In some family businesses this change in the FBL's hours has been seen by the FMEs as a change in work ethic culture, which applies to all FMEs. In these cases, the FMEs need to understand that the work ethic culture that applies to them is what the FBL did when he or she was building the business, not what the FBL is doing after he or she has stepped out of the COO role. The FMEs need to understand that the FBL is taking advantage of the opportunity he or she made with his or her own earlier efforts.

One FBL of a manufacturing company ran into a problem with his FME sons who started taking too much time off. When the FBL remarked to his sons about it, one son responded with, "But you do it, Dad." The FBL had a meeting with his sons and detailed the work effort he expected from them. He also reminded them that without being able to take time away from the business, it is less likely that he would want to keep the business. The FBL's sons understood his message, especially the threat of his selling the business. The sons subsequently returned to the work schedule they had kept before their father started taking a lot of time off from work. In most family businesses the work ethic culture for family members is simple: They should aspire to good work ethics. They need to give the family business the best that they can give.

The work ethic of the FBL is often different from the work ethic the FBL expects of the FMEs. I met a man in Australia, Elio, who proudly shared his story of coming over from Italy when 17 years old, owning only his packed suitcase. Elio, who looked to be in his seventies, commented that he still worked six or seven days a week, getting to the office early in the morning and staying late. I asked him if he expected his three children, who he had mentioned worked in the business, to work the same hours. He laughed when he said, "They would quit within a day if they were expected to work those hours."

Elio related to me that when he spoke with his children before they joined the business, he told them he did not want them to work the same long hours that had become part of his life. So he asked each child point blank what his or her expectations were about the number of hours and days of the week he or she would work. His children made it clear they loved the family business, but they had no desire to be working long hours, six or seven days a week, as they had seen their father do. The key is for the FMEs to know the work ethic expectations and decide whether they are willing to live with them.

Cultural Pothole 9. Lack of a Clear Policy for Evaluating FMEs

Virgil, who owns an advertising agency, had a policy of giving what he called "constructive criticism" to his daughter, Sarah, and his other top executives. Sarah was a vice president and director of marketing in the family business. The dynamics of her work relationship with her dad was causing her a great amount of emotional pain because he was as blunt with her as he was with his other employees. It was hard for her to accept even the slightest criticism of her work that he expressed during his evaluations, and she felt devastated when she received less than a glowing review from her dad. Pleasing her father was so important that taking criticism from him hit her many times harder than it would have if she had heard it from a nonparent boss because she felt she was failing her dad. At the same time, she felt unappreciated by him. Sarah could not separate her father-daughter relationship when it came time for her work review sessions. The situation with Sarah was further complicated by her low sense of self-esteem and her dual role as child and employee.

When Virgil came to understand this dynamic, he customized the way he worked with Sarah so he could evaluate her without harming their close father-daughter relationship. Virgil said he would not have done this for anyone else in the world but his daughter. Although the family business culture Virgil created to enable him to work with his daughter differed from the approach he used for evaluating the other employees, his inconsistency was okay because it kept the father-daughter relationship intact and Sarah was doing the best she could do at her job.

Be sensitive to how you evaluate your child FME, particularly if your child FME has psychological challenges, such as Sarah has. Very direct evaluations with a child FME in the business relationship can be a disaster for your FME when that FME already has low self-esteem. When your child FME has a good idea or accomplishes something significant, let him or her know. A little bit of praise to your child FME will go a long way. This can be as easy as a pat on the back and a simple "Good job."

Have a clear policy for evaluation of your FMEs that goes beyond the mechanics of how you do an evaluation. This cultural policy should include by whom the performances of family members will be evaluated. For example, many companies have a culture in which a family member can report only to another family member. Some family businesses have a policy whereby no sibling family members can be put in a position that requires one sibling to supervise or evaluate another sibling.

Cultural Pothole 10. A Parent Not Showing Proper Respect or Value to a Child FME

Many parent bosses do not show proper respect or value to their child FME at work, such as occurred in a situation I witnessed when I worked as an accountant for a manufacturer while going through law school. One day, I was given a tour of a factory by the owner of the business. While he was proudly showing me around, his son, the vice president of operations, approached us. He needed to discuss a work-related issue concerning something that had gone wrong. Upon hearing about the problem, the father became angry, calling his son "stupid," telling him he did not have a lick of brains in his head, and making many other derogatory statements. This took place in front of all the employees and me. The father turned back to talk to me and continued the tour as if nothing unusual had happened. His son cowered behind him. After the owner left, the operations manager who had been on the tour told me how sorry he felt for the son. While the father was kind to all the other employees, he constantly verbally abused the son. The operations manager confided in me that the son felt compelled to remain at this job for the money, which was an amount he wouldn't be able to earn at another job. I left work that day feeling quite sad for the owner's son.

Unfortunately, many parent bosses treat their child FME in a way that reflects badly on them as leaders and parents. This creates a culture in the business in which other employees are also disrespectful toward the FME children and possibly to each other. As mentioned earlier, an FME, especially a child FME, is far more susceptible to feelings of inadequacy when publicly criticized by a parent than are non-FMEs. It's not just the boss's expectations; it's also Mom's and Dad's. If you have a history of speaking disrespectfully to your children, retrain yourself to communicate respectfully. To do otherwise is almost asking for your non-FMEs to follow your lead and show a lack of respect to your FME.

Cultural Pothole 11. Lack of a Written Family Culture Statement

Claudine did volunteer work at a therapeutic horse center once a week, which meant that she had to leave work early on those days. She never needed to question whether it was going to be a problem with the family culture of the business because the family all had copies of a Family Culture Statement that said, "Family-member employees are expected to do civic volunteering and if possible to serve on the boards of local community organizations. The business will contribute to designated community organizations in which they are active."

Family business culture is like a time-honored recipe handed down through the generations: unless it is written down, successive generations of family members may lose track of a key ingredient. The way to steer around this pothole is to put the elements of the desired family culture into a written Family Culture Statement. The Family Culture Statement is a written declaration of the family members' rights, responsibilities, and behaviors, and it is exclusively for family members, unlike the Company Culture Statement, which covers the desired culture of all employees of the business and is available to all employees.

The Family Culture Statement is a powerful tool for establishing cultural expectations between the FBL and FMEs. It should clarify expectations and should address potential conflicting needs that typically arise in a family business, and it should also aid in the resolution of disputes and implementation of adjustments. The desired culture always stands a far better chance of being respected and adhered to by family members if a formal Family Culture Statement, which clarifies all the cultural rights and obligations of the FBL and FMEs, is written down.

In many cases, the written guidelines are started when a family member has become upset because of something that could have been cleared up with family culture guidelines. Putting these policies in writing before problems occur will keep many problems from ever arising. If statements are written during times of calmness, not after a heated argument in which emotions have taken over, a written Family Culture Statement will reduce the chances that family issues will contaminate the business. The more policies and procedures there are in writing, the fewer gray areas there are that can lead to problems. Instead of there being one Family Culture Statement, some family businesses have a series of memos that every FME receives.

The founder of one third-generation family business felt that perks should be restricted to only the top officers, while his sons, officers of the company, felt there should be a policy giving some level of special perks to all FMEs. They agreed to a written policy that states, "There may be certain perks, such as special mentoring or education opportunities for self-improvement that FMEs, who are children of owners of the business, will receive. Except for the stated extended family perks, family members will receive the same perks as management employees of the same level."

In an ideal world, the Family Culture Statement should be the result of collaboration between the FBL and FMEs based on a democratic consensus of unanimous decisions. In real life, it does not usually work this way because it is typically created by the FBL, although it may be modified with recommendations from FMEs. Best results are achieved when the FBL and all FMEs meet to identify and agree upon any important issues missing from the FBL's draft. The Family Culture Statement is a manifesto that can be challenged and modified, but only the FBL has the authority to make changes. In Second Reign and Dynastic Stages, the written Family Culture Statement is more likely to be modified after much discussion, negotiation, debate, compromise, and consensus. In these later stages of a family business, it is common for a Family Council or formal group of family members to craft these Family Culture Statements, which are not legally binding agreements.

All of the issues discussed in this chapter should be addressed in the written Family Culture Statement along with family policy issues discussed in previous chapters, such as whether family members, even the spouses or children of FBLs, are eligible to be employed by the business. The process alone of writing the Family Culture Statement will help you identify the culture that will be best for your family business and family dynamics. Once the culture is formalized in writing, it is easier to be proactive when a family member falls out of line with the desired family culture. Pointing to something specific in a formalized company document helps the FBL remove the subjectiveness of the criticism.

Cultural Pothole 12. Failure to Require Alignment

Often, the communication dynamics that exist in parent-child relationships spill over to their interactions at the family business. You have to be on guard that such a spillover does not contaminate the working culture of the business. One of the key challenges you face is staying tuned in to the early warning signs that FMEs are misaligned with your desired family culture at work. It is essential that you take quick action to resolve the situation. Some FBLs do not take action because they do not want to hurt the FME's feelings or they are concerned that their spouse or other family members will perceive them as being overly critical, especially when it involves a son or daughter. Other FBLs just look the other way because either they have too much to do or they do not want to be confrontational with someone they love.

Not being proactive in eliminating a family culture misalignment can lead to long-term problems. Upon spotting a problem, take immediate action to get your FME back in alignment. Without this action, problems are left to fester, additional family members tend to get drawn in, and the chances of the problem escalating increase.

Rachael, who works for her father in the family business, had a tendency to verbally blow up at her father in front of other employees when he gave her advice or constructive criticism. Her father, Boris, told her, "I won't let any other employee talk to me the way you sometimes talk to me at work. You must address me with respect at work." Boris made it clear that he would not tolerate this violation of the respectful culture he wanted at the business. He then suggested that Rachael create a computer file on anything she wanted to address with Boris that related to her being upset with him. She was to wait a day before she e-mailed any of these notes to him. This technique helped her take work-related criticism from her father without blowing up. It worked because by the next day, Rachael had often decided she did not need to send the e-mails. Rachael was able to separate the family history baggage from how she responded to the critical messages from her father. Requiring Rachael to comply with the respectful culture that he wanted changed things in a positive way. She now clearly understands that some of the conversations she may have with Boris at home are unsuitable in a business setting.

Many FBLs who have a dual role of parent and boss do not proactively address this fine balancing act when faced with a child who does not comply with the culture the FBL wants in his or her business. If Boris had not addressed the issue, it would have undermined the family culture Boris wanted in the business. There are a lot of unusual dynamics that exist between parents and children. One of your challenges, while you are assisting your child FME find his or her place in the family business, is to require your child FME to separate family baggage from the behavior that you want demonstrated at the business.

One of the most deadly violations of family culture deals with behind-the-back bad-mouthing of family members to non-FMEs. At the age of 45, Todd was running a business his parents had established. He greatly resented that his mother, Kelly, still owned 100 percent of the company stock, and he had discussed this resentment with his mother. At a meeting with his management team, he vented to them this resentment with such back-stabbing comments as, "It is good that my mother doesn't come to the office more often because she is so disruptive." Todd also complained that the business was paying his mother too much considering that she hadn't done anything to contribute to the business in over seven years.

No family business should permit a culture in which family members disparage other family members behind their back. Todd was clearly violating this type of family culture restriction. Upon hearing of Todd's outburst, Kelly requested a meeting with Todd. After the meeting, Todd found himself up against a brick wall. His mother told Todd that if he did not immediately eliminate expressing his resentment about her in front of others, he should quit the business. Todd did not get rid of his resentment and continued to express his unhappiness when he was with his mom in a private setting. This resentment continued for another five years until Kelly started to gift him small pieces of the company each year. But because Kelly was proactive, Todd at least stopped expressing negative feelings about his mother in front of employees.

Conclusion

Family businesses usually have in common the desire of the FBL to share a passion for certain activities of the family business with family members but within a culture framework for how the family members interact with each other. There is no family business with a utopian culture. Family businesses with greatly different cultures may run smoothly and might be equally successful. The issue is not how different they are from one another but rather how well the individuals working for these companies understand how their particular family culture is to operate within the business and work synergistically with one another in a way that is comfortable with the culture.

As the FBL and with the help of your FMEs, you should identify the Cultural Potholes mentioned in this chapter that may be impeding the development of positive family relationships in your business. Use my suggestions for moving around Cultural Potholes in the family business. Make sure your FMEs know your family culture and have guidelines or rules for what is expected of them. Use such tools as creating a TABenos communication atmosphere and developing a written Family Culture Statement to remove many of the Cultural Potholes in your family business. Using the tools and methods explained in this chapter to fill in the Cultural Potholes will allow for greater family-member harmony, stronger family relationships, and increased family business success.

Now you are ready to look at Chapter 7, which addresses the special relationship challenges that are faced only by spouses working together in family businesses.

Checklist for Aligning the Culture in the Family Business with the Company Vision

- Family relationships can create unique challenges to keeping communication open and productive. The TABenos exercise is an excellent method of maintaining good communication.
- All FMEs must understand the company culture as it relates to confidentiality of business information and which family members are privy to what kinds of information.
- While the FBL has the ultimate decision-making power, FMEs will resent and often defy the family culture if they feel their ideas are not heard and considered.
- The family business culture should not require the female FMEs to overcome more barriers than the male FMEs.
- Clear guidelines on lending and borrowing policies must be included in the written Family Culture Statement.
- Sibling rivalry can spill over into the business, creating a culture of bickering, if it is not eliminated.

- When more than one family owns the business, the owners must be sure to present one cohesive culture to avoid a split-personality culture.
- FMEs must be aware of the FBL's desired work ethics if the family business is to meet and surpass its goals and objectives. FMEs should decide if they are able to live with those ethics prior to joining the business.
- FBLs need to be sensitive to FMEs when giving work evaluations and ensure that the message is being heard with an employee's ears instead of a child's ears.
- Respectful interaction should be a cornerstone of the family business culture. This applies to how the FMEs address the FBL and also how the FBL addresses the FMEs.
- Cultural clarity will suffer if the desired family culture is not clearly defined in writing and shared and discussed with all FMEs.
- FMEs must be in alignment with the family culture. If FMEs come out of alignment, FBLs need to be proactive and correct the situation before the company culture suffers or changes.

CHAPTER 7

THE SEVENTH ELEMENT
Addressing Spousal Business Partners' Multiple Role Challenges

There have been a few occasions when I have heard business consultants make the comment, "Just because spouses own and work together in a business doesn't qualify it as a 'family business.'" I couldn't disagree more. After all, one part of the definition of "family" is a group of people who live together and are related by birth or marriage or adoption, and so on. Moreover, the number of spouses working together in a family business is very large. According to the National Federation of Independent Businesses (NFIB), there are an estimated 1.2 million husband and wife teams running American family businesses (NFIB, Nashville, Tennessee, 2003).

Spouses working together can, and often do, create family dynamics that are more awkward than other family business relationships. The challenges relating to spouses being family business partners are particularly difficult and can cause great strain, in part because the spouses not only work together but they also live together. When spouses work together, problems can be as mild as their running out of conversation to share or as extreme as their not speaking to each other altogether.

In this chapter, I present the 12 most common and potentially dangerous spousal business areas that, if not properly addressed, could bring about tremendous turmoil. I refer to these as Spousal Business Conflicts. I also show how to create the foundation for maintaining healthy spousal relations for each of these areas, by using methods for addressing the unique spousal needs present in each of these spouse business role relationship challenges.

Spousal Business Conflict 1. Having Conflicting Vision Statements

TAB facilitator-coach Steve Wolf, who is based out of Westville, New Jersey, has suggested that "in order to be a successful husband and wife team, both must be aware of and be in sync with the other spouse's Personal Vision, which includes the spouse's long-term desires involving the family business." Incompatibility often comes about from differences in Personal Visions regarding the willingness to take long-term financial risks. I too have often heard one or the other spouse make such comments as, "My husband wants to keep our company small and is fighting business growth." Such comments come with a lot of anger stemming from the feeling that there's no way out of the problem.

One husband and wife business partner team, Fran and Luis, had many discussions about Luis's desire to borrow long-term money for the expansion of their retail business into a second location and ultimately into a chain of stores. As a condition of receiving an expansion loan, the bank required both Fran and Luis to personally guarantee the repayment of the loan by pledging their home and other personal assets. Fran was concerned about what would happen if their company could not pay off the loan. Contrary to Luis's Personal Vision Statement, Fran's included an *explicit* desire to protect the couple's home and other assets from financial risk. She did not see the need to expand the business to become as big as Luis's Vision dictated.

Nevertheless, Luis understood the additional financial risk and wanted to go for it anyway. Fran refused to sign the personal guarantee. This difference in business philosophies rolled into their home life like a black cloud. Luis was furious: how could Fran put up a roadblock to his dreams for the business? Luis could barely look Fran in the eye, and they didn't talk to each other for *months* except to discuss pertinent business matters.

Luis and Fran could not reconcile the differences in their Personal Visions as to what they wanted from the business. Everything that they had enjoyed and had in common in their personal life now took a backseat to the tensions that filled their business life. Even after their kids, who did not work in the business, finally got them talking to one another again, Luis expressed his continued burning resentment over Fran not signing the personal guarantee. It was only after a desperate intervention from their children that Luis and Fran made a compromise. They finally reached an agreement in which they would personally guarantee a loan amount that was greatly reduced from what Luis had originally wanted to borrow. And this amount proved to be enough for the business to do some expansion, although not nearly to the extent Luis desired. Fortunately, they were able to reach a compromise, but only after a tremendous amount of distrust, anger, and resentment had built up—things that are not healthy for any marriage.

When spouses are running a business together, they have to reach a consensus regarding what they desire for the long-term future of the business. Reaching agreement becomes much easier when couples discuss issues in the context of their respective Personal Vision Statements.

In addition, spouses need to outline their common dream for the future of the family business in their Company Vision Statement. One way to bring differences in long-term desires out in the open is for the spouses to work together to develop a clearly stated written Company Vision Statement. Going through the process of creating and refining a Company Vision Statement helps illuminate areas that need mutual agreement. Mutually agreeing to the major elements in the Company Vision Statement will, at a minimum, reduce the intensity of disputes between the spouse partners relating to the future of the business or at least bring disputes to a head, which will help to reduce the undercurrents between the spouses.

Spousal Business Conflict 2. Not Clarifying for Employees the Areas of Spousal Business Authority

Regardless of how the legal ownership is held in businesses in which husbands and wives work together, in the minds of the employees of the business one of the spouses will inevitably be perceived as the authority in the business. It needs to be clear to both the spouses and the employees which spouse is the authority for which specific area of the business. This helps avoid crossed or missed communications.

I was in San Antonio, Texas, for a speaking engagement for my book, *Seven Secrets of Great Entrepreneurial Masters.* The event was produced by TAB facilitator-coach John Dini. He and I went out to dinner the night before the event, and I mentioned to him that my next book would be about family business. A big grin came over his face: "Well, here's a story for you. About 20 years ago, when my wife, Leila, and I were running a business together, we ran into a lot of problems. Luckily we learned a lot from that experience." I asked him about some of the challenges he faced. "First off, I can tell you that I hadn't figured on dealing with employee perceptions of which of us had authority over which aspects of the business. Our employees regularly made the wrongful assumption that talking to one of us was the equivalent to talking to *both* of us. I was regularly surprised when there were issues in my areas of responsibility—such as sales and purchasing—and I wasn't getting the information about things I needed to know to do my job. I'd ask the employee responsible why he or she did not give me the information, and the employee would say, 'But I told Leila about it weeks ago.' They'd tell her, but somehow the info wouldn't get to me. Leila would logically assume that since the information related to my responsibilities, that I had been filled in."

When John and Leila began operating their TAB business in 1997, they set out to clarify their areas of authority as well as the specifics of where and how information gets reported to them. "Now," John says, "if an employee asks a question or has information relating to the other spouse's responsibilities, we won't answer; we tell them they have to get the question or information to the appropriate person."

Spousal Business Conflict 3. Commingling Business Role Responsibilities

Some of the biggest problems among spouse business partners come about when both do the same things well but it is not clear what responsibility belongs to which spouse. Spouses should utilize the complementary skills of both while not overlapping into each other's area of responsibility. For example, even though both spouses may be talented in the sales area, only one partner should be in charge of that department.

In addition to reviewing each other's Personal SWOT Statements, both spouses should take a behavioral survey. Having ability in an area does not mean that you should be the one in charge of that area because it may not be a good fit with your natural personality or behavior. In the situation I mentioned earlier involving Luis and Fran, Fran's behavioral survey showed that she had an aversion to risk and was skeptical. Fran was careful, dependent, neat, and systematic. She would not be demanding, driving, ambitious, or competitive, and she would prefer to work independently. She was not particularly enthusiastic, inspiring, or demonstrative. Luis's survey results showed him to operate on the opposite end of the spectrum. Openly exploring each other's SWOT Statements will allow you to create mutually agreed upon written job descriptions that best utilize both partners' Strengths and avoid the Weaknesses so that you can perform expressly separate jobs. Ideally, each spouse should focus on different areas of the business that the other spouse would prefer to ignore.

A couple, each with an MBA specializing in marketing, had met while working for a large publicly owned company, and they had started a business. What attracted them to each other was that they both were interested in marketing and they had a similar way of thinking. Once they were running a business together, however, the challenge for this couple was to avoid stepping on each other's toes. To prevent commingling of responsibilities, they created job descriptions together for each of them with clearly defined sets of responsibilities. The husband was responsible for the operations of the business and development of a Web-based marketing division. The wife was in charge of getting new accounts and all other areas of the business. When they had this worked out with clear lines showing who reports to which spouse, they built it into an organizational chart that they gave to the employees of the business.

Make sure that you keep each other up to date on any important factors in your area that the other should know about. If you don't, your spouse may feel left out of something important. One method for doing this is to hold a standing weekly or monthly meeting that both spouses attend. During these meetings, both you and your spouse can bring the other up to date on what is happening in your individual areas of responsibility.

Spousal Business Conflict 4. Letting the Business, Rather Than the Marriage, Become the Center of the Relationship

One day, when Judi and I were in our late twenties, I smiled and ran my hand over the hood of my sleek, new, pumpkin orange Corvette with its black interior. Ahhh, how proud I was of being able to buy the car of my dreams at that time. I opened the door to my car and pulled out of my driveway. As I drove out of the neighborhood, I looked up and saw one of my neighbors, Carl, standing in his yard; he was leaning on his rake staring up at the sky. Carl and his wife, Angela, were one of the "older" couples on the block and were among the friendliest. For over 10 years Carl and Angela had owned and run a car parts distribution business together.

"Hey, Carl, how're you doing?" I called over to him. I was surprised when he walked over and blurted out, "Angela and I are splitting." *Wow*, I hadn't seen that coming. Just a few weeks earlier, he had been bragging at one of the neighborhood parties about how wonderful it was to be with the person he loved all day at work and then be able to be with her at home. "What happened?" I asked him. Carl began to tell me that Angela was turning every single business issue into a personal issue. "When I mentioned my concern about a shipment that didn't go out in time, she actually cried. She reminds me at home about things that I have to get done," he said. "Something negative takes place at the business, and it follows us home." He explained that "the 'place' of work for us is everywhere, almost all of the time. We share working and commuting together, but that has left us little else to share. We see the same people, sit in the same meetings, and even hear the same jokes. We listen to the same radio station in the car, read the same business publications, and deal with the same problems. Without realizing it, our home life has become a 'cone of silence.' There is just nothing to say that isn't a rehashing of our work experience. Since we didn't want the business to 'intrude' into our home, we have had nothing else to talk about except for the children, and now that they've gone off to college, we don't even have that!"

Over the years, many business owners, both male and female, have told me how their spouses bring home business problems and that doing this has destroyed the love in the relationship. It's not the same problem as when, early on, maybe they were doing everything they could just to make ends meet and get food on the table. Possibly, they got up with the dawn and left work after dusk.

But as the success of the business grows, many spouses want more. They seek romance from their relationship. When you work with that person you love, the line between business and personal relationships gets pretty fuzzy. In some business/marital relationships, tension from some business-connected irritant can linger for years. With some, the personal relationship destructs under the pressure of personalizing business interactions.

How do you *not* take business home with you? First off, both spouses need to make a concerted effort to recognize the potential for problems and work at not letting them happen. John Dini feels strongly that couples in business together need more than an initial vague conversation about keeping work in its place. John and Leila solved this challenge by making their home a neutral zone. John says, "We agreed to make decisions at work and leave them there. Within a few months of trying this approach, we noticed a marked change in our behavior at home. We were talking! We now keep separate offices at home, at opposite ends of the house. Our decision of whether or not we want to work from home at any given time is individual. If one of us is working at home, we respect the time decisions of the other. I will e-mail a question to Leila on a Saturday morning, knowing full well that she might not respond until Monday morning. Just like any other coworker, she has the right to her own time. Separating the offices also prevents us from overhearing partial conversations that may lead to wrongful interpretations and reactions that lead to trouble."

Simply stated, try to keep work conversations at work. This approach not only enhances personal conversations between spouses but it also helps keep possible bad feelings based on something that happened at the workplace out of the home. Make the effort to set aside the business things you are thinking about and focus on your partner or spouse when you are away from the business. This is particularly true when the two of you are working from your home.

Another rule to follow is to keep nonbusiness conversations at home. John Dini says, "With two teenage sons it is tempting to take time out of the workday to talk about the boys, school, or our families. But by keeping our workday focused on work, we have plenty of time to discuss our personal lives in the evening, and we are more inclined to do so. Our system, such as it is, works well in keeping the company from interfering or dominating our lives."

Just as it is recommended for any couple to make a "date night" away from the kids and responsibilities, it is important for married coworkers to make time away from the business to reconnect as a couple. Spouse business partners should set aside time that is clearly nonbusiness. Set aside play time as a couple and follow through. Do not make the mistake of constantly letting work get in the way of enjoying nonwork downtime together. Taking business calls or partaking in business text messaging while spending designated nonwork time together is not a cool thing to do. Agree with your spouse to leave the cell phones behind during this time together.

Keeping business secrets told to you by employees from your spouse can cause problems of trust. John and Leila Dini have made it clear to all employees that they will not be bound by employees begging confidentiality from the other spouse. John and Leila Dini's employees know that if an employee shares something about the business with John or Leila, they will share it with each other. John feels strongly that "keeping employee confidences from your spouse partner is an opening for all sorts of relationship trust problems."

Spousal Business Conflict 5. Letting Problems at Home Spill Over into Working Life

Problems in the home life of spouses working together all too often spill over into the family business. For example, Adele works with her husband, Sebastian; they each own half of the stock in the company. At home, Sebastian was easily frustrated with Adele and his behavior toward her carried over to their work environment. Soon neither of them was happy working together. At the time, they had been a married couple for 30 years and had shared a 27-year partnership running a business. Adele described her feelings by saying, "It seems that Sebastian is not capable of holding a rational business discussion before he just gets angry. It's one thing for him to get frustrated at home—not that I like it—but it's another to lose it in front of the employees. I feel like he's undermining the respect the employees have for me."

Adele attempted to tell Sebastian that he simply could not talk to her cruelly and that she was embarrassed by the way he spoke to her at work. He responded by bringing up some problems in their home life. Sebastian wouldn't change the way he was treating Adele until she finally broke down and told him, "I want to dissolve our business partnership immediately. I can't stand the lousy way you treat me at work. Just because I'm your wife, you're always saying sarcastic things about my work."

To keep the business running, Sebastian agreed with Adele to create a TABenos atmosphere between the two of them, at least at work. They used the same TABenos process that I explained in Chapter 6 to create a safe and open communications atmosphere at work. Adele and Sebastian agreed on very clear rules as to how they would speak to each other, particularly in front of employees. They are still together both in business and marriage. Many marriages among spouse business partners have been saved by doing the TABenos exercises and following the TABenos commitments.

Granted, Adele and Sebastian's story is a pretty extreme example of spouse–business partner unhappiness. However, you can see how far it can go when anger or unhappiness outside the business is left unaddressed such that it works its way into the business relationship. It took a conscious effort by Adele and Sebastian to stop letting their problems in their home life spill over into their business relationship.

Things are much harder to resolve when the relationship is abusive and the abusive party has no desire to change the communications atmosphere. Such was the case with Deana who owned and ran a business with her husband Irvin. She yelled at him at work when she was mad or frustrated with someone else whom she could not confront. Irvin knew and accepted that she would do this. He explained to me that he knew she was just getting anger and frustration out of her system and that the yelling was not because of him. Irvin was able to let things slide. When I asked Irvin whether the abusive manner in which Deana spoke to him at work had a negative impact on their marriage, he replied, "Just being with her is like being under a cloud of negativity." My response to him was that the problem was a lot deeper than just how she talked to him at work and that he should go to marriage counseling.

Spousal Business Conflict 6. Harboring Different Views on Who Should Be in Charge

The relationship of spouses working together is complicated by the fact that, even if they are equal partners in the business, it is rare for both spouses to actually run the business equally. Kevin Armstrong, a TAB facilitator-coach in Vancouver, Canada, shared his view that "when one spouse thinks he or she is more competent or more essential to the business, the spouse partners often run into special challenges." This situation often develops after years together in the business when one of the spouses becomes more assertive as he or she gains more business experience.

Kelly started a business based on her ideas and business know-how. Her husband, George, had very little business experience when they started out, but during the next 15 years, he became more and more assertive about how they should run the company and the changes he felt were needed in the company. George's increasing assertiveness manifested itself as tension in their business and personal relationship. It all came to a head with a screaming match during their twentieth anniversary party at which over 30 family members were present.

With a few beers under his belt, George publicly shared his feeling that "Kelly won't let go of the control. She makes hasty, extreme, and unbending decisions that I don't agree with. She makes instantaneous decisions and then doesn't revisit them or change her mind even when the decisions were wrong." Needless to say, a good time was ruined and the hard feelings were never totally eliminated. Several years after the party, Kelly told George, "I will never forgive you for ruining our anniversary party." But George's outburst at the party did open Kelly's eyes to the fact that she needed to get more buy-in from George on important business decisions. Instead of telling George what she had decided, she made an attempt to sell George on the reason for her decisions, just as she might try to sell her top executives on the reason for a business action.

It is natural for spouses to have differing views on key business decisions, just as it is natural for there to be differences of perspective among any executives about the operation and direction of any business. However, when dealing with a spouse, things are likely to take on a greater emotional edge. The best thing to do in these situations is to prepare an unemotional justification that focuses on facts when trying to convince your spouse why your decision for the operation or direction of the business is correct. A well-reasoned and well-presented case can overcome a lot of spousal resistance, even when it is in your spouse partner's "operating territory." However, you need to let it go if you cannot get your spouse partner to go along with the business decision you want. The challenge is how you, as a spouse, can just let it go if you really believe in your decision and your spouse partner does not. The time to "let something go" is when the damage to your spousal relationship outweighs the benefit to the business if you stick to your decision.

Jackie and Bruce Gernaey have a very successful TAB peer boards and coaching practice in Long Island. Once, when Judi and I went out to dinner with them, I asked them both what they saw as their secret for keeping a successful marriage when working together as partners. Bruce laughed, "It's because we both know she's the boss at work!" Jackie went on to explain her belief that the way to keep the stress out of their working relationship was for it to be clear who makes the final decisions. If there is no "boss," they will be at loggerheads constantly. The key to working well together is to not fight about final decisions. They are both at ease with the fact that she has the final say. They know couples in which no one has the final decision power, and without that, the couples are asking for trouble.

Spouses need to recognize that the personal relationship will be a lot better if one of the spouses has the final authority at work. The spouse with the greatest leadership strengths should assume this position. But it doesn't always work this way. Problems between spouse partners are usually worse if there is no designated spouse to have the final say in the business if the spouses cannot come to an agreement. When neither spouse is willing to give the other the "final say," the spouses should use a neutral third party as a mediator to give a nonbinding decision without the potential emotional baggage of the decision being forced on one spouse by the other. This person should be an independent professional who understands the business and is trusted and respected by each of the spouse partners. The mediator should understand the dynamics of family business. A mediator certified by the Academy of Family Mediators can also do the job if you and your spouse do not have a relationship with a third party who is able to resolve key business-related issues by bringing objectivity to the table. When neither spouse has the final business decision authority, business problems are often never resolved or even dealt with, and conflicts grow out of control because of spite. In such situations, the spouses should bring in a neutral third party as the designated tie-breaker.

Spousal Business Conflict 7. Not Making Time for Themselves

My sister, Sheelah, and her husband, Stan, work together at their Missouri Merchants and Manufacturers Association business. Years ago, Sheelah told me how important it was for her to set aside time for herself for karate and swimming. Spouses need time for themselves in which to pursue their personal passions. Many spouses get rid of work-related tension and focus by engaging in some form of exercise or a hobby that does not involve the spouse.

Some spouses who work with each other create time for themselves by going to the movies or visiting family or friends before going home to a spouse they've just spent the day with. Making time to do the things you like without the person you work with every day is a great way to make a marriage and a professional relationship work.

Sheelah and Stan also drive to work separately because it gives them some time alone to unwind and think about the day. There are times that Sheelah will visit our mom or her grandkids before going home. Driving separately also allows them to better schedule their time as it fits their particular responsibilities, instead of going to and from work based on the other's need to be at work at a particular time. John Dini and his wife, Leila, also drive separately to and from work. He says, "There is no guilt if one of us needs to go in early and the other is catching up on some sleep." Even though driving separately may be a waste of gasoline, the benefits of keeping the marriage strong far outweigh the energy concerns.

Spousal Business Conflict 8. Blended Families

Spousal conflict is particularly hard to handle with a blended family. Nikolai and Irena worked well in their family software company until Irena's son joined the business. Nikolai's two sons from a previous marriage also worked for the company, and they brought a great deal of value to the company; his elder son was being groomed to run the business. Irena's son, however, was not as motivated, nor was he innately talented in areas that could help the business. The only reason he was employed by the business was because he was a family member and needed work.

Complications arose between the spouses over the compensation of Irena's son and Nikolai's sons. Irena was upset with the discrepancy in pay between her son and Nikolai's sons. She thought it was unfair that her son was not making the same salary or getting the same perks as his stepbrothers. Irena pressured Nikolai who then felt obligated to put all of their sons on the same pay level. Nikolai's older son, who served as the COO, felt that his time and efforts were not properly valued by his father and stepmother, so he left the business. When the older son left, the father had to step back into the COO role and work much longer hours with much more stress. He blamed this on his wife, and their happy marriage became miserable and full of resentment.

This type of blended "his, hers, and ours" family has become much more common in recent decades, and it makes more challenges for spousal dynamics when the various kids enter the family business. Don and Carole own a kitchen and bath store; they are facing the challenge of a blended family. They each had one child from previous marriages, and when they married, they then had a daughter together. All the kids eventually joined the business. Their daughter, whom they had together, entered the business several years after their first two children joined the business. Their spousal relationship became stressful and difficult as a result of how they dealt with the three different children and their very different skills and passion for the business. Don expected their daughter to have a high aptitude for mechanics, but she is not mechanically inclined. Carole told her husband that he was not treating their daughter the same as the other two children at work. She resented what she perceived as much greater expectations for the work results of their daughter. Don vehemently disagreed. It took the intervention of a third party to get both Don and Carole to see things through the eyes of the other, accept the differences of the children, and manage each child differently without being unfair.

Tom, whom I met while lounging by a pool in Port Douglas, Australia, has a blended family business that he described to me as "working together splendidly." Tom was on vacation from his electrical engineering business. He shared his pride about the business's employing his wife and him, her two sons from her first marriage, his two sons from his first marriage, and his daughter's husband. I told him I was writing a book about family businesses, and I asked how it was working with them. He said the key to keeping any family member from thinking that he was playing favorites was by his making it clear "that at work I am not family." He told them, "When you walk through the door, I am not your husband, father, or father-in-law. I am your boss." He explained this to each of the children and his wife before they entered the business.

As blended families have become more common, the number of family businesses that bring in both the stepchildren and the children that couples may have together has increased. Dealing with the dynamics of simply bringing two families together is challenging enough on its own. Then add business involvements, and you have the recipe for a powder keg. Blended families often involve great differences in ages, and this adds an even greater challenge to the roles of parents-spouses-business partners because the business experience of the children may range as much as the age range. Blended family businesses can work out if the spouse partners understand the importance of not allowing any possible interpretation that any member of the family is getting special treatment compared to the others.

Spousal Business Conflict 9. Firing the Spouse

The issue of firing a family member close to you is difficult, but it's a much tougher situation when you know you need to fire your spouse. Firing a spouse is much more difficult when the spouse helped start the business, but as the business has matured, the spouse's skills have become antiquated and he or she is no longer the correct person for that position. The efforts the spouse put forth to help start the business were greatly appreciated, but what now, when the spouse no longer meets the needs of the business? In the optimistic glow of starting the business, it would be highly unusual to discuss what should happen when a spouse becomes unnecessary, even detrimental to the business. But the more successful the business, the more highly skilled the FBLs need to become. While you cannot read the future needs of your business, you can set out clear criteria for the employment of a spouse, just as you would any FME, just as you should for any employee.

Theodore, whose spouse joined his business a few years after he started it, wishes he had had such a conversation with his wife. He said, "Like many business owners, hiring my wife seemed to be an ideal solution. I needed a controller, and my wife was fully qualified. I figured, what was the sense of her working for someone else and coming home each day to an empty house. We could commute together, see each other during the workday, and even eat our meals together at whatever odd hour we left work." But the impact of her joining the business was not what he expected. "My wife's working for my company was a disaster for the business and for our relationship. She was arrogant and condescending to our employees. I tried talking to her about it, but she couldn't accept that this was how she came across. I knew she had to go, so I fired her." When I asked how it affected their home life, Theodore responded, "Today we can joke about it, but for years after I fired her, it was pure hell at home."

There are a lot of marriages that have been destroyed because they couldn't survive working together. This is a hiring decision that not only impacts your business but also your own domestic happiness. A lot of thought should be given to the challenges mentioned in this chapter before bringing a spouse into a business that is already in operation. Without an up-front understanding that one of the spouses may have to leave the business, you need to have an approach that minimizes the negative impact if the spouse has to leave. Taking no action can be the worse decision because when spouse partners conflict at work, both the business and the relationship are in jeopardy and something will have to give. Too often it is the marriage relationship.

Sergei was given a management position at the family "holding company" by his father-in-law. The holding company, which controlled several businesses, did not do well under the son-in-law's management. Upon the death of the father-in-law, Sergei's wife took over ownership of the holding company, and conflicts with Sergei at work were so great that she fired her husband. She assumed operating responsibility and returned the family business holdings to profitability. But the impact on the marriage was extremely bad, and ultimately the marriage dissolved.

When there is a spouse who is not a good fit for the business, one solution I've seen applied successfully is for the spouses to work together to help the spouse start a new entrepreneurial venture. When Oliver's painting company was in its infancy, he brought his wife, Betty, in as a company bookkeeper. As the business grew, the position outgrew Betty; she simply was not qualified to handle the more sophisticated accounting needs of the business. By mutual agreement, her role was reduced to working in, but not running, the accounting department. Despite this adjustment, other difficulties arose. The most persistent problem involved her resisting and sometimes outright rejecting her husband's initiatives, such as his decision to hire a CFO to, among other things, run the accounting department. She put up such a public fuss that each of the two CFOs he had hired for the job quit within months of starting work. The reason they both gave for quitting was that they did not want to work with Betty. They pointed out that she didn't follow through on assignments delegated to her and she interfered with their managing of "her friends" in the department.

In a non–family business environment, Betty's actions wouldn't be accepted. But how could Oliver reprimand his wife? Oliver was in a bind for more than one reason. To keep the peace at home, Oliver could not fire her. He realized that not only was he struggling with Betty's actions but his reactions to the situations were being watched by the other employees to see what he would do about it.

Oliver asked his business coach, a trusted advisor, what he should do. Together, they first focused on why Betty was so resistant to doing her assigned role in the accounting department. It turned out that Betty had a Personal Vision in which she saw her role in the business as much more important—at the same level as it was when the company was starting up and she was the sole bookkeeper in the business. She missed having more power and felt threatened that Oliver wanted to remove her altogether from the business. She was in fear of losing her identity, her purpose, and even her work relationship with her husband.

Her behaviors caused her to resist Oliver's progressive plans for the business. Oliver and Betty discussed their respective Personal Visions Statements. Their dreams for the future of the company were extremely different. It became clear that they wanted things that were in conflict with each other's Personal Vision in fundamental ways. When the coach suggested that they assess what the best role for Betty would be at the company, Oliver responded that instead of finding Betty a new role, what they needed was to find a graceful way to get Betty out of the business. As it turned out, Betty had a strong interest in the travel industry as she enjoyed arranging the many trips that she and Oliver had taken over the years. Oliver purchased a very inexpensive travel agency franchise for Betty that allowed her to operate out of their home. Between the travel business from the company and some outside business she developed, the travel agency gave her a little money, a lot of enjoyment, and, most importantly, got her out of the primary family business. From Oliver's perspective, it resulted in a more successful business and a better relationship with his wife. Betty's leaving the business has actually healed the damaged spouse partner relationship as the excitement of regaining passion for her work has been renewed. Old resentments have been forgotten, and the couple is walking together into a new future.

Spousal Business Conflict 10. Disagreeing about Firing an FME

Having a child in the business who is not meeting expectations adds an additional layer of spousal tension on top of that which exists in any family unit. It is never easy for a parent boss to decide whether or not to fire an FME child. It becomes further complicated when the other spouse does not agree with the decision, as it happened with one couple who owned a food distribution company.

While the business was owned equally by George and his wife, George worked full-time and ran the business while his wife worked part-time. They had a son and daughter employed full-time in the business as well. The son was not performing satisfactorily due to a drug dependency. The husband felt the best thing to do was to fire the son. The wife was against the firing. She made it clear to her husband that if he wanted to have a pleasant home life, he was going to have to find a way to keep the son employed. Her son was her "baby," even though he was 32 years old, and in her mind he had to be protected. On the other hand, their daughter FME begged her father to fire her brother. She was tired of working hard while seeing her brother's problems damage the business. The tension created by having the son in the business almost resulted in the daughter leaving the business.

George spoke to his son and told him he would pay for a recovery program, but the son could not work for the business until he was clean. Against his wife's wishes, George fired his son. His wife was furious, and relations between them remained chilly until the son got help and pulled his life together. Interestingly, the "chill" went away when the son, after graduating from his recovery program, credited his father's "tough love" as being important in his improvement.

Another situation involved a daughter-in-law who worked in the medical supply business owned by her husband's parents. The daughter-in-law was the vice president of sales, and she was personally responsible for all the big sales decisions. The father-in-law, Carmelo, was informed by his son during an early morning coffee run that he planned to leave his wife. He told Carmelo that his wife had to be let go. Carmelo loved his son, but he also loved his daughter-in-law, and he was extremely pleased with the development of his daughter-in-law in her job. So he said, "No!" Carmelo's wife, who worked as the controller of the business, then demanded that Carmelo fire his daughter-in-law. Carmelo hated to lose his daughter-in-law, but he felt he had no choice, even though it would be disruptive to the business. He let his daughter-in-law go with a big pay-off package and a big apology. Losing the daughter-in-law turned out to be as detrimental to the business as Carmelo feared. Several important clients left because of what they felt was unfair treatment of the former daughter-in-law. Carmelo's sacrifice to please his wife and son almost destroyed the business that he and his wife had developed over three decades. Moreover, Carmelo harbored deep resentment at being pushed into this position.

Spousal relations are severely tested when spouses cannot agree on the horribly sticky situation of firing an immediate family member. It is easy to see how this challenge can put daggers into a happy, healthy spousal relationship.

Spousal Business Conflict 11. Having the Spouses of Your Children Working Together with Your Children in the Family Business

Before I first discussed with Jason, who is married to my daughter, Lynette, the possibility of my bringing him on board at TAB, I first had conversations with Lynette. She had started with TAB several years earlier, and she was an officer of TAB helping to develop new training products for our facilitators and helping to add new facilitators as TAB expanded into new areas. I explained to her that I didn't want her to be working with Jason in the same business. I told Lynette that she would have to decide whether she would be willing to leave her full-time involvement with TAB if Jason joined TAB. I pointed out that she might find good use for her creativity and passion at Direct Communication Services, Inc. (DCS), another of my family businesses, where she would not need to do any out-of-town travel. At the time, Lynette was pregnant and had already expressed to me that she did not want to be traveling out of town for work after her child was born. After a week, she told me that if Jason joined TAB, she would be willing to move over to DCS so that the two of them would not be working for the same company.

Think hard about whether it is a good idea for the spouses of your children to work with your children in your business. The potential for problems between the two of them at work generally outweighs the good that might come from their working together. The challenges are so great that many FBLs restrict spouses of their children FMEs from joining their family businesses, even if they have demonstrated skills in other businesses that could help the family businesses.

If you are going to permit your children and their spouses to work for you, make sure that they are working as far away from each other physically and bureaucratically as possible. Also, arrange it so that none of their responsibilities overlap.

Spousal Business Conflict 12. On the Way to Becoming Ex-Spouses

Unfortunately, spouses in some family businesses will face the unpleasant situation of becoming ex-spouses and then have to deal with the negative impact upon the business. Disagreements between divorcing spouses have tied up the legal control of many businesses with ownership disputes. Troy equally owned 50 percent of the family restaurant with his wife, Annika. For many years they had been living in an atmosphere of tension, and after years of arguing about business matters, they arrived at an emotional and traumatic breakup of the marriage. Eager to move on, Troy asked his wife to name her price for her stock in the business, and he told her that he would pay the price if it was fair. The price Annika wanted for the buyout was tied to the emotional nature of the breakup rather than the fair market value of the business. Troy told her that he would sell to her for the same price she wanted and she said no.

While in the midst of splitting, Troy remarked how damaging their divorce was becoming to the business they had built together over the years. Working together while getting divorced was "awful," but neither of them was able to work out a price to buy out the other. Troy complained, "We don't have a legal mechanism to unwind the ownership without mutual consent, and we are spending money on attorneys that could be used to improve the restaurant. There is nothing in our shareholder agreement to handle our situation without fighting it out legally." Things got so bad at work that Troy eventually took what he referred to as a "discounted value" for his stock to get away from the situation.

All too often, ex–spouse partner conflicts wind up in court. It makes good sense for business ownership and potential rights to ownership between spouses to be structured from the beginning in a way that assumes the worst: a divorce. Addressing these issues when the business is formed or before a spouse enters a business has prevented a lot of problems for spouses down the road when the marriages dissolve.

The key is to acknowledge and address the situation right away, preferably through an objective third party. If possible, spouse partners who are on their way to becoming exes should avoid bringing business ownership and control issues to court. First, try alternative nonlawsuit dispute-resolution approaches, such as mediation. Litigating business ownership and control issues makes the already difficult experience of divorce worse and causes major rifts throughout entire families as well as the businesses. When a marriage is dissolving, the sooner the spouse partners can resolve a dispute involving spousal ownership, the better their chances are of avoiding a knock-down, drag-out family feud that may cause the downfall of the business and the disruption of the families.

Conclusion

I have never heard a spouse partner say, "Wow, working in the business with my spouse has helped our marriage improve" or "Working together makes our relationship more loving." There are significant challenges to working with a spouse, so that the magic of the marriage is not destroyed. Spouses need to recognize the danger areas mentioned in this chapter, and they need to proactively address them in order to balance their spousal work and home relationships.

Checklist for Addressing Spousal Business Partners' Multiple Role Challenges

- Both spouses should take the time to review each other's Personal Vision Statements and discuss any conflicts to avoid future disagreements.
- Both spouses and employees need to fully understand who has final authority, and there needs to be a clear line of reporting.
- Both spouses need to focus on their individual strengths and avoid commingling their professional roles.
- Both spouses need to leave business matters at work so that the marriage, not the business, is the center of the relationship.
- If there are any negative habits in the way the spouses communicate at home, those habits cannot spill over into

the business. Open, safe communication must exist in the business environment at all times. Creating a TABenos environment is one way to do this.

- Spouses must come to an agreement on which spouse has final authority on business decisions.
- Spouses need to spend personal time away from their spouse partner.
- When stepchildren come into the business, they must be granted the same considerations as any biological children belonging to the couple.
- If one spouse is no longer an asset to the business, steps should be taken to help the spouse discover a new beginning outside the family business.
- If an FME needs to be let go, sensitivity must be given to how the other spouse feels about letting that person go.
- FBLs need to think long and hard before agreeing to allow their children's spouses to join the business. If the children's spouses are allowed to become FMEs, the FBL should try to avoid having the children and their spouses work together.
- If the marriage dissolves, steps must be taken so that the business doesn't dissolve too. Bringing in a neutral third party to mediate is the best approach to take.

CHAPTER 8

THE EIGHTH ELEMENT
Recruiting, Retaining, and Inspiring Non-Family-Member Employees in a Family Business

Recruiting and retaining talented employees are challenges for any business owner. But with the added factor of the family dynamics, there are more barriers in family businesses to hiring and holding onto talented non-FMEs, particularly in the executive ranks. In this chapter, I will show you seven of the most common barriers that have kept most family businesses from successfully adding and retaining non-FMEs and the ways to overcome these barriers.

Non-FME Barrier 1. Concerns about Career Development Opportunities

Gustave, who owns a car dealership, had three of his kids in the business. He hired Cheryl, a CFO who was experienced in accounting and finance. When Cheryl was interviewed for the CFO position, she expressed her concern by asking, "What influence will I have on the overall operations of the company or the company's achieving its long-term goals?" Gustave explained to Cheryl that she had expertise and aptitude in an area that his three child FMEs lacked. Gustave explained that he recognized the value that she brought to the company and how her voice should help grow the value of the company. He expected her to challenge everything that she saw, such as whether the company should continue with certain initiatives based on the projected return on investment. Cheryl was made aware of opportunities for potential leadership positions in the company as the company grew. Cheryl joined Gustave's family business and is still a valuable factor in its outstanding growth.

Unlike Gustave, many other FBLs overlook the needs and aspirations of non-FME executives working for their family businesses. There are two important keys to locking in top-level non-FME executives in your family business. One way to keep these executives is to let them know there is a future for them in leadership positions and that you will give your support to training and educating them in a way that will help them develop their abilities, skills, and responsibilities. The second way is to develop a creative compensation reward program tied to the results of the business.

Let's start by looking at the first key to keeping these executives, which is to show them future leadership position growth. Many non-FMEs leave careers with family businesses because they find that there are limitations on how far their careers can go. Paying well may be enough to keep these executives as employees. But if you want to keep your non-FMEs motivated and operating at the top level of their abilities, you must bring about the opportunity for the professional development and happiness they seek. Creating a healthy environment for their growth means they can gain more responsibility and income potential, if they demonstrate a high level of productivity and efficiency within the family business.

Most non-FMEs recognize that they are not likely to attain the top leadership position in the business. However, their needs and aspirations require that they have important leadership roles, based on how their contributions help the progress of the company. Giving them leadership opportunities will help propel them to make the greatest positive impact in your business. They need to see the long-term growth potential for themselves in your family business. Your challenge is to help create a future for these key employees that is not severely limited because they are not family. Without being shown this vision of their future in the business, non-FMEs become discouraged and end up underachieving in the business.

The challenge non-FMEs face regarding career opportunity is compounded by the number of FMEs in your business. Bernard ran a business with 50 employees. He had two executive non-FMEs who had been with the company for decades. Bernard surprised everyone by bringing in his 30-year-old daughter, a lawyer, as general counsel—a highly coveted position. Basically, she just showed up at the business without any advanced announcement to the other executives. The two nonfamily executives were highly concerned, but they didn't leave the business.

Then, the next year, Bernard brought his nephew into the business in an executive position. Within months, the non-FME executive vice president (EVP) quit. "Look," he said, "I can see the writing on the wall. They may have lower positions than I do right now, but when the daughter and nephew get enough experience, they're going to become leaders in the company, and there will be no important leadership position for me. As each family member joins the business, I can just see the loss of growth opportunities for myself." After decades of working for the family business, the threat was palpable. "Do I really want one of them as my boss down the road? No, I don't want to have to one day be in a position of reporting to them."

If he had been open to his non-FME regarding the opportunities available to him in the future, Bernard might have been able to keep him. He should have challenged himself to see what he could do to neutralize the EVP's concern about growth limitations, thereby retaining and motivating the EVP. Bernard should have tried to map out a clear career path within the business that could have satisfied the EVP. By not doing this, he created a major leadership gap in his company that lasted for the several years until his daughter and nephew were able to step up.

Even though the other non-FME executive stayed with Bernard, he too expressed concerns about what the two FMEs joining the business meant to *his* future opportunities in the business. And he was no longer inspired. His motivation and work effort were never the same. However, in spite of his concern about his long-term opportunities, he stayed with Bernard's family business, explaining to Bernard that he liked working for a good family firm with good values where he was treated well. One way that Bernard addressed this lack of motivation was to develop a creative compensation reward program tied to the increased financial results of the business.

I once met the very successful owner of several car dealerships and a real estate development company. His sons held all the top positions in his companies. I admired his success and asked him how he handled the challenge of attracting and retaining outstanding non-FMEs. He told me he put in place a compensation program for the few "difference makers" among his top non-FME executives that gave them the potential to make more than the competitive level of compensation for their positions. Financial incentives gave his non-FMEs an opportunity to participate in the success and growth of the family business. He said he had never had a non-FME executive quit the business who he felt was important to getting his business to the next level of success.

Financial incentives based on long-term results of the family business are the most effective way to knock down fears of uncertain long-range job opportunities. This is not to say you can abandon communicating plans for what the executives will be doing in the future, but as the old saying goes, money talks. Of course, financial incentives for key executives must be measured on the future success of the business. One way this can be done is by offering stock without voting rights. I have only given stock options to a non-FME once. I did this based on the contributions the man had made to TAB before I gave him the stock options and my belief that his creativity and extreme work effort would be of major value to TAB in the future. The nonvoting stock, however, contained restrictions on his ability to transfer the stock to anyone but my company, and it contained a formula for valuing the stock when it came back to the company. Having ownership was very important to this "difference maker" and his results for the company. According to a survey of TAB members running family businesses, fewer than 3 percent of them allow non-FMEs to have ownership in their businesses. One of the most common reasons given for not granting stock ownership to non-FMEs is the desire that only family members be owners in their company. Others have avoided giving ownership to non-FMEs for fear of litigation from them as stockholders.

I was on a nonprofit board of directors along with Irene, a top-level executive with a family business in the IT field. For years, Irene mentioned that she was part owner of the business and proudly talked about the success of the business. When I met the CEO of the business and explained that I knew his co-owner, he smiled when he pointed out to me that he was happy Irene referred to herself as an owner of the business but that Irene did not have any ownership in the business. Instead, she had a financial incentive based on having 3 percent growth of the book value of his company as compared to the previous year. His company will owe Irene this amount when she leaves the company, provided that she stays there a minimum period of time. He said that he was happy with the results of the incentive because it had helped him to successfully retain three key executives, including Irene. This incentive is often called "phantom stock." Phantom stock is not really stock or ownership but is a contract that provides a formula for the non-FME to benefit from the increased long-term value of the business without having to make any investment in, or owning any part of, the business. You have to wonder whether both of Bernard's executives would still be with his business if he had used phantom stock or any other creative way to retain key non-FME executives.

Some family business owners have been successful in keeping non-FME executives, who are indispensable to their businesses, by rewarding them according to an annual bonus plan that is based on profit growth over some benchmark year. For example, the VP of one intellectual property business has an annual bonus that rewards her with 5 percent of all annual profits that exceed the $750,000 in profits that the company earned the year before she started to get the bonus. This has a long-term impact because the level of the bonuses becomes so substantial that the non-FME is being rewarded greatly above the going rate for his or her services.

Another way to give key non-FMEs financial incentive rewards without giving them ownership in the business is to allow them to invest in outside ventures financed by the family business. This allows key non-FMEs to grow their own wealth as a result of their employment by the family business, although the ownership is not directly in the family business. One example of this approach took place within Diego's trucking company when he set up an affiliated company to buy and lease trucks and equipment to the parent trucking company that employed his three top non-FME executives. Diego invited his three executives to buy ownership in the truck leasing company. Years later, he allowed the same non-FMEs to invest in a limited-liability company that bought a two-story office building. The building was easy to finance because the first floor of the building was leased by the trucking company.

Non-FME Barrier 2. Concerns about Long-Term Job Security

Put yourself in the position of a non-FME executive. Having a family member join the business with no advanced announcement can be very disheartening and bring up fears about long-term job security. The threats to the career opportunities felt by nonfamily executives are typically less if they are highly skilled and experienced in areas in which FMEs lack aptitude or passion. However, even if this is the case, there still may be a concern about long-term job security, such as the concern of Janet, a merchandising manager. She had been working for a family retail business for over 20 years when the owner brought in his son, an accountant. Janet put in her resignation because she feared that down the road the son would fire her and eventually want his own family member in the position.

What to do when a non-FME feels that he or she will no longer be needed once an FME comes on board? Bernard, whom we discussed above, surprised his executives twice by having family members show up for work without any advanced announcement to his executives. One thing Bernard *should* have done was give his executives significant notice of his intent to bring FMEs into the business. Even though it had been a part of *his* Personal Vision for the future, he failed to share this with them. Having the two relatives show up for work without any advanced warning to his top executives was a mistake that made his executives fearful of the next big surprise. Bernard should have outlined what the long-term roles of the executives would be as the family members developed and how the involvement of the new family members in the business would affect the executive team in the future. It would have been productive if Bernard had also let his executives know that the business of his Vision holds a future for them as well. Moreover, he should have discussed future training and education that would help to develop his executive's abilities, skills, and responsibilities. He then might have been able to hold on to his executive vice president.

Because family members are competing for company training and development resources, it might be difficult to develop this training and education objective. In addition, it is natural to focus your training and development budget on your family members. This is why FBLs must set up a budget for executive training and education for non-FMEs that helps to improve their abilities.

Don't wait for your non-FMEs to discuss their concerns about long-term job security with you because by then it may be too late. While it's natural for them to have concerns, it is not unusual for non-FME executives to remain tight-lipped regarding job security fears. The best way to alleviate this fear and keep non-FMEs dedicated to their work is to open up the communication. Francine, a non-FME senior vice president of a family business that owns a chain of dog boarding facilities, was prompted to look for another job after her friend and fellow non-FME executive was left jobless when the family business brought in a nephew to take over the friend's job. She saw the grief her friend went through, and she didn't want that to happen to her. Upon receiving a job offer from a company that seemed to provide better job security, Francine made the decision to leave and never discussed her concerns with the FBL. The loss of Francine might have been avoided if the FBL had explained to her how poorly Francine's friend had been doing her job and that the friend needed to be replaced regardless as to whether the person who replaced her was family or not.

When you bring a child into the business as the future successor, all employees will be checking the competence of the new family member, and they will wonder what the change means to the survival of the company. Non-FMEs' concerns about job security are to be expected since the family member will eventually be responsible for keeping the business successful. Recognizing that the non-FMEs might have this insecurity is important. Discuss with your key executives the new family member's prior experience and how it will help the company achieve its goals. Communicating to non-FME executives how the family member will be prepared for the new role is important for addressing their fears.

Somewhat ironically, it often helps to allay this fear among non-FMEs if the chosen successor actually has the ability and desire to take over the business because then there is less likelihood that the company will be sold to outsiders, which may mean the termination of the non-FMEs. Those FBLs who have Personal Visions that include keeping the business in the family for future generations should share this dream with their non-FMEs.

Saul anointed his son Irvin as the future leader of their clothing distributorship. The problem was the non-FMEs didn't think Irvin was capable of doing the job. Their fear was that Irvin would run the business into the ground (as many successors have done), thus destroying their work security. One by one, each of the two longtime non-FME executives quit the family business. As one stated, "I wanted to leave well before the ship goes down." As is very common for FBLs to do, Saul told his two executives about his succession decision without being sensitive to the security fears that would keep them from comfortably remaining with the family business. It's a shame that the two executives did not discuss their concerns with Saul when Saul was working on his succession plans.

Right after Jason and I reached an understanding that he would be coming on board at TAB, I informed my non-FME executives about the decision, explaining that Jason would be groomed to one day take over as president. I explained my belief that this would increase their job security because they would not have to face the unknown impact of new nonfamily ownership of TAB. These executives know that working for even the largest public company has job security risks, such as the company merging or being sold and executives being laid off. To a large extent, this approach helped neutralize their concerns about how Jason's joining the company would affect their long-term job security.

Many non-FMEs assume that ownership of the family business will ultimately be transferred to some family member unless told otherwise. Your challenge to overcome job security fears and retain non-FME executives is much greater if you plan to one day sell the business to outside parties rather than keeping the business in the family. Even if your sale includes employment contracts for the executives, there are typically limits as to the number of years involved. So the employment contracts will not provide the long-term security most non-FME executives seek.

One question I repeatedly hear from FBLs is, "How much should I share with my non-FMEs about my Vision of not keeping the business in the family and instead selling it to outsiders?" Jim planned to sell the business to outsiders 5 to 10 years in the future. He intentionally did not share this Vision with his non-FME executives because he was afraid that doing so would result in losing his top talent. Jim kept this part of his Personal Vision as a Pocket Vision—that is, he kept this information "in his pocket"—to prevent losing good people because he wasn't sure what impact sharing this information would have on his ability to retain the nonfamily employees. Sharing factors that impact on non-FME executives' security is too often held back. You can't keep your plans to sell hidden forever. The day came when Jim had to reveal the truth because someone outside the business knew of Jim's interest in selling and mentioned it to one of Jim's employees. To these nonfamily executives, it seemed clear that Jim had jeopardized their long-term job security, and it caused them to be angry and distrustful of Jim. It is understandable that these non-FMEs were very reactive to what they viewed as having been misled. Even after Jim explained that he had changed his mind about selling to outsiders, the trust level never returned.

In another situation, when Wayne decided that he wanted to sell his business, he discussed in confidence with two non-FME executives that he did not intend to transfer ownership of his furniture parts manufacturing business to any of his three children. He explained that he would try to get the executives five-year employment contracts but he also wanted to come up with a program that would reward them with a percentage of the profits over a certain sales price. They worked this out, and the two executives helped him get a top price for the business when the time came to sell it.

In contrast to how Wayne handled things, you make yourself the victim of your own secretive fears of losing your executives if you do not share information that can greatly affect their job security. You do not want valued non-FMEs to lose faith or trust in you because you were not up front about your dream about selling the business sometime in the future. Discuss your future plans with them, and explore ways you can provide some benefit to them beyond employment contracts. Talk to them about it, and be open to their input and ideas. Non-FMEs also need to know you cannot protect them against everything, but you can help. Many, like Wayne, have made their non-FME executives helpful participants in accomplishing the sale of the business by negotiating employment contracts that provide them with several years of job security and, for a select few, give them a piece of the sales pie.

Non-FME Barrier 3. An FME Reporting to a Non-FME

Don Schlueter, a TAB facilitator-coach in Chicago, Illinois, related to me a story about a $16 million Dynastic Stage business.

Don worked for this family business for 15 years as a non-FME executive. Don said, "I found myself caught in the middle of many family struggles that always seemed to become my problem to solve." One of these problems was caused by the fact that both the CEO's nephew and his son-in-law were reporting to Don. Don felt both of these FME executives were "overqualified" in their positions and as a result were "underperforming." It was hard for them to passionately work in jobs that did not offer them the challenges they were capable of handling. "I persevered, the company grew, and I was able to convince the CEO to move both of his relatives out from working for me into positions in which they were running smaller companies owned by the family business."

Don's situation is an example of a non-FME who is able to accept that FMEs, whether executive level or not, are reporting to him or her and, as he said, "persevere." Most non-FMEs view having FMEs reporting to them as a no-win situation. They realize that the FME generally has "the ear" of the FBL. So if an FME has a gripe with his or her non-FME immediate supervisor, the FME will probably take the complaint directly to the FBL. Sharon, for example, is a non-FME who supervised an FBL's daughter who was interning at the family business. When Sharon found out that the daughter didn't like her and was expressing her unhappiness directly to her dad, the FBL, Sharon decided that she had better quit the company, even though she had been working for the business for 10 years. In her resignation letter, Sharon explained that she resented being balled out by the FBL for matters that were brought up by his daughter. She felt that she couldn't do her job well while being "spied" on.

Maggie, a non-FME director of operations for a pet product manufacturer, was told that the son of the founder would be joining the business and would be reporting to her for the next few years. The FBL told Maggie, "Make sure that my son gets qualified in the operations part of the business because he will need to know this area well when he one day takes over the COO position." Put yourself in Maggie's shoes: a non-FME who knows that she will, at some time in the future, report to the FME who, for the next few years, will be reporting to her. What an awkward position it is when she has to write up performance reports on the son! Maggie tried to express her concern over having to report on the man who would one day be her boss. The FBL then explained to Maggie that he expected her to give objective performance reviews to his son as if he were not the son of the boss. Under these circumstances, Maggie didn't feel she could honestly do her job well.

Maggie decided to bring up again her concern and that she was thinking of leaving the company because of it. With the threat of losing Maggie, the FBL changed the rules and clarified the expectations of interactions between Maggie and his son. Maggie was no longer expected to do reviews, and the guidelines even included a section that said the son could not go over Maggie's head to discuss complaints directly with his father. Fortunately these expectations were discussed and put in writing early before the son FME started working for the company. This avoided the potential damage from Maggie becoming an unmotivated, unhappy employee or leaving the company.

Other FBLs feel it best to ease FMEs slowly into the company so that non-FMEs can see the value of the FMEs. Tom, the FBL of a carpet company, wanted to quickly move his younger son to become the director of warehouse operations. However, he held off because his older son Eli expressed reservations about the plan; Eli felt that it would offer too many complications for his younger brother to report to a non-FME warehouse manager and then end up supervising the warehouse manager. Eli, who was president of the company, felt that it would have a negative impact on both of his warehouse managers who were doing excellent jobs. Eli felt strongly about requiring his younger brother to prove himself in the warehouse before he was promoted over the two people who were then running the warehouse (as first- and second-shift managers). He also felt that it would be unfair to his inexperienced brother for him to take over managing an area in the company with which he was unfamiliar. Gradually, the younger son was eased into responsibility in the warehouse, and, about a year later, one of the warehouse managers mentioned to Eli that the "young buck" was good at warehouse operations. It was an easy transition from there to making him director of warehouse operations without the barrier of resentment from the warehouse managers.

Ben, who owned a sporting goods store, grew concerned when his daughter was laid off from her job after years of working in the stock market. Even though she didn't have any experience with sporting goods, he put her in charge of a department where she managed a non-FME who had been working in sporting goods for over 20 years. The non-FME deeply resented that Ben put his daughter in the management position. This resentment could have been at least partially neutralized by Ben if he had scheduled meetings with his daughter and the long-term non-FME so that they could talk out the situation in advance. Instead, Ben informally said, "Hi, my daughter's name is Jane, and she is now your boss." It took a long time before the non-FME manager really got to know Jane and even longer until he understood how she operated and created new opportunities for her team. The right kind of meeting early in the game could have made the non-FME manager feel more secure in his future and helped Jane become part of the team more quickly.

Another type of problem can arise when an FME must report to a non-FME. Ron was a longtime non-FME executive vice president. Ron worked for Mike, the owner of a $90 million family business. Mike had recruited Ron from a bigger company to help bring a higher level of professionalism to his company. It worked, and the company grew much more profitable under Ron's tutelage. Ron's involvement even allowed Mike to focus on his strength and passion for developing the marketing and sales end of the business. They had a great synergistic working relationship.

All of that changed when Mike's son, Dan, joined the company. Mike asked Ron to mentor his son, and Dan started as a manager who reported to Ron. Soon, Dan wanted major changes to take place in the marketing model of the business. The problem was that Mike didn't agree with Dan's changes at all, but Ron did agree with them. When Mike told Ron that he could not approve Dan's changes, Ron pointed out the authority given to him in the written FME job description that was signed off on by Mike. Mike said that, in spite of the job description, Ron should realize that his orders to Dan were really coming from Mike via Ron since Dan was his son. Ron was not happy about being in a position where he would be managing Dan but had no authority to approve Dan's changes because of Mike. Ron was so uncomfortable being caught in the middle between the father he worked for and the son who was supposed to be working for him that he took an early retirement.

Should it be necessary for a family member to report to a non-FME, they both will need to be schooled on what their relationship should be, or resentment will build up. Part of the schooling is letting FMEs know that they cannot come back to the FBL and complain that they are not getting a fair deal. They know that the relationship with the FME will change eventually and that they, as non-FMEs, may in the future report to the FBL or another FME. These non-FMEs fear that even normal criticism of the FME by them could result in jeopardizing their long-term security when the FME gets more power and has the chance to get back at the non-FME. The FME who is reporting to the non-FME could be promoted to a parallel position or even become the boss of the non-FME. The non-FME can therefore be torn by a conflict of interest since the faster the FME develops, the sooner the non-FME becomes vulnerable to resentment from the FME that may have developed from his or her working for the non-FME.

The bottom line is that you are putting your non-FMEs into an uncomfortable position if you have any of your FMEs reporting to them. The problem is that when your FMEs are working lower in the family business hierarchy, particularly when the FMEs are inexperienced, it is difficult for the FMEs to learn and develop effectively without reporting to non-FME supervisors. But the question is, how do you minimize the discomfort of the non-FMEs?

Paul, who owned an electrical contracting business, minimized the discomfort of Tom, his project manager, when his son finished his apprentice program and was assigned to work for Tom. Paul met personally with Tom to make sure that he was sensitive to the challenge for him since his relationship with the FME would change in the future as his son moved up. Paul recognized that he was putting the project manager into a tough position. Paul then met with Tom and his son together to discuss what he expected from his son and the importance of understanding how awkward things might be for the project manager. Paul explained that he would not tolerate resentment toward Tom stemming from his son working for him now or in the future when his son moved into a parallel position or would be put in charge of Tom.

When an FBL is grooming a successor, the FBL has to realize that to have the FME report to a non-FME puts the non-FME in a position of training someone who may cause the non-FME to lose his or her position after the FME is trained. I chose to go another route when bringing in Jason. I created an organization chart that, from the very first day, showed Jason as the COO and the non-FME executives as reporting to Jason. I met with the executives more than a month before Jason started work to explain to them that I would need their help to develop Jason as an eventual successor. I let them know that I wanted to surround Jason with talented non-FME managers but I would not put them in the uncomfortable position of having Jason report to them while he was being trained. I expected them to work with Jason to help him develop but at all times I made it clear as to who was reporting to whom.

Non-FME Barrier 4. Inability to Know and Work with Family Business Dynamics

Rachel searched six months for a CFO to join her family manufacturing business, which also employed her son as the vice president of sales. It hadn't really occurred to Rachel to discuss how family dynamics would affect the CFO's role during the interviews with the nonfamily members applying for the CFO position. When Mitch was hired as the CFO, he had no understanding of the unique dynamics of the family for which he would be working. Within Mitch's first month of work, he realized that Rachel was not holding her son accountable for his failure to meet sales commitments. This resulted in the company overspending in areas supporting the projected sales. Mitch discussed this problem with Rachel, who elected to do nothing about it. She defended her lack of action by saying, "I will always have a different standard for dealing with my son. That's nothing I'm going to change." Within three months of being hired, Mitch quit.

Rachel should have explained to Mitch the dynamics of her relationship with her son during the interview process. She should have been up front and explained the truth in a gentle and smart way. During the interviewing stage, Rachel should have had a frank discussion with Mitch about the positives and negatives of working for her family in the business. She could have said something like, "You need to understand how I manage my son and decide if you are amenable to it." Explaining what values her family stands for and her goals and aspirations for her son would have reduced the chances of hiring a non-FME who did not share the same view.

The family message does not need to be all negative. There are many benefits to non-FMEs working in Rachel's business that nonfamily businesses might not provide. For example, there is a great amount of stability and loyalty that exists in Rachel's business with the consistency of her leadership. Also, if her son were to take over the business, he would be much more likely to keep the CFO who had been part of his mom's team. This is unlike publicly owned businesses in which the stockholder-elected CEOs change and each new CEO is likely to bring in his or her own people.

You are not going to go into a lengthy "family business realities" discussion with every non-FME job applicant. Most family businesses do not feel the need to discuss the family dynamics in the business with applicants for employee positions that are lower than executive level. Discussions relating to family dynamics generally should not take place until you have determined that you have a serious interest in hiring a potential non-FME executive.

Rita, who has three child FMEs, has learned to ask non-FME executive candidates if they would be uncomfortable working for a company that grants some favoritism toward FMEs as well as special privileges. Rita discusses future advancement potential in the business with these executives prior to hiring them by explaining that her family employees come first but there will be important leadership positions available to non-FMEs. Before Rita started discussing the realities of her family business situation with executives she was recruiting, Rita wasted a lot of time and money hiring employees who did not stay long-term. This was because they didn't embrace the statement "Blood is thicker than water." Rita has found that addressing such concerns with a prospective employee before making an offer has "turned off" some good prospects, but it is better to lose them before they become employees than afterward when you have invested money in their learning curve.

If you have a strong interest in the candidate, you need to discuss the family dynamics specific to your company. You should not make an offer unless the executive has both an understanding and an acceptance of the dynamics and privileges that family-member employees have because the family owns the business. Clarify what the applicant's interaction will be with your FMEs. You will eliminate the guesswork and frustration that many non-FMEs go through when attempting to understand their roles within a family business. This guesswork and frustration has caused many well-qualified executives to leave the employment of family businesses. After explaining the family dynamics and how family members may be treated differently, try to verify that the recruit understands how his or her specific role may be affected by the family dynamics. As a result of this approach, you will greatly increase the chances that your new executive hire will stay with your family business as a long-term employee.

Mary often felt frustrated at work when she found she had a different opinion than a peer-level executive, whom she referred to as the owner's "kid." When there was a difference, Mary knew that the "kid's" opinion would always win out. Mary didn't mention this to her boss because, she said, "I did not feel secure enough to bring up my concerns with this type of problem. I know that when there is a conflict between a family member and the best interests of the business, the decision will usually be for what is in the best interests of the family." However, Mary stayed with the family business saying, "I loved working in the cosmetics business and not having to travel." However, this type of conflict can (and has) lead to non-FME executives resenting the ownership's attitude to side with family right or wrong, and it has caused executives to leave the family businesses.

Another area of family dynamics that must be understood and dealt with involves mixed signals coming from the FBL and the FMEs. Marcus, the FME son of the founder and CEO of the family's successful health-care business, constantly put Brook, a non-FME director of operations, into an awkward situation.

Marcus was desperate to escape from the shadow of his father. He was driven by a need to differentiate himself from his father and surpass him. This resulted in Marcus challenging everything in operations that was his father's way of doing things without first looking at why these ways were working. Sometimes he pushed Brook to make changes that had been tried by his father years before that didn't work and resulted in the current way of operating the business.

Marcus's attitude was causing confusion and concern for Brook, so she talked to the CEO about Marcus. She explained that it would be best if Marcus would learn from the mistakes of his father without the need to rebel against the traditional way things are being done in the family business. Brook pointed out that some of the things that Marcus wanted to try had been already tested in some manner in the past and had not worked. The CEO expressed to Brook that he was sorry that she was caught in the middle and expressed to his son, "Let's do things the way we have been doing them, but do them better." Sadly, the CEO did nothing to follow through in correcting the family dynamics problem. The unhealthy family issue between Marcus and his father became increasingly more embedded into the business environment. This familial dysfunction made it very challenging for Brook to understand the direction she should be taking. So she responded by playing it safe whenever she could. She says that she avoids making any decisions that could indicate that she is backing one family member over the other.

When a non-FME becomes caught between two FMEs, this is called *triangulation*. Triangulation problems are not limited to mixed signals between an FBL and an FME. Non-FMEs are often caught between co-FBLs, such as one tug-of-war that Tammy, a non-FME accounting vice president, found herself involved in. During a wedding, I happened to be seated next to Tammy. During dinner and after a few drinks, Tammy vented to me, "I am so sick of having to get in between the brother and sister co-owners of the company I work at! They have different Visions for the company, and somehow I'm stuck between the two of them. It's so damned stressful!"

Tammy went on to explain how the brother and sister own the business equally, and no one has final control, so they try to use her as the tie-breaking vote. "Susan belittles and undermines her brother, behind his back. She says that she does not have faith in her brother's abilities. Susan calls me into her office to obsessively talk about issues she has with him. Susan doesn't agree with her brother's Vision for the future of the business or the goals needed to reach the Vision. It's a real pain when we have management meetings, and after hours of discussion and brainstorming, we still have not come to an agreement about the direction of the company!" It got to the point where Tammy *dreaded* talking to Susan for fear of hearing her launch into yet another derogatory story about her brother. The way she handled it was to tune Susan out. It became increasingly difficult for Tammy to operate effectively with Susan because she felt caught in the middle if the brother told her to do things that she knew Susan would disagree with. She would complete an analysis that Susan would veto, and she could hear the two of them yelling in one of their offices. That was about the only time she ever saw them talking to each other. As she was talking, I thought of how difficult it must be for Tammy to be in the middle of this tug-of-war. I asked her what she was going to do about the problem. Tammy said, "Keep my ears open for other opportunities."

Every family business should have a policy regarding any employee, family or not, expressing negative views about family members to other employees of the family business. You should make it clear that it's not acceptable to make disparaging comments or share personal family matters about any FME, including the FBL. One manufacturer has a policy that makes it clear to non-FMEs that it's not acceptable to make negative comments about the FBL to any FMEs, and if they have a view about what the

FBL is doing or not doing, it needs to be expressed directly to the FBL. This did not take place with the brother and sister business because the violator of this principle was Susan, one of the co-FBLs.

At TAB, we show a written TAB Culture Statement to employee applicants whom we have an interest in hiring. The statement says, among other things, that TAB is a family business and that certain guiding values, principles, and traditions of our family are infused into the culture of our businesses. It explains that, like all family businesses, decisions will sometimes take into consideration their impact upon the family as well as upon the business. After the applicant has read the statement, our head of HR answers any questions about what this statement means and explores the alignment of these new-hire candidates with our family business philosophy and family dynamics. The TAB Culture Statement refers to our belief that TAB employees must deal truthfully with those they come into contact with including, without limitation, TAB franchisees, members, resources, suppliers, and their fellow employees. One franchisee sales prospect we interviewed laughed when he read the truthfulness requirement and said, "But we all know salespeople say what they have to say to make the sale." He wasn't hired. TAB is better off without an employee who does not fit with our family philosophy. Having a written Company Culture Statement helps recruits determine whether or not their values are aligned with TAB's and whether they believe they can be productive, effective contributors in TAB's culture. Recruiting executives who both accept and fit in with your specific family culture will be one of your best retention tools.

Non-FME Barrier 5. Resentment over Privileged Treatment

Ted, a nonfamily director of finance for a family-owned electrical distributorship, described the challenges he faced having to deal with his boss's daughter, Jessica. Ted resented her poor work effort and particularly that Jessica was protected from having to meet her commitments by her father. Jessica had no accountability for the budget items she submitted every year. Ted's boss always had an excuse for his daughter's lack of results and felt he had a perfect right to treat his daughter with different expectations than nonfamily members. However, no one else in management was granted any leeway on their commitments. Ted felt outside the "family cocoon" and, therefore, unprotected.

After a while Ted began complaining to other executives about how Jessica was treated in comparison with other executives. The leeway given to Jessica for accountability was only part of the double standard. Jessica did not have the same work ethics or productivity of other managers at her same management level. She did not set an example for a high level of commitment for non-FMEs to follow. This double standard resulted in Ted feeling a tremendous amount of animosity toward Jessica and giving less than his best at work. Double standards may be exhibited with treatment of performance accountability, work hours, vacations, and even restrictions on outside work. Just think how frustrating this situation was for Ted and how it impacted on the work culture of the family business Ted worked for.

Some double standards that upset non-FMEs may seem petty to a family business owner, but these issues may still cause real morale problems. For example, Jill, the owner of a hair salon, brought her 23-year-old daughter into the business. Her non-FMEs resented that her daughter was able to leave work early to walk her dog when they were kept to a stricter schedule. Jill responded to the expression of this resentment by saying, "It gives me pleasure that I can provide an environment in which my daughter can leave work to walk her dog." She then offered the same option to her other hair stylists recognizing that most would not give up income to leave their stations.

Gabriel, a son-in-law of the FBL of an IT business, started working for the company as its executive vice president. When he first arrived at work, he found he had been assigned by the director of operations, a non-FME, to a tiny office that did not have a desk or telephone. The office was filled with file boxes and a folding table that had no drawers. This situation occurred in spite of the fact that the company's executives knew for months when Gabriel would be starting work. The situation happened because the director of operations resented Gabriel coming in at a position that the director of operations felt should be his. He expressed to other executives his resentment of Gabriel getting the EVP position because of privileged treatment. The morning of his first day at work, Gabriel asked the director of operations to have the boxes removed from his office. When they were not moved several hours after his request, he finally moved the boxes himself. It was not until later in the week that Gabriel was provided a desk, and it had to be put together. The director of operations made no effort to have any other employee assemble the desk, and it took a day for Gabriel to put it together.

Gabriel did not tell his father-in-law about the passive-aggressive attitude of the director of operations. Instead, Gabriel bided his time, and when he was ready for a bigger office, he took the office of the director of operations. Doing so sent a clear message to the other employees of the company that it was not smart to make things difficult for Gabriel. I mention this example of the passive-aggressive actions of a non-FME against an FME because resentment often exists when a family member receives privileges or is treated differently. You need to recognize this barrier in order to overcome it. It is one that is not expressed to the FBL but instead is shown by passive-aggressive behavior such as the extreme example of the actions that were taken by the director of operations just to frustrate Gabriel.

It is often easy for an outsider to see why there is resentment about privileged treatment of a family member. Billy walked into his company's executive vice president's office and announced, "Good news, Cal. I'm moving my youngest son from sales to working directly for you. He's had some problems, as you know, so I want you to help me make a man of him." Cal reacted to this uncomfortable situation with a sigh, and he was not happy about it. He did not feel that it was his job to babysit a "really incompetent adult kid." Over the next six months, Cal sat on the kid's tail, but he was angry that so much of his time was being diverted and wasted. At the end of the six months, he gave his resignation. Billy was surprised. Apparently, he was not conscious of causing the resentment of his EVP by putting his son in such a privileged position.

Dean worked for his father in the family business manufacturing plant as a purchasing agent. Dean's performance was so poor that the non-FME operations manager went to Dean's father and complained about how Dean was paying too much for materials. Dean's father acknowledged the problem, but he did nothing about it beyond telling Dean to negotiate harder on price. This double standard was resented and perceived correctly by the non-FMEs to be the result of special privileges being given to Dean because he was a family member. In turn, the resentment resulted in a "self-corrected" situation of lower productivity, reduced quality, and increased absenteeism. Ultimately, it caused the resignation of the operations manager.

Family members are often put in key positions even though they do not have the skills or abilities to handle the positions. The amount of skill and experience a family member must demonstrate in order to be promoted within a family business is usually less than that which is required from a non-FME. Most of the time there is a belief among non-FMEs that family members will move up the ladder unless the person proves incompetent. You should be sensitive to how you would feel if you were nonfamily and saw a family member being promoted based solely on family relationships. To get around this barrier, be careful that your family members have the natural aptitude, skills, passion, and behavioral nature to do an assigned job.

When I was writing my weekly nationally syndicated newspaper column *Business Insights*, I received a letter from a director of telemarketing for a computer company. He complained that he and other non-FMEs were not being allowed to take on any work outside the business. However, the son of the business owner was allowed to open and run "on the side" a computer software start-up business that was not part of the family business. Not only did the business owner permit the diversion of her son's attention but she also shared with the writer of the letter her pride that her son was an entrepreneur. This only exacerbated the problem because what her son was "doing on the side" was not allowed for other employees. This is another example of a family business owner not recognizing resentment brewing for legitimate reasons—in this case, allowing the FMEs to do something that the non-FMEs are not allowed to do—among the non-FMEs in the business. The double standard was also used by some to justify breaking the company rules: the director of telemarketing confided in his letter that he was consulting for other businesses on the side. He justified his secretive behavior by saying that his boss's son was being allowed to have an outside job.

If you are okay with your family members having professional commitments outside your family business, just remember that it sets an example for non-FMEs to follow. A lack of full focus on a business is not good for any business.

Double standards in employee perks can also be a source of resentment among non-FMEs. At one manufacturing company, a warehouse manager made the mistake of being too vocal regarding his resentment toward the boss's son. The son was learning the business by working in the warehouse. He drove to work in a company-leased Corvette. Ed, the business owner, met with the warehouse manager and explained that the manager needed to be realistic. He said, "The company profits are my money, so it is none of your business as to the type of car I give my son."

This approach stopped the warehouse manager from sharing his resentment about the car. However, the resentment did not go away; it only turned inward. Months later, the problem resurfaced when the warehouse manager was reviewed and he complained about his $2,000 raise by bringing up the fact that although the son reported to him, the son drove a company-leased Corvette. The warehouse manager pointed out that the idea of the son driving a $50,000 company-rented car, when he got only a $2,000 raise for all his hard work, was "absurd." Ed told him, "This is the way I want my family to live. I care about you, but you aren't family. Live with it or leave the company."

Ed's actions were defensive and did not create goodwill. The next day he got back to the warehouse manager and apologized for the way he had responded. Ed realized that he should have given his son the money for the lease privately instead of giving his son a company car while he was working in such a low-level company position.

In another family business, a daughter, who headed up the marketing department in the home building business, became pregnant. She was given a flexible work arrangement by her father, William, which began during her pregnancy. She had a son, and everyone in the company knew her flexible work schedule would continue until her son started kindergarten. While the non-FMEs may have been happy for the daughter because she had this flexibility, it would not have been human of them if they failed to harbor some level of envy or resentment. After one of his managers mentioned the double standard, William met with his non-FME managers to talk about the situation. William said, "I want my daughter to have the flexible schedule because she is caring for my grandchild. It makes me feel good that taking the risk to start a business allows me to do this for my grandchild." William's non-FMEs like him and appreciate his honesty. With the truth laid before them, they accepted the situation.

Conclusion

Regardless of the stage of a family business, in order to keep top-level non-FME management intact, the FBL must recognize and knock down the barriers to hiring and retaining good nonfamily employees, especially key executives. Family matters need to be kept out of the business. Family members should not pull non-FMEs into family dysfunction by sharing things with them relating to the personal lives of other family members that should stay within the family. FMEs have to set boundaries with non-FMEs regarding sharing personal information about other family members. Family dynamic issues play themselves out in the business, but the real issues usually go far deeper. Family relationships often get strained, but family members need to avoid fueling the fire of employee dissension and sort these issues out separately from the business. FBLs need to be careful to not let double standards toward family members cause too many problems among non-FMEs.

Now we are ready for the final chapter, which happens to be the last chapter of one stage of a family business: Chapter 9 deals with the transition of the ownership of the business to other family members.

Checklist for Recruiting, Retaining, and Inspiring Non-Family-Member Employees in a Family Business

- Attracting non-FME talent and keeping these employees inspired and happy are essential to the success of a family business.
- Keep non-FMEs focused and motivated by giving them honest feedback regarding career development opportunities within the company.

- Provide non-FMEs with creative financial incentives as one way to show them that they are an important part of the future of your family business; such incentives will also help neutralize job security fears.
- Be proactive in neutralizing the potential problems in a situation in which an FME reports directly to a non-FME; be sure to communicate clearly regarding roles and expectations.
- Before they come on board, non-FMEs must understand and agree to work with the existing family business dynamics. Sharing with prospective non-FMEs a written Company Culture Statement is one way to impart this knowledge.
- Keep family issues and work separate to avoid pulling non-FMEs into family dysfunction.
- If possible, avoid double standards between non-FMEs and FMEs. If double standards need to exist, an honest explanation for them can dramatically reduce non-FME resentment.

CHAPTER 9

THE NINTH ELEMENT
Transitioning Ownership to Family Members

Sometimes the successor chosen to run the business will become the future owner of the business, but many times there are other family members who are chosen to be the future owners of the business. When there is a difference, one challenge is getting these parties in sync with one another. The film industry is a close analogy in that the groomed successor could be compared to the director of a film, while the owner of the business could be compared to the producer of the film—the one who has final say. Therefore, every business owner should clearly identify who will direct the business and who will oversee it as the owner.

The decision most privately owned businesses have to make is whether or not to take the business public; in contrast, the first question most FBLs generally ask is, "Do I want my business to be kept in the family, or do I want to sell it to an outside party?" It is very difficult for most FBLs to decide whether to sell or gift the family business to family members or sell it to outsiders.

What the question boils down to is, will the chosen family members help successfully build the business, or will they run it into the ground? The answer will help determine if it should be given to family members to manage or eventually sold to others. Also, the FBL has to keep in mind that even if the business ownership is given to another family member, it is extremely difficult for an FBL to cut the emotional attachment to the business. For those who determine that they do want to keep the business in the family, there are specific challenges to be considered. The following are seven common challenges to consider for the future transition of your business ownership to family members and how to prepare for and overcome each of them.

Ownership Transition Challenge 1. Percentage Split of Ownership

Family businesses are generally more successful if one person has the right to make final decisions. It is understandable that two or more people, even if they are family, will not agree on all the major decisions that need to be made relating to the business, and this leads to dissension. Although some family owners with equal ownership work effectively together, more often there will be conflict, and in some cases it can even destroy the business. Many FBLs choose to give their children equal ownership in their family businesses, whether through gifting or allowing siblings to buy the same amount of company ownership. However, TAB facilitators coach their FBLs to write Personal Vision Statements that provide for tie-breakers.

Brian, for instance, retired after selling his retail chain to his two FME sons, with each buying an equal 50 percent of the ownership. He felt that equal ownership was "only fair." What he didn't foresee was that inevitably many important decisions were delayed because neither son had more decision-making control than the other. Not only did this greatly harm the business, it also broke up the siblings' once very close friendship. They became enemies, although they eventually did agree to use a third party to arbitrate the problems they could not resolve on their own.

Family business owners have to think about the ramifications of designated ownership on the successor they are grooming to run the business. Phil's six children were employed in his family metal fabrication business. His daughter Cindy had been the designated successor for several years. One day, Phil called for a Family Council meeting. During the meeting, he announced that he was going to offer to sell to each of his children one-sixth ownership in the business, which would make the six siblings equal owners. Phil explained that allowing each sibling to own the same amount of the company was the only "fair" way. Cindy was outraged. She pointed out examples in which controlling ownership of certain family businesses had gone to the successor family member who would be taking over the reins. Phil explained, "This isn't going to be the case with *my* business because I love you all equally."

Cindy let Phil know she would not stay in the business as the designated successor if she was going to own only one-sixth of the business and had to battle with her siblings over the big decisions she would inevitably have to make. Phil did not change his mind, so Cindy quit the business, which was probably a wise decision for her since it is usually very difficult to effectively manage a business when all owners have equal control.

Phil thus found himself in the undesirable position of having to choose and groom a new successor from among his remaining children. He then had to continue working for his company while the newly designated successor got the needed experience to run the business. As a result, Phil had to stay active full-time in the business three years longer than he had intended. Tragically, Phil and Cindy never spoke again. The friction between the two of them greatly impacted extended family relations, especially at family functions they both attended.

Phil could have avoided a falling-out with his daughter if he had allowed Cindy, as his successor, to buy voting stock equal to one-sixth of the company while the other five siblings could have been offered nonvoting stock. This would have granted all six children the equal economic ownership Phil desired, but it would have given Cindy the final say in all matters. One of the most effective methods for avoiding equal control problems is by separating voting ownership from nonvoting ownership. It is very difficult to effectively manage a business when all owners have equal control.

Determining how or whether you want to spread ownership of the family business among your family members requires you to look closely at emotional considerations. FBLs tend to leave the lion's share to their spouses—regardless of the spouse's little or no involvement in a leadership position in the business. FBLs also tend to disregard how much time the spouse actually intends to put into the business, be it on a daily or big picture basis. The lukewarm commitment of the FBL's spouse can be demoralizing to the motivation of the FME who is being groomed to run the business.

Your decision regarding how much to give to each of your family members may involve such things as whom you get along with best or trust the most. In one situation, the father gave stock to his grandchildren because he wanted to help support them financially in the future. Derek, an owner of a hugely successful oil business, had three children, each from a different marriage. When his third child was a toddler, he announced to his two adult children FMEs that he had added a provision to his estate planning that stipulated if anything happened to him, the two grown sons would share voting power with his third child. He added that his third wife, whom the grown sons intensely disliked, would vote the third child's stock until the child turned 21 years old. Up in arms, the two adult children called for a meeting with their father. At the meeting, they explained the reasons why they felt their father was not being fair. They pointed out their fear that the toddler may or may not show any business judgment when grown or may not even have any interest in working in the family business. The dispute was resolved by the father changing his will to provide that his two adult sons would inherit the family's voting stock ownership in the business. The toddler would not have voting rights but would be treated as a financial equal with nonvoting stock equal to that of the older brothers. The problem was solved by separating voting control from financial benefits.

If you are looking at what will be best for the results of the business, one family member should have controlling interest, while other family members receive nonvoting interest. This approach allows the economic benefits to be distributed, thus preventing the types of problems that can take place when the person running the business does not have control of the business. Remember Thomas, the brother from Chapter 3, who was upset because his brother, Kendall, was being paid an equal salary even though they had significantly unequal responsibilities in the family business? Thomas, the COO of the business, was even more upset about his father's decision that the family business ownership be distributed equally between Thomas and Kendall upon their father's death. Only after Thomas threatened to leave the family business did his father commit to changing his estate plan to reflect that Thomas would inherit voting stock while Kendall would receive an equal amount of nonvoting stock.

I control some of my family businesses by owning all the voting shares, which in some cases are 1 percent or less of all the shares in the companies but I have all of the voting rights. The two are mutually exclusive. Voting rights stocks are not the same as owning stock. All the rest of the ownership in these family businesses consists of nonvoting stocks. This approach allows me to keep control of these businesses while giving my children the economic benefits that I want them to receive. This two-tier ownership structure was created at the time I formed these businesses—that's the key! This ownership setup can be put in place for a business at any time as long as you keep in mind that you need to be sensitive to the tax laws including estate and gift taxes. If you establish this two-tier ownership structure later when the stock in the business is doing well, the stock will then be worth more and the taxes will be higher because of appreciation than they would have been when the company was first organized legally.

It can put a lot of strain on non-FMEs when FMEs have equal ownership. Under such circumstances non-FMEs get pulled in different directions as one sibling fights for control over the other. Virgil, the owner of a retail chain, sold the ownership of the company to three people equally, resulting in each having an equal amount of voting stock. One-third was given to one son, one-third went to another son, and the other third went to a non-FME. Virgil believed that adding the non-FME would provide a tie-breaker. Virgil didn't foresee one major problem: The structure of the distribution put undue pressure on the non-FME to side with one or the other, and he constantly felt caught in the middle when the brothers didn't agree, which was often. When he agreed with one brother, the other brother was upset. Before the first year was over, the non-FME asked "out" by exercising his right to sell his stock back to the company.

Ownership Transition Challenge 2. Purchase Price and Financing Terms

The most common approach for transitioning family business ownership is to sell the business or transfer it through inheritance. This leads to the questions, "What is a fair price for family members to pay for the family business?" and "What is the business worth?" Negotiating the price of the business is a very delicate subject when one generation is buying from another. Emotions get in the way when there are differing opinions of the price of the business. Having your business valued by a valuation expert helps provide a range of prices for the negotiations between the family members. It is important to do a valuation of the business because if it is worth more than the sale price to your relatives, the IRS may view the difference as a gift that can be taxed.

Often, business owners get a higher price when they sell to someone outside of the business, and one reason for that is that the owners tend to give their family members a "deal"—that is, a price lower than the free market value. One woman, Lucy, determined the price she wanted for her family retail business by meeting with her accountant. Together, they determined what amount would provide her with sufficient after-tax proceeds to meet her retirement lifestyle needs. She also sought tax advice from the accountant because she had to be sensitive to the potential tax impact of selling the business for less than she might be able to get on the open market. She wanted to keep the cost of acquisition low for her kids by taking a payout for most of the price using a note signed by her kids and secured with some assets of the business.

When a business is sold to family members, the determination of a fair price is often affected by whether the price is paid at closing or involves seller financing, as was done when Lucy sold her business to her kids. Lucy sold her business at the very low end of the reasonable price range for the business. On the other hand, some family business sellers require a higher price if they have agreed to seller financing for part of the purchase price. They feel this is justified because they risk not getting paid in the future versus the certainty of getting all the money at closing.

Seller financing is typical with the sale of family businesses. But seller financing has resulted in many owners never getting the full payment for the businesses they sold to relatives. So when seller financing is being considered, it is especially important for you to realistically judge the capability of the family member to successfully pay off the note for the purchase price of the business. You should not take back seller financing as part of the purchase price unless you feel totally confident that the business will be successful enough for all the future payments to be made.

Dan is the owner of a successful distributor business. His son began working with him 14 years earlier. Both of them assumed the son would take over ownership of the business eventually. After 14 years, with no clear statement from his father concerning pricing for ownership transition, the son asked Dan to be specific about his future intention regarding ownership of the business. Dan told his son that when he was ready to sell, his CPA firm would prepare an analysis of the range of market-value sale prices for the business and he would sell for the low price of the range.

Dan knew that his son could not pay for the full value of the business at closing. So when he was ready to plan an exit date, he engaged a CPA firm to prepare cash flow projections to make sure that the payments could be made by his son to him, after taxes, over several years without hurting the cash flow of the company. The analysis showed that the business needed to grow to another level of income to support payments to Dan for his seller financing, to pay his son the compensation he desired as the new owner, and to still have the cash flow to grow. Dan knew compromises needed to be reached to ensure the future growth of the business. So Dan stayed on with the company a few years longer to get the business up to the needed profit level to satisfy the cash flow needs, including the payments to him for the sale of the business.

In another situation, Barry, who owned a car dealership, explained that he would sell his company to his son who worked for him, but he wanted full value from the business based on what he could get on the open market. Barry added that he would allow his son to pay the purchase price in 112 monthly payments. The sale was made, and his father retired to Arizona. The son now owned a business that was required to make payments to the father for the purchase price. Within months, the son purchased new auto shop equipment with a bank loan requiring 60 months of payments. For years, the son had thought that the business could operate very well without his father. He was therefore surprised to find that he needed to hire a couple of new executives to replace his father's work effort and that they cost more than he expected.

The result was that so much cash flow was being used for payments to the father, payments to the bank, and payments to the new executives that the company, although profitable, fell into a difficult position of not having the cash flow needed to expand. This created a lot of personal and professional stress for the son. Consequently, after only two years, the son offered the business back to his father, Barry, who refused to take it back or do away with the seller financing secured by certain assets of the business. The son ended up selling the business to an out-of-town company for an amount that only cleared his debt to his father and his bank loan. When there's not enough cash flow to support the needs of the business and the payments to both current and former family owners, the end result is nearly always disastrous for family relationships. A cash flow analysis before the sale along with restrictions on incurring new large debt could have avoided the auto dealership ownership problem.

Fred no longer wanted to have any day-to-day involvement in his New Jersey–based distribution business. He wanted to live most of the year in Florida. His son, who had worked in the business for 25 years, had been president of the business for the last 10 years, and he wanted to buy the company from his parents. Fred engaged a professional business evaluator to determine the market value of the business. The son offered to pay the fair market price for the business with a down payment of 20 percent and promised to pay the rest of the purchase price over 10 years. Before agreeing to the seller financing, Fred made it clear to his son that he and his wife needed the payments to be made on time to support the retirement lifestyle they wanted. The sale agreement stipulated that until the seller financing was paid off in full, the son would not compensate himself or his family beyond the $100,000 a year he had been earning from the business. Fred required this condition in order to increase the chances that the business would succeed and the seller financing would be paid off. Fred knew that he would, if he and his wife felt they did not need the money, forgive the note through gifts to the son each year, not to exceed the annual gift exemption. After several years, Fred and his wife started forgiving the note payments up to the amount permissible without gift tax consequences.

If a family member takes on ownership and then drives the business into the ground, it can hurt the family member providing seller financing. Herb and his brother Ken bought a technology support business from their father. Under their father's leadership, the business had been very successful. Their father was counting on the money from his seller financing to his sons as a major part of his retirement program. After a few years without the father's leadership, the company began doing poorly, which resulted in Herb and Ken not making payments to their father. The parents' retirement lifestyle had to be greatly reduced. The father and mother were so angry at their sons that their relationship was permanently damaged.

Ownership Transition Challenge 3. Income to Support Retirement Lifestyle

In many situations involving the transition of ownership to a family member, the owner is looking for continued income that will support a retirement lifestyle. However, monies going to the retired or semiretired former owner can be greatly resented by the next-generation owner. It is important that the transitioning owner and the new owner discuss the income expectations of the current family business owner before any final transition agreement is made. This will reduce, but may not eliminate, the resentment from the next-generation owner of the business. Long-term acceptance of paying an income to the former owner is more of a problem when the owner is selling versus gifting the business.

Many sell their businesses to family members with a contractual structure providing that the selling family member will receive lifetime consulting income from the business, even if he or she no longer makes much contribution to the business. These consulting contracts sometimes provide for payments to be paid to the seller's surviving spouse in the event of the death of the FBL. The resentment of family-member owners who are active in the business about the payments to the former owner who is no longer active starts creeping up as each year goes by.

Zach really opened my eyes as to how complicated this type of situation can become. Zach explained that, 18 years earlier, he had bought the family business from his father at a price that was very attractive to Zach, but with a written contract between the business and his father that called for his father to receive an income for consulting services for as long as he lived. He stated that he both loved and respected his 85-year-old father. Then he went on to lament about how his father comes to work for a few hours each weekday. He loves to chitchat with everyone, but he doesn't contribute anything of actual value to the business. Zach said that the company had a strong cash flow and had no problem making the consulting payments to his father. However, he felt it was unfair for his father to continue to draw income from the business after so many years of providing no real services to the business. He said he probably would never share his feelings with his father on this matter because he would not want to hurt his feelings.

Resentment directed at the parent who is still getting the same pay while no longer as active is not limited to transitions of ownership through selling the business to family members. When a stock gifting program is put in place, the parent who is committing to the ownership gifting and those family members who will receive the ownership gifts need to have a meeting of minds on any "strings" that will be attached to the gifts. Three years before Donald semiretired from the company he founded, he met with his son, Bill, and daughter, Riley, to discuss his plans to start gifting to each the maximum amount of ownership in the family business that he could give them annually within the tax-free gift allowance amount. The two siblings worked hard as officers of the company and the company prospered under their leadership. Donald told his children that even though he would be gifting them the ownership, he wanted them to understand that he expected his compensation from the business to continue at the same level, "even when I stop coming to the business every day." The distribution of profits from the company is based on their percentage of ownership. Donald's percentage of ownership would decrease each year with the annual gift of ownership in the business to his children and Donald realized that his income from annual profit distributions would decrease unless company profits increased enough to offset his decreased percentage of ownership.

A few years after Donald semiretired, his annual profit distributions actually increased because the company had tripled in profits. "It wouldn't have happened without our efforts," Riley said with a sardonic laugh during her monthly TAB board meeting. "So, as you can imagine, I'm a bit resentful that Dad's taking his full compensation while semiretired and also getting increased profit distributions—even though he's no longer regularly involved in the business." One of the older members of Riley's TAB board said to Riley, "Did the stock your father gifted to you result in increased distributions to you from increased profits of the business?" Riley acknowledged that her increased percentage of the ownership in the business was already resulting in an increased portion of the annual profit distributions. He then asked, "Did you understand that your father would be enjoying a continuation of his income and getting ownership profit distributions when he discussed his gifting program and his desire to eventually semiretire? Riley mulled this over and said, "Yes, I guess I did." Riley left the meeting more in touch with the fact that her father was entitled to live the good life he had brought about, and that she and her brother were still living a very good material life they were able to enjoy.

Riley's father's attitude is not unlike many business owners who transition ownership little by little to their children and don't see any reason for their income to be reduced when they are no longer fully active in the business. They view their compensation as a return on the years of efforts they invested to move the company to where it is. They see their continued compensation as a fair return for what they did, rather than what they continue to do. Over 90 percent of family business owners have little or no income diversification, deriving the majority of their income and security from their business. Based on this, it is not surprising that even if they have sold or gifted ownership of a family business, they expect to receive a salary or consulting income from the business. Often this ongoing income from the business is needed to provide them with their desired level of lifestyle.

During my *Seven Secrets* book tour, I met Bill, who owned a retail chain. He shared a story of how he had brought about an embracing of his ongoing income when ownership was transitioned to his daughter. Bill told me how, at age 70, he had revised his Personal Vision Statement to reflect his desire to have his business provide him with a $100,000 yearly "consulting" income for his retirement. His daughter had been working for the business for 20 years, and she wanted to have some ownership of the business. He told his daughter he was willing to start gifting the business to her with the provision that he stay on as CEO of the company without day-to-day involvement in the business. He explained that if she wasn't okay with his continued income of $100,000 a year, he would need to sell the business to an outside party. He had engaged a professional to prepare a valuation, and based on the result, Bill felt that he would be able to sell the business to an outside investor for a price that, when invested in high-grade bonds, would generate passive income of at least $100,000 a year. So his daughter said, "Sure, okay." So Bill started gifting his business to his daughter with an annual gift that has continued over many years. In case his death should happen before all the ownership is gifted to his daughter, Bill's will provides that his daughter will inherit the remaining amount of ownership he has in the family business.

Under Bill's agreement with his daughter, Bill is spending a limited amount of time working at the business and is working mostly out of an office in his home. He works only on things involving his Strengths that have potential for Big Picture impact. Furthermore, he explained, his income is tax deductible for the business, so it is not really costing the business $100,000 after taxes. Bill proudly told me that since his daughter took over running the company, the business is "earning several times what it did when I was working six days a week running the business" and that his CEO income has increased from the original $100,000 so that it is much more now than it was when he worked full-time. Bill told me his daughter generously expresses to him how much she enjoys having him involved, even if in only a semiretirement type of CEO position.

As with the payments for seller financing, the selling or gifting family owner and the new family-member owner need to look at whether or not the business has the capability to generate the desired salary payments or consulting income to the former owner, the compensation desired by the new owner, and enough remaining cash flow to grow.

Ownership Transition Challenge 4. Gift and Estate Taxes

Many family business owners dream of gifting their family businesses to designated family members or providing for the family members to inherit the businesses when the owners die.

For these family business owners, the purchase price is obviously not a driving force. There is no template to use when it comes down to whether and when to gift. The gifting decision has to be tailored to each owner's financial and psychological needs.

When one owner of a family optical store died at 72 years of age, he left his stock to his wife, who was then 68 years old and worked part-time in the business. She already owned 50 percent of the stock before receiving the remaining 50 percent when her husband died. Their son Ray, the COO of the family business at that time, was given none of the stock in the family business when his father died. Thirty years later, when his mother was 98, Ray and two of his sons were then running the business. Ray's mother still had all the ownership in the business and refused to start gifting any of her stock. I asked Ray, "Why on earth hasn't she gifted or sold her stock to you or your sons?" Ray commented to me humorously that she didn't do any gifting because she wanted financial protection for her old age. He would not have been human if he had not been a bit frustrated with the situation. Although Ray continued to run the business for decades after his father's death, he never got any ownership in the business until his mother died at age 99. By then, Ray was older than his father was at the time of his death. Getting the stock at that time was not the best estate planning move. He had to work on transitioning the stock to his two grown sons who were working in the business.

It is important for parents to come to grips with the fact that if they leave a business that creates a large estate, their inheritors will face major estate taxes when both parents die. Victor shared with me the problems he faced when he inherited the business after his mother, who had been the owner and driving force of the business, died suddenly. He commented, "She *was* the business." Not only had she failed to do any exit planning but she had all the key client relationships. When his mother died, the business took a nosedive. Victor, who inherited the business, had to pay the estate taxes on the business. The IRS considered the value of the business to be what it was on the day of his mother's death, but Victor felt that the real value was much less without his mom leading the business.

As family business owners get older, many initiate a policy of making annual gifts of business ownership to family members of the next generation in order to take advantage of gift tax exclusions. There are tax laws that need to be considered to determine how much you can gift each year and still avoid any gift tax. Gifting a certain amount of ownership each year can be an effective method of reducing, or even avoiding, potential gift and estate taxes.

Wes and his wife live in a joint property state. Wes's plan is to transfer some ownership of his business to his children before he and his wife die and the children find themselves with estate tax concerns. Based on the then current laws, they each gifted to their daughter and her spouse $11,000 per year in stock in the family business for a total of $44,000 tax free. If the tax laws change, as they are known to do, the annual ownership gifts by Wes and his wife will change accordingly.

Before Wes started the annual gifting of ownership in the family business, he engaged a firm to complete a valuation of the family business. This provided Wes with the information he needed to determine exactly how much stock he and his wife could give each year without any tax liability. Gifts of stock based on professional business valuations are more likely to stand up to legal scrutiny. Furthermore, if Wes should die still having ownership in the business, the professional evaluation that was prepared for him will help determine the value of his estate and business. Wes knows that Uncle Sam will value his business and collect taxes based on its value the "minute before you die." An additional benefit Wes realized from having the professional evaluation prepared was that it alerted him that the value of his business was so high that it could turn out that his heirs might not be able to pay the inheritance taxes from their own pocketbooks. This led Wes to have his business buy "key-person insurance" on his life in an amount that would pay the estate taxes, which would protect his company from being sold to outsiders to cover the taxes. He reviews the face amount of the policy on a regular basis because, whenever the value of the business changes, he wants the policy value to be changed as needed.

Some have used conversion of common stock to preferred stock to reduce the exposure to estate taxes. Charlie wanted to semiretire and get the ownership assets out of his and his wife's estate, but he wanted to be sure that he would receive a specific minimum amount of income from the business without relinquishing full control of the business. He recapitalized his business by exchanging some of his common stock for preferred stock that provides for a specific return on his investment to be paid as a dividend each year. The amount of the dividends would satisfy his ongoing needs for semiretirement income. Recapitalization to create the stock classification with its dividend preferences was accomplished tax free because it was structured such that the fair market values of the preferred stock Charlie received and the common stock he surrendered were equal. Additionally, with his preferred stock, he retained voting rights so he did not relinquish final voting control of the business. The exchange of his common stock for preferred stock was structured to ensure that Charlie will receive a minimum amount of income from the preferred stock. At the same time, it will keep future appreciation of the family business separate from his estate as a preferred stockholder because future increases in the value of the company will go to his children, who are the remaining common stock shareholders.

Ownership Transition Challenge 5. When and How Partners Must Sell Their Respective Ownership to Other Family Partners or Back to the Business

When more than one family member has ownership in the family business, it is important that they have a written agreement that covers circumstances that can be anticipated, such as a partner's retiring, becoming disabled, or dying, or the disintegration of the partners' working relationship. For simplicity, I will collectively refer to agreements that have these types of terms, as well as other terms, as "Family Partnership Agreements." Family Partnership Agreements can specify when and how partners must sell their respective ownership to other family partners or back to the business.

When Tara and her sister Alice started their catering business, their attorney drew up a Family Partnership Agreement with buy/sell provisions that defined how they could sell their ownership. They both agreed that although they loved and enjoyed working with each other, there was no guarantee that they would want to work with or enjoy working with any other family member. In order to keep ownership in the business from winding up in the hands of people who might be undesirable as family partners in one of their eyes, their Family Partnership Agreement restricted Tara and Alice from transitioning the partner's ownership to anyone, even a spouse or child, unless the company first had a chance to buy back the stock. This provision covered any reason for transitioning ownership, including a voluntary situation, such as a desire to sell, or an involuntary situation, such as the death of either sister.

One provision in the agreement between Tara and Alice provided that if either elected to no longer stay active full-time in the business, that sister must allow the company to buy back her stock. Years later, Tara decided to retire from full-time work, but Alice did not exercise her rights to require Tara to sell back her ownership. Things changed, however, when Tara told Alice that she wanted to sell her stock in the business to her daughter. Alice pointed out that the agreement required that the business had the right to redeem Tara's stock based on a predetermined formula and that Tara could not therefore sell her stock directly to her daughter. Because this had been agreed to so many years earlier,

Tara honored the intent and kept a very good relationship with her sister after the business bought back Tara's ownership.

Sometimes Family Partnership Agreements go a step further relating to retirement and provide a specific retirement age when the family partner has to offer the stock back to the business to redeem. In one business, Adolf, who at the time was in his early forties, agreed with his two younger brothers who were in their thirties, to a mandatory retirement age of 75. Funding for the buyouts of their ownership interests was backed by life insurance taken out when the three men were young. It was not pleasant for Adolf when he turned 75 because he did not want to retire, but his brothers required the enforcement of the mandatory retirement provision that all of them had agreed to many years earlier.

Sometimes the reason for transitioning ownership is that the family-member owners of the business don't get along. Even though you hope that family-member relationships will work when family members collectively own a business, it is wise to stipulate in the Family Partnership Agreement just how things will be handled if one family-member partner does not want to stay in business.

Stevan Wolf, a TAB facilitator-coach in Westville, New Jersey, shared a story with me about a father and two sons who began their business making candy in the family kitchen just after World War II. Their business grew as they were able to create cellophane bags (newly invented) and make preweighed packaged candy for stocking grocery store shelves. This new product replaced the need to have bulk candies in barrels from which the candy was weighed out for purchasing. As the company grew and prospered over the next several years, the relationship between the family members remained strong. Then, suddenly, trouble began when a dispute between the father and the older son escalated into a nasty situation and their personal relationship went sharply downhill. The younger son stepped in to help solve the problem and instead was drawn into the dispute between his brother and his father. The three of them were unable to solve what became a very bitter problem among the family-member owners of the business.

Fortunately, they had a Family Partnership Agreement that specified that each of the three family members, in a specific order starting with the father, had the right to buy the ownership in the company from the others. The father was interested in buying out his sons, but he could not obtain the needed financing. The older son wanted out of the business and did not opt to buy the ownership. The younger son wanted to buy out the ownership of his father and his brother, and he was able to secure the financing. Sadly, the father was so resentful of what took place that he did not communicate with his sons, their spouses, and their kids for the next 20 years!

Family members who collectively own a family business should consider a "right-of-first-refusal" clause that gives the current family owners of the business the right to buy the ownership of any other family member before that ownership can be sold, gifted, or bequeathed to any other person. Some Family Partnership Agreements do not have a broad right of first refusal as such but instead cover any change of ownership other than the ownership being sold, gifted, or bequeathed to the children of existing family-member owners of the business.

Mike and Joel were cousins, who had been friends from the time they were very young. When Mike was 38 and Joel was 40, they started a consumer electronics retail store together. Within months, they realized that they had totally different ideas on how to run their new business. Mike didn't like confrontations and was extremely frustrated by the anger that his cousin showed when they disagreed. Mike realized that when it came to business, his cousin Joel had work ethic expectations that were greatly different than his. Joel felt Mike had financial goals that involved them taking too much out of the business too soon and that Mike wanted to take too many financial risks with the business. All of these things should have been discussed and resolved before they started the business. But, as with many family partnerships, this was not the case. They had never discussed ground rules or philosophies for running the business because, as Mike said, "we had always gotten along." Soon their friendship turned into a bitter relationship and, unfortunately, they did not have a Family Partnership Agreement with a buy/sell provision that identified what happened if one of the partners wanted the other partner out of the business. There was no provision that detailed what would happen if they didn't get along. As with many family partners, they had greatly different views of the market value of their family business and, as a result, they stayed together in an unpleasant business relationship for several years until Mike sold his interest to Joel for what he felt was, "way less than it was worth."

A formalized meeting of the minds needs to address what will take place if family business partners don't get along. Family Partnership Agreements should contain a formula or method to determine how to buy/sell the ownership of other owners of the family business. Will the other partner be required to buy the exiting partners interest, and if so what will be the formula or method for determining the purchase price? Family Partnership Agreements should outline the procedures that will be used to determine the value of the business when the sale of ownership by one of the family partners is involved. Some agreements have provisions that explain how to select and engage a professional to provide a valuation of the business. Instead of an outside market price valuation, some Family Partnership Agreements require that the partners exchange offers to purchase each other's ownership with some agreement as to how the buyer will be determined. One common approach is that the highest offer determines which partner will be the buyer and the amount that will be paid for the other partner's ownership interest in the business.

When Adam took on his brother-in-law, Derek, as a 50 percent partner in the weight-loss business that he started, he required that they enter into a Family Partnership Agreement that covered a situation in which they didn't get along and wanted to dissolve the partnership. Their Family Partnership Agreement was designed with a provision that is a version of what some call the "one cuts, one picks rule." The provision required the partner who wanted out to allow the other partner to draft all the terms of the dissolution, including price, distribution of assets, and any noncompete provisions, with the understanding that the other family partner could choose to be either the buyer or seller under those terms. After several years, Adam wanted out, and Derek submitted a draft of all the terms he wanted in the dissolution, including the price that he would pay Adam for his 50 percent ownership. Derek knew that Adam could elect to use these terms to buy Derek's ownership. To Derek's relief, Adam declined to buy out Derek's ownership for the same terms and Derek bought out Adam.

Ownership Transition Challenge 6. Factors and Terms Unique to Ownership Transitions to Family Members

The terms of the sale or gift of family business ownership to family members tend to include some factors and terms that are not typically included in the sale of a business to nonfamily buyers. For example, one of the terms that commonly must be considered involves the continuation of personal guarantees by the selling or gifting parties for bank loans or credit lines involving the business. Nonfamily parties purchasing a business would typically not consider asking the seller to continue with his or her personal guarantees for the loans to the business. But it is a common request, even a need, when family members take over ownership of the business. The conflict is that the seller or the person gifting ownership generally wants to be taken off the personal guarantees that he or she gave to get the bank loans and credit lines for the business. When transitioning their family businesses to family members, the need to get out of the business guarantees, whether to lenders or suppliers, and retire with peace of mind is essential to many.

Tina decided to retire and sell her nursing uniform and equipment business to her son and daughter, who had been executives in the business for years and were happy to buy the business, particularly at the attractive price asked for by Tina. However, Tina was adamant about removing her personal guarantees on the business's long-term bank loan. The bank said no to eliminating the personal guarantee because it felt that the two children did not have the personal assets to protect the bank if they could not operate the business at a high level without Tina in the business. In addition, three of the company's key suppliers wanted to continue to look at Tina's assets for security versus the assets of her two children. The children found that they could not get these suppliers to keep giving their company the same dollar amounts in their lines of credit without Tina's personal guarantee.

Tina finally agreed to sell half the business to her son and daughter and stay on as a guarantor. She gave her two children the option to buy the other half if and when they could arrange for a new bank loan and trade credit from the same suppliers or alternative suppliers without Tina's personal guarantee. The sale of the last 50 percent of Tina's ownership was delayed for two years, until refinancing could be worked out with another bank that did not require Tina's personal guarantee of the business loan and the key suppliers finally agreed to remove Tina's personal guarantees.

Another issue specific to transitioning ownership to family members involves this one: How do you protect family members who will have ownership when they are not at an age at which you feel they are ready to responsibly vote their ownership of the stock? The age of being able to assume adequate responsibility may differ greatly among the minds of business owners transitioning ownership to young family members. You can protect young family stockholders from themselves by creating a trust to hold the stock. A trust will be controlled by a trustee until the beneficiary reaches a predetermined minimum age, at which time the beneficiary will take over from the trustee the right to vote his or her stock in the business. Of course, a trust agreement should also include such things as how the trust is to pay the beneficiary.

Another issue involves the request of a dying family member to never sell the family business to outsiders. When his sons were very young, Jeremy told his wife, Sara, that he wanted his two sons to run the business when they were older. He made Sara promise that if anything happened to him, the business would ultimately go to the boys. But the boys were still young when Jeremy passed away, and the task was left to Sara to keep the business going until the boys were older. Unfortunately, she was not able to successfully manage it. Sara would have preferred to sell the business and use the money from the sale of the family business to help raise the boys. Because of her promise, however, Sara did not sell the business even though it put the business in jeopardy and consumed a significant part of their family savings before she got the hang of running it. It goes back to the maxim, "Don't try to manage from the grave."

Don't put your family members in a risky financial and emotional situation with such requests. They should not be left to deal with the emotional burden of going against your wishes. In keeping with this belief, I have told my son-in-law, Jason, and my daughters, Michele and Lynette, that they have my okay to say goodbye to the business if I die or I'm incapacitated. It's okay for them to play it safe and turn the business into assets that can continue to give them a good quality of life without the risk of business ownership, if that is what they want.

Another term specific to the sale of a business to family members is the requirement that the new owner provide employment and income to other family members, such as another child of the seller who may not have the ability to earn as much working for an outside business. The longer the new family-member owners own the business, the more likely they are to resent these terms requiring their business to continue supporting FMEs who are not carrying their weight or who have gotten used to getting paid more than market value for their jobs. It is surprising that there is often a backlash of emotion by the new family-member owners after a number of years of their supporting one or more nonproductive family members. The new owners start to feel resentment about having to make these sacrifices that often reduce the amount of money the new owners can take out of the business or even the amount of money available for financing business growth. This very unique request or requirement from the selling family member needs to be discussed fully before the transition of ownership, and both the selling and buying family members need to be objective about how they may feel about this need to employee family members years down the road.

Another term often involved when businesses are sold to family members with seller financing involves ongoing control by the selling party. Many FBLs have elected to maintain a controlling role in the business until the financing debt to them is repaid. This role also meets the FBL's emotional needs to still be involved while allowing the selling family member to get away from the day-to-day involvement in the company. It allows these FBLs to retain the purpose and passion they have for the business. But it also sets the stage for resentment by the family member buying the business.

When Augusto's father sold him the family landscaping business with a long-term payout of the purchase price, he said, "I want a final voice in the business until the note is paid off so I can make sure it does well enough to make the seller financing payments to me." Five years later, Augusto was frustrated over the fact that the only time his father stepped foot in the business was when Augusto was trying to implement a change that he felt would potentially grow the business. Augusto said, "Dad wants nothing to do with day-to-day operations, but just try and change or innovate on any of his obviously set-in-stone policies, and, boy, he is suddenly back in the picture in a flash." Augusto loves and respects his dad, but he resents the fact his dad is keeping him from growing the company that he now owns. The solution to Augusto's challenge was paying off the loan to his dad with funds from a new bank loan, even though the interest on the bank loan was twice that which was involved with the seller financing given by his father.

Ownership Transition Challenge 7. Negative Repercussions from Family Members Passed Up as Owners

A decision to sell to outsiders because of a concern about the competency of family members to run the business is not uncommon. In fact, according to a Laird Norton Tyee survey, 25 percent of majority shareholders in family businesses think the next generation is not competent enough to take the reigns. If you decide to sell to outsiders, be prepared to accept the potential repercussions from FMEs who were passed up as owners.

When Randy started working for John, his father, in his successful cattle ranch business, John told Randy that he hoped Randy would be able to own the ranch sometime in the future. John then surprised the heck out of Randy when John announced, *seven years after Randy joined the family business,* that he had changed his mind. He had come to the conclusion that Randy was not capable of running the business himself and if Randy owned the business, he would need to hire a professional to run it. John said, "Randy would destroy it because he's not going to hire someone to run it and he would change everything I had done to make it successful." John decided instead that it would be better to leave money to Randy from the sale of the business to an outsider. When John sold the business to a very large company with many successful cattle ranches, John gave Randy a large gift from the sale proceeds. But Randy and his father never had the same relationship after the sale.

Sometimes, unlike the situation with Randy and his father, no promises have been made to the children about the future ownership of the business, yet the children assume they will eventually own it. Most of the time, the negative repercussions will not be as severe as those displayed by Simon, who had been on a fast career track at a public company when he joined his parents' pharmaceutical business as a senior vice president. Simon's parents never overtly expressed to him that the business would one day be turned over to him. But in Simon's mind, it was a forgone conclusion that he would get the business since his parents would not otherwise have encouraged him to leave the public company at which he had been working. Simon was completely taken aback when he showed up at work one morning to find his parents having a meeting with a public company that was interested in buying the business. There had been no mention to him ever about their one day selling the business to outsiders. Simon could not understand why his mom and dad had kept him in the dark about this. When Simon spoke privately with his father, his father explained that he and his wife had changed their minds about gifting or selling their business to Simon after receiving an unsolicited offer from a public company that they considered "too good to turn down."

A few days later, Simon expressed his surprise at what his parents were doing since he had thought he would someday own the business. He asked that he be given the opportunity to buy the business. Simon made an offer to his parents to buy the business for the same amount offered by the public company. His offer, however, involved his parents providing seller financing with a series of equal payouts that would take place over 10 years, rather than his parents being paid the entire price at closing, which was the deal with the public company. His parents looked over Simon's bid and discussed it at great length with each other. Then Simon's father got back to him and explained that they were firm in their decision to sell the family business to the public company.

"Look, Simon," his father told him. "I appreciate that you want to keep the company in the family. But the public company has offered us the entire asking price *at* closing and with no risk. It will secure us financially for our retirement, and we don't want to take any risk of not getting the payments." This need for security was not surprising since Simon's parents had been war refugees. After coming to America, they had finally made their way financially. But they still lived in fear of "being without." They put great importance on their secure retirement, and getting payments of the purchase price over 10 years was not guaranteed if the business did not continue to be successful. "I'm truly sorry, Simon, but we are getting a really great price for the business with it all being paid when we sell the business. The money's going to provide a well-financed retirement for me and your mom. And we've negotiated an employment package for you—it's worth several hundred thousands of dollars. We know you must be thrilled to hear that."

Simon was anything but pleased. His parents felt that the money their son would receive would help provide for Simon and his family, even if his future employment didn't pay as much as he had been paid by the family business. But Simon's thoughts were, "What do my parents think I will do now for a job?" Simon, who had three children, was concerned that "at 52, it'll be hard to find an executive position somewhere else and several hundred thousand dollars will not support my family without another income to help out." Both Simon and his wife took the sale badly and never again attended family gatherings, and they denied the husband's parents any interaction with their three grandchildren. Several years later, the father expressed remorse over not getting to see his grandchildren grow up and he resented his son's "failure to understand why we did the right thing."

When Simon's parents decided to sell the business to a public company, they should have shared their intent with Simon and explained why. Not informing Simon by essentially declaring "It's this way because I say so" was not likely to smooth things over. Be honest about why you are selling to outsiders if you have a change of heart and you will have a better shot at neutralizing negative family repercussions.

I know of several situations in which the decision to change who was to get ownership of the business was not that of the owner but that of the spouse of the owner. One situation involved Doug who, for years, planned to sell his business to his daughter, Kathy, who was an executive in the business. However, when his wife, Carol, got wind of his plans, she was furious. Carol was adamant about his not selling the business to Kathy! Carol told Doug, "If you sell to Kathy, you will keep your foot in the business to feel confident that it does well." She reminded Doug about how obsessed he gets with his business and that he tends to think about it all the time. Carol talked to her daughter Kathy and said, "It would be better for us and for your dad's health if we sold to an outside party." Doug then explained to Kathy, "Mom's pretty convinced that I'll never be able to get my mind off the business if it stays in the family. She wants me mentally and financially free from the business, and now that I've had some time to think about it, she does have a point." Fortunately, his daughter was supportive of the eventual sale to an outside company after hearing the concerns about Doug's mental and physical well-being.

Conclusion

It's important to discuss with your family members how they may feel about ownership or equity in the family business. You may be surprised to find out that they feel entitled to or expect to receive some level of ownership. This discussion should not be limited to your FMEs since family members who have never worked for or contributed to the family business may feel they should be given some ownership purely because they are family.

The terms of family business ownership transition to family members will differ for every business based on such individual factors as economics or health needs. Consequently, the timing of the transition needs to be discussed at some point or you will be compromising the well-being and future growth of the business. Don't allow this matter to get shunted to the bottom of your list of important things to do and put off until a time when you no longer have the mental or physical capacity to keep running the business. Even some of the greatest business leaders have fallen victim to procrastinating about dealing with the inevitable.

Don't delay thinking about transitioning ownership until you are ready to move into semi- or full retirement. Your timing of the transition of your family business ownership should be planned so that it is accomplished with your best interest in mind and within a time frame that allows you plenty of time to emotionally prepare for a new future away from the business. You do not want the family business to be left to fate because you did not make or implement the necessary transition plans. Create and put a plan into action that addresses the transfer of business ownership to family members when there's plenty of time for the new family-member owner to learn the ropes under your mentorship. This is a long, complex process. Throughout the journey, keep discussing developments with family members potentially affected by the plan. If your desire is to keep the business in your family, decide who will become the new owner, how the ownership will be transferred (that is, will it be sold, gifted, or bequeathed to the new owner), and above all, get up-to-date advice from qualified professionals.

Checklist for Transitioning Ownership to Family Members

- The decision to keep the company in the family after the FBL's retirement is loaded with questions such as to whom, when, and how the company ownership will be transferred. The answers are the bedrock of a succession plan and cannot be avoided or delayed.
- Even if the leadership role is granted to a sole heir, there are creative ways of distributing ownership in the business to other FMEs to reduce tension and resentment.
- When transitioning to a family member, the appraised value of the business often takes a back seat. Protect yourself and your successor by knowing the tax laws and structuring the transition accordingly.
- If you desire a semiretirement salary of consulting fees, you must discuss the details of the arrangement with your successor before the transition takes place.
- Businesses that are gifted to or inherited by family members fall subject to varying tax laws. Always consult a qualified attorney or accountant.
- If you co-own the business with a family partner or partners, have a Family Partnership Agreement that stipulates how and when you can sell your share in the business.
- Never force family members to make promises to the grave such as, "I'll never sell the business."
- If you are an FBL who is selling or gifting a business, you should have your name removed from any personal guarantees.
- Put in writing any additional terms of sale, such as providing future employment for family members.
- Seller financing can present risks to retiring FBLs who are dependent on proceeds from the sale of the company. As the FBL, you may wish to maintain a minimal role in the business

after the ownership transition to ensure that the business continues to prosper.

- Plan for the timing of the transition well before the plan will go into action. Give yourself time to get used to the idea and to properly groom your successor.

Conclusion

The nine elements of family business success shared in this book address the unique challenges of family businesses and provide the proven formula that will enable you and your family to enjoy a greater family relationship while maximizing the potential for success of your family business. The hundreds of stories I have related in this book provide lessons of what other family business leaders have done wrong from which you can learn. But I have also shared stories that show you the best processes and techniques to use for handling these family business challenges. These methods will help your family develop more harmonious interpersonal relationships and help your family business leader become more successful.

As the founder of a family business, The Alternative Board, in which my son-in-law, Jason, is president, I'm often asked by TAB facilitator-coaches and TAB members if I look forward to one day seeing a third generation of my family leading The Alternative Board. The truth is I don't know if any of my grandchildren will grow into adults who will have the passion for TAB that they would need to have to be effective leaders of the company. If any do decide to take TAB into a Dynastic Stage, that would be wonderful. But if not, that's okay too. What I wish most for my grandchildren is that they each live fulfilled lives that include work that is meaningful to them because they have a passion for it. My hope is that each of my grandchildren will embark on a safe and happy journey to his or her respective dreams. You shouldn't force your dreams on others.

I look forward to hearing any stories you want to share of how the *Nine Elements of Family Business Success* has helped the family relationships in your family business and helped your family business go to the next level of success. Please send your stories to afishman@TABBoards.com.

Enjoy the journey!

Allen E. Fishman

APPENDIX
Exhibits

Exhibit A

Jason Zickerman's 2001 SWOT Analysis

Strengths

- Financial acumen
- Multitasking
- Goal oriented
- Deadline sensitive
- Extremely strong work ethic
- Ability to motivate employees
- Never-ending desire to succeed

Weaknesses

- No knowledge of the franchising business or of franchise law and contracts

- No experience dealing with likely adversarial resentment from those who will feel I have the position because of nepotism
- Lack of experience in growing a company in a COO capacity
- No experience in motivating nonemployees, such as franchisees
- Unfamiliar with the thinking, or mindset, of a franchisee
- No connections or relationships in the franchise industry
- May see things too black and white rather than seeing gray areas

Opportunities

- If business could be successful, my life could be significantly changed financially, and I will be better able to provide for my family.
- I will be able to become a more participating father and husband who is home rather than working nights and weekends.
- I could make a positive difference in the lives of many people, whereas in past and current work, I was not making a difference.
- I would gain personal satisfaction from seeing a business grow and ultimately become the biggest in the world at what we do.
- The successes would go way beyond monetary if I am able to make TAB succeed.
- I would have the opportunity to develop high-level negotiating ability and experience.
- I would have the opportunity to become more business savvy from having run a large business.

Threats

- Potential for major displeasure and resistance from both franchisees and current TAB employees to position appointment with their thinking that the appointment is strictly the result of nepotism without first viewing my ability to perform.

Exhibit B

Information to Be Shared with the Successor

- *A financial summary of the status of the business and a projection of its financial future.* Support for the assessment should be provided via financial statements for the current and recent years. Although it should include a cash flow chart, in the case of most small businesses, there will be no cash flow projections. The summary should include the names of the company's bankers, the lines of credit, and average balances. It should also list the names of your company insurance carriers and types of coverage.
- *A legal and administrative profile giving information on the structure of the business such as Family Partnership Agreements, corporate records, buy and sell agreements, and royalty agreements.* This profile should include all information on patents, licenses, contracts, and leases. It should also list the names and addresses of attorneys, accountants, and any other outside professionals retained by the company.
- *An operations report containing an inventory of major equipment, manufacturing specifications, and process and scheduling procedures as well as quality control measures and production standards.* This report should include a brief analysis of the efficiency of plants and equipment currently in use. This information should be given in an informal presentation by the FBL

and include the FBL's operating philosophy and state the Company Vision.

- *Sales and marketing overview.* This information would include such things as current and future plans involving major clients, advertising programs, and information about competitors. This overview should outline your basic buying procedures and list inventory levels, present contracts, and suppliers.
- *Management systems information overview.* This information would include such things as the IT procedures manuals and flowcharts.
- *Human resources overview.* This information would include an organizational chart with positions, titles and names, and job descriptions. The overview should include a list of needs for potential new position hires with brief job descriptions and the skill levels required. FBLs need to make sure that the successors are familiar with the basic responsibilities of the people with whom they will work the closest and that they know the strengths and weaknesses of all employees.

Exhibit C

TABenos Exercise

One family provided the following answers to the first TABenos question, "What does communication armor look like?"

Trying to control the discussion
Combative, unreasonable, or argumentative
Negative body language
Disingenuous
Hurtful sarcasm
Not listening or disengaging
Anger

Condescending
Defensive
Disrespectful
Abusive language
Deflection
Arrogance
Repetition
Blame game
Reacting to the messenger, not the message
Excessive humor
Throwing things
Crying
Questioning for reasons other than understanding the person
Being political
Dominating
Lying or withholding material information
"You" messages versus "I" messages
Accusing
Boredom
Denial
Trying to manipulate
Fear of retribution or retaliation for expressing views
Impatience
Interrupting
Attacking style

The same family responded as follows to Question 2, "What causes or triggers you or other family members to put down your armor defense mechanisms?"

Confidentiality
Trust
Not viewing the same set of facts differently
No yelling

Positive tone
No threats of reprisals
No one's trying to take advantage of you
Others' respect for your self-esteem
Ability to compromise
Shared positive experiences
No presumption of malice
No hidden agendas
Nonjudgmental
Desire for win-win
No sarcasm
Being factual
Sincerity
Empathy
Being open to the outcome
Being fair
Desire for synergy
Compassion
No history of passive-aggressive behavior
Knowing role
Honoring needs of others
Balance short- and long-term objectives
Mutual Vision for future of business
Allowing time to process
Not taking things personally
Knowing commitments will be kept
Respect
Nonterritorial
No negative body language
Patience
Not overreacting
Collaborative
Supportive attitude
Honesty

The same family responded as follows to Question 3, "What would be gained if the family communicated within a TABenos environment?"

Greater growth and prosperity for the family business

Ideas and suggestions of family members will be heard to a greater degree

Will enjoy being around each other more, whether inside or outside the business

Business initiatives will be executed in a timelier manner and with greater clarity

Greater fairness

More teamwork

Will feel more respected

Enjoy life more

Greater collaboration

Better understanding of short- versus long-term objectives

Family members will present their ideas, views, and interests without being intimidated

Needs of other family members will be honored

More respect to family-member employees from non-family-member employees

Glossary

DISC   An acronym for a behavior profile: Dominance, Influence, Steadiness, and Conscientiousness. A high D personality would be demanding, driving, ambitious, and competitive. A high I personality would want to work with people and would be enthusiastic, inspiring, and demonstrative. Someone relaxed, resistant to change, predictable, and consistent would be a high S personality. High C personalities would be careful, dependent, neat, and systematic. People who score low in any of these areas would have very few of the traits that define that particular personality type.

Dynastic Stage   The third-generation, or more, ownership of the business; usually at least one family member is acting as the family business leader (FBL) or is being groomed to become the FBL if there is an interim CEO.

family business   Any business employing more than one family member.

family business leader (FBL)   The leader of a family business.

family-member employee (FME)   An employee of a family business usually related to the family business leader (FBL).

family partners   When I refer to "family partners," I am referring to situations in which more than one family member has ownership of the business, and I am not limiting this term to legal partnership relationships. I include, for purposes of this book, ownership of the company as a corporation or any other legal entity.

Founder's Stage   When the founder of the business is the family business leader (FBL) and he or she is actively involved in the business.

non-family-member employee (non-FME)   A family business employee who is not a family member.

partner   When I refer to "partner," I am using the term conceptually, not legally, so that stockholders may be referred to as "partners."

Personal Vision   Your long-range dreams of success and happiness. These aspirations should remain relatively constant for 5 to 10 years into the future.

Second Reign   The second-generation ownership of the business; usually the business is being run by siblings or a child of the founder.

spouse   I am including domestic partners within the term "spouses" or "couples" when I talk about couples that work together in the family business.

Index

About the Author

Allen E. Fishman is the bestselling author of *Seven Secrets of Great Entrepreneurial Masters: The GEM Power Formula for Lifelong Success*. He is the founder and CEO of his family business, The Alternative Board (TAB), the world's largest business peer board and coaching franchise system. As a noted expert on privately held companies, he has been featured in numerous media venues, including CNBC, Bloomberg, *The Wall Street Journal*, and *USA Today*, and he is a featured speaker at engagements around the world.